Childhood Social, Legal and Health Studies

Emma Zara O'Brien

and

Margaret Prangnell

Gill Education
Hume Avenue
Park West
Dublin 12
www.gilleducation.ie

Gill Education is an imprint of M.H. Gill & Co.

© Emma Zara O'Brien and Margaret Prangnell 2015

978 07171 6813 2

Print origination by O'K Graphic Design, Dublin
Printed by GraphyCems, Spain
Index by Cliff Murphy

ized her mistake. "Oh là, Monsieur, for that, there are a lot of other things one would like to do. Set up a little shop, for instance, in Rue St.-Honoré. But it's very expensive, a shop. Monsieur might perhaps lend me the money?"

"Call me Blanco."

"Monsieur Blanco. You understand, all this business involving Madame, Mademoiselle, and the apartment seems to me very complicated. I don't understand it. I ought to ask Madame what she thinks of it. I could go to her in the clinic. I believe it's in Fontenay-aux-Roses."

"I wouldn't advise it."

"But perhaps I wouldn't, if Monsieur lent me the money to open a shop. Then I could forget about Madame and the apartment and move away to live over the shop in Rue St.-Honoré."

"I could lend you the money, but I don't think it would be a good idea. I don't think you have a shopkeeper mentality."

"Mentality?"

"The thieves' instinct. All merchants are thieves."

"Oh, that, Monsieur Blanco. There you have reason."

"I'm sure you're very good at some things. Blackmailing perhaps. You could live in the lap of luxury if you chose. It's all in playing your cards. You're clever enough."

"Monsieur is too good."

"No I'm not, and neither are you. I think you'll do."

"Do?"

"But you must pay attention and do exactly what I tell you. And say nothing to anyone. Hermine says you're the soul of discretion."

"Oh là. What is that, Monsieur Blanco? Why, it's a hundred-franc bill."

"Here's Hermine."

"Oh là là. Would you imagine, Mademoiselle, what Monsieur Blanco's been telling me."

Claire's stay in the clinic, delayed by minor complications and by the indecision of Dr. Simon, had lengthened to ten days. Now it was about to end. Hermine had come almost every day to visit her but had said nothing about the arrangements for returning to Paris. The two of them had come out to Fontenay in a horse-drawn voiture with a couch in it on which Claire could recline, with Hermine at her side to attend to her needs. There was no need for this now that she was better; a simple cab would do, or the train from Sceaux which ran through Fontenay on its way to Paris.

Instead Claire looked out the window from her bed and saw a hired landau drawing into the lane, an old-fashioned vehicle with glass windows and a leather top. On the bench sat a cabman in a coat with gold braid and an Irish cap with ribbons. He got down and opened the door, and Hermine got out, followed by Blanco carrying a bouquet of roses and a bottle of champagne in an ice bucket. They disappeared from view, and there was a disturbance of some sort in the anteroom. She could see Blanco waving and gesticulating over the coifed heads of the Sisters, who were attempting to bar the bucket of champagne from the sickroom.

Hermine fled in to her looking pale and distraught. "Dear Maman, how are you feeling? I hope you're well enough for our little journey. We're going the—long way around. It may be somewhat tiring."

"Hermine, what are you talking about? I'm perfectly well. I've just got a sore finger. What is Blanco doing out there, the idiot? And what did he come along for anyhow?"

"Oh Maman, it's all right. Don't excite yourself." She had an expression on her face that Claire remembered well, as though she had got into the jam in the kitchen and was hoping her mother wouldn't know. "Leave everything to Blanco. He's a perfect gentleman and he's been very nice to me while you've been in the clinic."

"Nice to you?" Claire wasn't aware that Hermine knew Blanco, except for the single occasion when she met him in the café. "What *is* he doing?"

She pushed herself up on the bed to look; Hermine pushed her down again. A beaming Sister came in with the roses arranged in a vase. There was water on the vase and she wiped it off with the skirt of her habit before she set it on the table, in her excitement lifting the skirt high enough to show her leg. Out in the anteroom, Blanco had persuaded the Sisters to allow the champagne as well, quoting St. Paul to the effect that a little wine was good for the stomach and arguing that it would lift up Madame's spirits.

The Sisters scurried about to get glasses and found a linen napkin to wrap around the bottle. All these things were brought into the room in a procession with Blanco following them. He loomed over the others in the room. His reddish-brown cheeks were touched with pink; he looked as though he had been sitting by an open fire. He radiated cheerfulness, energy, and light. He looked around for a place to put his hat, found none, and set it on the foot of the bed.

"Hello, Claire. A happy winter solstice to you. You're not well enough to go to a party, so we've brought the party to you."

The Sister set the napkin-wrapped bottle on the table and he seized it and unscrewed the wires. It had been jiggled on the journey out from Paris and a fountain of foam sprang out. He filled a glass for Claire, pressed it into her hand, and distributed the rest into his own glass and those of the Sisters, including the Matron who had come in to see what all the fuss was about. He even poured a little for Hermine, but Claire pretended not to notice.

"A votre santé," he said, clinking his glass with hers. "Santé, santé, santé," chanted the Sisters each holding her glass with its tiny drop of champagne.

Blanco took a rose from the bouquet on the table, shook off the drops of water, and set in on the pillow beside her. Lancelot, she remembered, had only promised her roses in the summer. "Wherever did you find roses at this time of the year?"

"It's nothing. The florist at the Palais-Royal can find anything. They're from a hothouse in Nice. They came up by fast train."

"Maman," said Hermine, "Boris is so anxious for you to come home. I take him for a walk every day. He likes his new—" She stopped, flustered again. "And Professor Souteran spoke to me after the chemistry lecture. He asked if it was true that

I was your daughter. You know, Maman, we came out from
Paris in a landau. In fine weather you can put the top down.
It's ever so much nicer than a cab." She rattled on as though
she wanted at all costs to fill up the silence.

"Hermine, why are you going on about Boris and Professor
Souteran and the landau? Have you been getting into the jam
in the kitchen? Stop chattering for a moment. I can't hear myself think. Since we've drunk all the champagne," she said
crossly, "now I think I'll get dressed and we'll go back to Paris."

The Matron, an enormous woman who nevertheless seemed
light on her feet, as though her bosom were a cumulus cloud
inside her habit, finished her glass and set it on the table. "I
will wink at champagne," she said, "but you will all have to
clear out of here while Madame changes. Tout le monde fiche
le camp." With this salty expression she looked with special
firmness at Blanco. A sister appeared with the clothes Claire
had worn when she came out from Paris, including her time-
worn black dress which looked even shabbier as clothes always
do when one isn't wearing them.

A half an hour later the landau was going at a trot down
the road toward the Porte d'Orléans. Claire was still a little
giddy from the champagne and feeling quite cheerful, although half asleep. Her right hand, still in its bandage, rested
on a pillow donated for her comfort by the clinic. On the floor
of the landau was a little pot of coals like a Venetian scaldino
to keep her feet warm. It was dark—she wasn't sure of the
hour but it seemed to be early evening—and the elegant brass
lamps on either side of the landau were illuminated. The
streetlamps floated by like disembodied heads, the landau
lurched along smoothly on its rubber tires, the signs of shops
drifted past the window, a baker, a locksmith, a cobbler's. Where
were they? She recognized the Boulevard Raspail, then the
cemetery where poor Paul was buried, the green patch of the
Square des Ménages, and the Rue du Bac. They seemed to
have passed Rue de Vaugirard where they ought to have
turned. What had Hermine said? Something about going the
long way around. They were somewhere in the Faubourg St.-

Germain; it was certainly not the way to Rue François-Villon.

The landau drew up before a house in a street she didn't recognize. It was a narrow street of town houses, each with its polished brass door plate and its pair of lamps beside the entry. The cabman got down and opened the door of the landau.

"What's this?" she said faintly. "Why are we coming here? Why don't we go home?"

"This is home, Maman. We moved while you were in the clinic. This is our new apartment."

With Blanco and Hermine helping her, one at each elbow, she was lowered to the pavement and guided across the sidewalk to the door. The cabman followed behind with her valise. Inside was a hall with onyx walls and electric bulbs gleaming in little alcoves. She was spirited up a staircase, Hermine and Blanco still at her elbows, and through another door. Blanco gave the cabman something folded tight in his hand that evidently pleased him greatly.

Lamps glowed softly on tables and buffets, illuminating strange massive pieces of furniture. Boris, who for some reason was wearing a red bow instead of a collar, barked twice and then stood panting at her, his button eyes sparkling. There in a doorway was Mme Lacrosse done up in black alpaca with a white apron, and from behind her came the smell of cooking. It was one of those dreams in which all the figures of your waking life appear but in costume and transformed into other roles, your old aunt a witch, the tobacconist at the corner the King of Prussia, as though they were playing parts in a grotesque drama. Even a dog identical to Boris was set down on the stage to mock her with his resemblance to the Boris of real life.

"What is this? What have you done? Blanco, take me home. I don't like this. Hermine! Where are you?" Hermine had strayed away into another room.

"Now Claire, you don't want to live down there by the slaughterhouse. It was picturesque, perhaps, but not very suitable. I never saw anyone in that neighborhood that I'd care to know. It's too far out of town, and the apartment you had was dingy."

"But we're comfortable there. We've always lived there."

"Well, you don't anymore. You live here."

She felt faint and sat down on an Empire side chair covered in dove-colored velvet. "I can't afford it."

"As for the expense, and I was sure you'd get to that point, I've paid for it all, but don't worry, you can pay me back if you like. I've had a talk with your banker. He tells me you've got lots of money. You keep putting it in the bank but you never take any out."

"My banker?"

"Well, he's my banker too. He's become quite a good friend of mine. He and I have a talk now and then and he's full of praise for you."

"He talks to you about me? Blanco, I don't care for this prying and probing into my private life. Take me home now. I don't care for this place."

Hermine appeared, still with a guilty look on her face which she dissimulated as best she could. She lifted Claire up from the velvet chair. "Here's your room, Maman," she said smoothly. "Blanco can't take you home to Rue François-Villon because we don't live there anymore. The furniture is gone and all our things are here."

Claire found her meager collection of clothes in a wardrobe in her new room. They didn't fill a tenth of it. The furniture was all in a heavy Empire style that Blanco seemed to favor, dark mahogany with inlays of ivory and ebony.

"In architecture," said Blanco, "I prefer the eighteenth century, but the furniture isn't very practical. It's too spindly and fragile for everyday use. This furniture is right out of Balzac. You can imagine César Birotteau sitting in one of those chairs."

"Where's my furniture?"

"It's all been sold. Maman, you can't believe how Blanco and I had to rush around doing all these things to surprise you."

"Sold?"

"Aren't these lovely linens?"

"Linens?"

"Maman, why do you repeat the last word of everything I say? Are you afflicted with echolalia? See how nice they are."

She showed her mother the bed linens, lilac-colored damask

with lace on the pillowslips. Claire thought of the old bed-sheets that she and Paul had bought when they were married. As far as she could remember they had never bought any others. When they began to wear out, she cut them apart and sewed them together again sides-to-center.

"I don't care for this, Hermine. We must go home now." Even though she had heard Hermine telling her that the furniture was gone from their old apartment, in her deepest mind she refused to believe this and told herself that if she went on speaking as if it hadn't happened, the furniture would come back into place and everything would be as it had been before. She knew now that she was deeply attached to the shabby apartment where she and Paul had lived when they were first married, where Hermine had been born, where Lancelot had come to tell her that Paul was dying. She recalled every detail of it with a piercing clarity, even to the brass lion's paw at the end of the lavoratory chain and the coppery taste of the water from the kitchen tap. But the memory wavered now like a photograph seen underwater; she had to close her eyes to capture it at all.

She ran her fingers one last time over the damask. The scent of lilac clung heavily in the air; it was almost oppressive. Without a word she went back into the salon with Hermine trailing after her.

Blanco was on his hands and knees by the fireplace, laying a fire of newspapers, kindling, and coal. He accomplished this without getting a smudge on his immaculate white suit. In only a few minutes the flames were licking up and the coal was making a snapping noise.

"In our old place, it was always I who laid the fire." As soon as she said this she realized that she had spoken of the apartment in Rue François-Villon for the first time in the past tense. It diminished rapidly in her thoughts. She saw it now as a set of empty rooms, tawdry and worn, a place where she had once lived.

"Come and lie down, Maman. You're tired. You should rest a little before dinner."

* * *

After dinner was over and Blanco had gone, Claire went into her new room and shut the door. A pair of lamps glowed softly on the dressing table, and Mme Lacrosse had turned the bed down while they were still at dinner. She felt as though she were in a hotel, a strange and luxurious one in a foreign city. And yet her own clothes were in the wardrobe, her daughter was in another room, and Mme Lacrosse, transformed from concièrge to housekeeper, was rattling pots and turning water off and on in the kitchen. Lying on the bed with her bandaged hand on her chest, she communed with her dead husband. Oh Paul what shall I do. Here is this American who follows me about, giving me apartments and making me drink champagne. He claims he loves me but he does nothing about it. And there is Lancelot who is also difficult. He wishes to use glowstone to blow up cities. I believe he loves me too but he doesn't know it himself. I don't wish to have suitors, what am I to do with them. Even though I was crushed with grief when I lost you, I thought it would be easier being a widow, since there would be only one person and it wouldn't be so complex, but it's like a one-legged man walking a tightwire. And Paul, a rat bit me and I've been sick. I'm not used to being sick. Please tell me what to do.

Many times she had spoken like this to Paul, but now he wouldn't come out of the shadows at the bottom of the room where he was hiding, watching her but silent. Even he seemed sinister now. That was what it meant to be dead, the dead were sinister. Among the phantoms that beset me, how can I find my friends, she wondered. And yet she had many; she was admired by all, the workers at the Institute were loyal to her, she commanded the respect of Lancelot and her daughter loved her dearly. (She blundered on over the question of whether this was true, that all daughters loved their mothers dearly.) She even had suitors. But that was not really so. She would not have allowed such a thing, out of respect for the memory of Paul. And yet she had told Paul it was so, and so it must be true.

At that point, as she lay on the bed in the half-lighted room, she had an extraordinary revelation about herself. The idea occurred to her that there must be something about her that exerted a powerful attraction on the opposite sex, even though this had never struck her before and it seemed unlikely on the face of it. Her whole life had turned around these men who had abruptly singled her out from the others and treated her specially, dropped everything else to concern themselves with her: first Professor Desiato in her schooldays, then dear old Puisson-Lepuy at the Sorbonne, then Paul himself. And then of course Lancelot and Blanco. She examined herself in the private mirror of her mind trying to discover what extraordinary quality, previously unknown to her, could account for this. She remembered that her mother had been a famous beauty. She was left to conclude, somewhat unwillingly, that she must be beautiful. She had never before seriously considered this.

She got up from the bed, feeling a little prick of mortality from the half-healed hand, and sat at the dressing table in the subdued glow of the lamps on either side. She looked at the image in the mirror. It was startlingly clear; even in the lamplight she saw every line of her face, every turn of eyelid and nostril, every detail of the faint down on her cheeks, as these things might be seen in the most expensive of microscopes. With her scientist's mind she puzzled out why this was so, why it was that she was seeing her own face as though for the first time, as though previously she had seen it only through a fog or veil that blurred the details and cast a pall of gray over everything. After a few moments of thought she realized that it was because she had never possessed a good mirror before in her life. The one in Rue François-Villon was splotched and dim, and the one in the lavatory of the Institute was worse. Now she saw the image of a woman who was almost a stranger to her: an elongated face made more striking through the pallor of sickness, the bun of dark hair that contrasted sharply with her paleness, and yet was reflected in the dark eyes with their gleam of penetrating intelligence, of questioning intelligence, at the corners. She imagined this face being looked upon by a man, not just any man, but a man of sensitivity and austerity, of character, of calm and refined insight, a man who

floated just out of reach in her secret thoughts, her half-dreams,
a man who was Paul and was not Paul, who was not sinister as
Paul was now that he was dead, but who was alive and watching her, about to speak. As for the image in the glass, it was
silent and grave, yet something at the edges of the lips made
it seem as though it was about to smile at any moment.

"Comme tu es belle," she murmured to herself in the light
and singsong French she had learned as a child in Belgium.

Hermine no longer took the omnibus to the University; she
could walk to her lectures at the Faculty of Sciences in ten
minutes, down the Boulevard St.-Germain and across the Luxembourg Gardens. Her way took her past the pond where,
later in the day, children watched over by their nurses would
play with toy boats. Now, in the morning, the pond was a deserted gray disk with only a shimmer of breeze wrinkling it at
the edges. On the other side of the gardens, where she came
out onto the Boulevard St.-Michel, was the kiosk of the man
who sold crêpes. She had never bought a crêpe from him and
her parents had never bought her one when she was a child,
even though she had been coming to the Luxembourg all her
life and all the other parents bought them for their children.
She had never had a toy boat to launch in the pond either.
She gave the kiosk a fleeting glance as she went by, then stopped
and turned. She had never before looked at the thing clearly.
It was a small octagonal wooden building, painted green,
something like an illustration for a children's book. She stepped
up to the counter, with a timid but determined smile, and said,
"A crêpe."

"Normal?" he shouted. He was a hairy man wearing only
blue cotton pants and a singlet, even though it was a cold December day.

"Normal."

"We also have jam."

"No jam."

"Or with chestnut cream. Very good."

"Normal."

"Very well, Mademoiselle."

Fixing her with a basilisk stare instead of looking at what he was doing, he poured some batter onto his smoking-hot griddle from a ladle. Then, seizing a wooden paddle (he still hadn't taken his eyes from her and could evidently do all this blindfolded), he spread it around skillfully until it formed a circle as large as a tea tray, bubbling and browning at the edges. After only a few seconds (my eyes bore into you, Mademoiselle, I see your most secret thoughts) he lifted the edge with his paddle, seized the half-liquid disk with both hands, and flopped it dexterously over onto the other side. The top was a delicious-looking filigree of brown on a background of beige. Another few seconds and he whipped the crêpe into the air, not even bothering to use the paddle this time and snatching it from the griddle with his bare fingers. Flopping it onto a wooden board, he applied melted butter from a can and sprinkled it with sugar. Then he folded it up like a napkin in a restaurant, so rapidly that the eye could hardly follow his motions. The whole business had taken less than a minute. He handed her the crêpe wrapped in a paper and she gave him twenty centimes. He folded his arms and stared at her as if to see what she was going to do with it, eat it, put it in her pocket, or feed it to the ducks on the pond.

Nibbling at the edges and holding it so the butter wouldn't drip, she went on toward the Sorbonne. It was delicious. The batter was toasted to a golden brown in a pattern of intricate tracery; it was crisp on the surface and slightly rubbery underneath, and it had the savor of things that are hot and freshly fried. Because of the way it was folded, as she bit into it her teeth went through several layers of the papery substance separated by butter and sugar. The sugar was sweet and gritty and the butter soaked through onto her fingers. She thought that she had never had anything so good. She knew now why her parents had denied her this heavenly sensory indulgence, which surely ought not to be permitted to any mere mortal.

"Mademoiselle is privileged," said Professor Souteran as she entered the lecture hall still eating the last of it. "Ordinarily

185

we don't eat crêpes in the august halls of the Sorbonne. May we all have a bite?"

"Pardon, Professor. I didn't have time to have breakfast, because my mother isn't well and I have to take care of her."

"Ah, your sainted mother. My excuses, Mademoiselle Savarin. The rest of you," he told them, "all bear witness that we have not caused Mademoiselle to go hungry during the illness of her mother, and that we have waived the rule that one doesn't bring food into the Sorbonne by allowing her to eat a crêpe during the lecture on the characteristics of organic molecules."

Hermine was embarrassed, and also appalled to think that the arrangements of her private life had been brought to the attention of three hundred students. Still the crêpe was good. She had noticed something about her fate in the world that was previously unknown to her, that she was able to sin without being punished for it.

And can we really believe this—not that Hermine ate a crêpe in the lecture hall, but that she connived with Blanco, whom she had first seen as an enemy in the drama of her life, to despoil her mother's home and callously sell her furniture, while she lay sick in a clinic, and remove her clothes and her most personal possessions to a perfectly strange apartment in another part of the city? What could possess a well-brought-up young lady to behave in such a rude, a cynical, an unfilial way, and in a series of actions that brought her into daily intimacy with a man twice her age, who was unmarried and lived in a hotel, and a foreigner to boot?

Hermine could hardly believe it herself. Blanco's notion had been something of a shock when he first proposed it. But in the end she fell in with his plans. In spite of his native courtesy and good manners, he was a person of a metallic inflexibility when it was a question of something he wanted to do. His will was even stronger than her mother's, though it wouldn't have seemed so at first. So how could she, a mere girl, without experience of the world, her character still tentative and unformed like a half-baked crêpe, possibly stand up to him? And besides (all this was a dialogue she conducted with herself, an elaborate exercise in self-justification), his plans had a certain logic to them, for she had known all of her life that the apartment in Rue François-Villon was shabby and out-of-the-way, and that her family could afford better. And then, for some reason it was harder to say no to a man wearing white than a man wearing black. Possibly this was because he had white ideas rather than black ideas, thought Hermine, allowing this purely literary conceit to dominate her practical thinking. She had no difficulty at all in resisting Carlo and Lancelot, whose clothing was somber and whose designs on her were sinister (assuming that Lancelot was able to design in his sleep). And her mother didn't really seem to object to the new apartment. Or rather, she seemed to object, but she didn't really object. In time she would come to see that it was all for the best, that the new apartment was nicer, that Blanco was a noble gentleman motivated only by altruism and a clairvoyant insight into what was best for everyone. Dear Maman! It was all for her good. She was aware in a part of her mind at least that Blanco had designs on her mother, but they were white designs that corresponded to his clothing. Hermine had never met anyone who was so obviously a walking symbol, an assembly of abstractions, in addition to being a real flesh-and-blood person. His knighthood was indicated by his argent hair, his alabaster brow, his genial and elaborate courtesy, and his armor was his shining white clothing. So reasoned Hermine. Perhaps she was a little in love with him. Perhaps she herself had designs on him; white designs of course.

What is my opinion of all this? I have no opinion. Hermine was still a very young girl, as she herself knew, and she used this as an excuse for her own self-indulgence. I believe I know her better than anybody, and yet I myself only half understand her, the Hermine of eighteen that is. (No, I am not ready to reveal myself yet). Like all young girls, she was a medley of tragedies and butterflies, of solemn virtue and the most depraved of reveries, of timidity and sporadic impulses to flaunt her superiorities, her wit and keen intelligence, her sly ermine beauty, before the whole astounded world, which could only fall at her feet and concede her all the privileges she so imperiously demanded. We have all been young girls, or else young men; presumably their impulses and confusions are more or less the same, like the turning inside-out of a glove. (This is how Hermine at the age of eighteen imagined the male anatomy.)

The fact is that my knowledge of my subject is imperfect, because I am at least partly making up this story as I report it. I can tell you that Hermine bought a crêpe in the Luxembourg Gardens, but I don't really know how it tasted or the precise kind of joy it brought her. Here I start creating a fiction. No matter if I have eaten the crêpe myself; as soon as I start telling you about it, it becomes a story and not a crêpe. I tell you how crêpes *ought* to taste, and perhaps do in the real world, but if they do I have forgotten it, the taste buds in the mouth have no memory, we can only reconstruct the sensation by imagining crêpe, butter, and sugar and then combining them together in the mouth of our recollection. And so it is with everything; Proust's madeleine, Joyce's cake of soap, the curds that were inside Don Quixote's helmet so that when he squashed them onto his head he thought they were his brains. Cervantes never did that to himself, and if he did he soon forgot it, and remembered only the story he told himself about it; and told the others also; and so he became a great author. I am not a great author, and I tell you frankly that I don't know a hill of beans (to use Blanco's expression) about what went on in Hermine's mind at the age of eighteen, but I have a pretty good idea of what to tell you about it. So you'll have to put up with me. (I slip behind a classic column before you catch a glimpse of who I am.) Storyteller and reader, we play chase and tag. I am still chasing Hermine, and in a moment I will let you know what I find.

Here she is in a dialogue with her dear Maman. She has come home from the Sorbonne but has not told her she has eaten a crêpe or been subjected to the irony of Professor Souteran.

"Maman, how is your poor finger?"

"Oh, my poor finger. How are your studies coming at the university? I'm sure you don't apply yourself enough."

"We can't all be like you, Maman."

"Like me! What nonsense. At your age I was a perfectly ordinary girl. There was nothing in the least remarkable about me. Then I met your father and he transformed me. It is he who deserves the credit for anything I've achieved, even in the years since he is gone. He invented me, just as he invented glowstone. I wouldn't have existed without his love and his teaching, without his example of character. Hermine," she went on by a connection that took place effortlessly in her own mind, "do you have any young men?"

"Have any young men?" she repeated innocently, playing for a time. "How could I have any young men, Maman?"

"I mean, aren't there other students at the Sorbonne, or—" she couldn't imagine anywhere else Hermine would go, so it would have to be the Sorbonne—"who seem particularly friendly, or who speak to you after the lectures, or who invite you—" But that was impossible too because Hermine never went to cafés.

"Of course, there is Carlo, Maman."

"Oh, Carlo. What a fool. Do you know, Hermine, what I think about Carlo?"

"What, Maman?"

"He's very romantic, like all Italians, but his romanticism is hopelessly mixed up with his ambitions. He wants to win the love of a beautiful woman, and he wants to become an important person in science, but he's lazy and wants to do both these things in a single stroke. Do you know what I think, Hermine? He would like to marry you, and then when I'm no longer here he would be the director of the Institute."

"Exactly what I think myself, Maman."

VII

Claire's bank was in Rue Castiglione, near Place Vendôme. She went there once a month to take care of her financial affairs, which she knew very little about, preferring to leave them in the hands of her personal banker M. Géricault. This, of course, was the perfidious banker who had revealed all her secrets to Blanco. She did know that she had two accounts, one in her own name and one in the name of the Institute. There was a lot of money in both of these accounts, and as she thought about it she was puzzled what to do with it. Even after she had paid Blanco back for the apartment the sum in her own account was astronomical. It wasn't like the old days when she and Paul had worked in the dingy and cramped laboratory at the Theosophical Society and were always short of money. M. Géricault said she should invest it in territorial bonds or British consols. She didn't know what either of these things were. What would Paul do about the money? It was the question she always asked herself when she had a decision to make. Probably exactly what he had done when he was alive, ignore it and devote himself to the scientific work of the laboratory, going about in threadbare old clothing. If there was enough money to buy new equipment, or pay a little more to the assistants, he did so, otherwise they went without.

It was a gray and piercingly cold March day about three months after she got out of the clinic. Having finished her business at the bank, she set off down the sidewalk. But out of absentmindedness, or moved by some demon, she turned the wrong way, toward Place Vendôme instead of back to the omnibus stop in Rue de Rivoli.

She had never before been in this square even though it was one of the most famous in Paris. It was not a part of the city where she had any reason to come. There was Napoleon on his column, and across the square was the Ritz. She paused before the window of Cartier's, wondering why people wanted to possess these hard and glittering bits of mineral which had no merit other than that they were very expensive. A necklace cost enough to run the Institute for a year, and a diamond ring as much as a spectroscope. And a diamond was only a scrap of igneous carbon. A mad idea seized her: to go in and buy the ring, take it to another shop and sell it, and use the money to buy Delvaux another spectroscope. Was she going out of her wits? She was perfectly well now; her hand was healed and she had no fever, although she hadn't regained the weight she lost at the time of her sickness. Dr. Simon reproached her for having mislaid a great many red corpuscles and not being able to find them again. She had lost so many things when she moved to the new apartment. Perhaps she had left them in Rue François-Villon.

She passed on from Cartier's to a hatter, a furrier, a glover. The last shop before the end of the square was small with a front of white-enameled boiserie. The windows were silvered on the inside and reflected back only the column in the square and the elegant hotel behind it. On the door, which was also of silvered glass, there were two words:

Collaveri
Modes

GLOWSTONE

She pushed open the door and went in. From the rear the middle-aged modiste came forward with a little smile. Claire ignored her and looked around the room. The shop was shrewdly designed. On the sidewalk outside the mirrored glass reflected the viewer's present clothing, in Claire's case her old paletot and plain black dress, in the grayish light of the winter day. Inside the lighting was pink and the eye was caressed with a hundred springtime hues. Brocades, satins, ribbons, and egret feathers were in fashion. The dresses in the room—which were of course only models and possibilities, anything could be made to order—were displayed on headless wicker mannikins. She found herself staring at a gown of wine-colored satin with fine needlework on the shoulders. Looking closer, she saw that the needlework was actually eyelet embroidery through which the bare skin of the shoulders and bosom could be seen. She felt a warmth spreading into her face. She had known there were such dresses, she had even seen women wearing them in the streets of Paris, but for some reason it had never really struck her that they were for sale in shops, that anyone could walk in from the street and buy one.

Another dress caught her eye, more practical and suited for her age: a mauve moiré afternoon dress, perfectly plain except for frills on the bodice which were really for modesty rather than decoration, narrow at the waist, with a long skirt which caught the light in the swirls of its almost invisible pattern. It was fastened at the throat with a brooch of violet amethyst, a stone exactly the color of the glass vessels in the laboratory that had been tinted by the effects of glowstone.

Amethyst, she knew, was a perfectly ordinary mineral, a variety of quartz which owed its color to the presence of manganese. But this scientific thought was only an effort of her mind to suppress the swell of covetousness that rose in her blood. The desire she felt to possess the dress and brooch made her feel a little faint. Was it possible that a responsible and eminent scientist could be tempted by a piece of violet glass on a dress? She broke away from the modiste's smile and hurried out the door, leaving behind her this trivial summons to an unworthy and superficial pleasure. Outside in the square,

this time she turned in the right direction, toward the omnibus stop.

   In the apartment in Rue de Bellechasse she wandered around
listlessly doing the things that people do when they come home
to a house after being out. She patted Boris and tried to calm
his joyful barking, she went into the bedroom and put away
her bank passbook, she visited the kitchen briefly to see if Mme
Lacrosse had dinner underway, and she pulled open the curtains of the salon to let in the gray afternoon light. Then, with
a glance toward the kitchen and this interloper she still wasn't
used to—she really didn't care for servants living in the same
rooms with her—she went down the passage, opened the door
at the end, entered the small white-painted cubicle and switched
on the light, closed the door, and latched it.

   She set her reticule down onto the shelf, which also had
combs, brushes, and hairpins on it. Only women lived in this
house, Claire, Hermine, and Mme Lacrosse. It was a nunnery
forbidden to men, a gynaeceum. There were no shaving brushes
or razors, no lingering odor of pipes. She felt secure and protected in this room, inviolable and at the same time remote, as
though some part of her was left outside the door when she
entered, the part that had to do with the world of men. She
didn't know whether she enjoyed this sensation or not. She
rather thought that she did.

   One of Hermine's more thoughtful acts was that when she
had moved the things out of Rue François-Villon she had
thought of the brass lion's paw on the end of the lavoratory
chain and brought it along to the new apartment. There Blanco
or someone else had fastened it to the chain of the new WC,
a splendid apparatus of white porcelain with a varnished oak
seat and an oaken tank to match on the wall above. Opposite
the WC was the varnished oak counter with a washbowl of the
same porcelain and a cake of translucent English soap in a
saucer. Above it was a shelf for one's things. There was a bronze
rod with a towel hanging from it and a vase with a single rose,
replaced daily by Mme Lacrosse. She didn't really care for this

lavatory; she was too used to the old one. But she was consoled by the fitting on the end of the chain; four times a day she clasped the lion's paw that had so often been clasped by the hand of Paul. It was a link with the past, with her memories, with the happiness of her youth and the years when Paul was still alive, a kind of little household god that had carried the protective spirit of the family from one household to another. She could not really have accepted the new apartment as her own without the brass paw.

Turning around, she hitched up her skirt and pulled down her drawers. Then she sat down. After a moment there was the plashing of a tiny silver thread, like a brook in a fairy tale. When this ended there was a final soft plop or two, as if drops had fallen from some nodding flower into a pond, and then silence. She went on sitting for some time. The light overhead cast a pattern of shadows on the walls, projections of the flutings of its glass, a kind of moiré that played on the white surface of the room and tremored imperceptibly. Moiré; she tried to remember how that word had come into her thoughts. Directly in front of her and below, her drawers were pushed down on her legs. In her field of vision she saw a pair of finely modeled white knees, each with a tiny dimple at the top. They might have been the knees of a girl. It struck her that as women age it shows chiefly in the face. There the lines of worry and laughter, the ravages of sunlight, the small sags of gravity take their daily toll. But the rest of the body was miraculously preserved as though sealed under a glass bell, or covered in transparent wax that protected it from the air. And this no one knew about, because the part of her body that remained young was precisely that part of her body that was hidden in clothing from throat to ankle.

Her arms were a darker pink and covered with speckles. And her hands—she kept them under the fold of her dress where she had it tucked up over her waist. On their backs were liver spots, and on the palms the scars of glowstone burns crisscrossed like a basket. The hands hung at the end of her arms, useful tools for functional tasks but no more a part of her than the other apparatus of the laboratory. She went on sitting for some time, spellbound by this new spectacle of her knees. She could scarcely take her eyes from them. With reluctance she stood up, pulled up the drawers, and let the skirt fall into place. She grasped the brass paw. From overhead the waters fell with a soft rushing and declined into silence.

The next day, leaving the laboratory on a pretext, she went to Place Vendôme and bought the mauve moiré dress, furtively but under the spell of a powerful and irresistible compulsion, as though she were visiting a house of assignation.

Blanco sat in the dressing room of the Folies-Bergères talking to Zoë Brooking, sitting in his usual style, straddling a reversed chair with his arms resting on the back. His hat he had set carefully on the other chair, first dusting off the light film of face powder on it. Zoë was at the table removing her makeup. The room was illuminated only with a circle of bare electric bulbs around the mirror. In their light the flesh of her shoulders and bust, through the filmy dressing gown, appeared like a strange tropical fruit, pulsing warmly where a vein appeared in her throat.

"I haven't seen you since the last time I was in Paris, but you haven't changed a bit. You seem to be immortal. All things change and pass away, the Arc de Triomphe will in time crumble and turn to dust, the sun will grow cold, but Zoë Brooking remains the same."

"I am immortal, Blanco. Besides I spend a lot of money on cosmetics."

"I'm surprised to have a moment alone with you. The last time I was in Paris this room was as full of people as the Gare St.-Lazare."

"Oh, I still have plenty of admirers. They flock about me like sharks. Can one speak of a flock of sharks? I think not." Although she was English, from long years of residence on the continent she had developed a light French accent or oddness of phrase, probably an affectation. "But I can manage them all, you know. Men are nothing to me. Only to a few do I offer the gift of my affection. When your card was brought up, I told the maid to admit nobody but you."

"The gift of your affection. You phrase yourself so delicately."

"I suppose you've come to request it again. That's the usual reason people come after the show."

"You're a terrible cynic. As a matter of fact, at the moment I'm in love with another woman."

"In love? What a strange expression. You sound like a schoolboy."

"I feel like one."

"Is she—someone like me? I mean in the theater."

"She couldn't be more different. She's a scientist. I don't know whether she'll have me. She's too grand for me, I'm afraid. Not the kind of person you'd be likely to meet."

"And you've taken a vow of chastity on account of this person?"

"I wouldn't put it that way. Surely you know what being in love is, Zoë. You must remember it from when you were a girl."

"Then why have you come to see me?" she asked with a trace of irritation.

"Just to renew old friendships. I intensely admire your dancing, as I do all forms of art. It ranks with Cézanne and the Impressionists, I would say, taking one thing with another. I wouldn't go as far as Wagner, you're still a cut below that, but you're at least the equal of Rodin."

"Oh, bother Wagner."

"Tell me something. How did you do that trick with the flower? Your partner, that ominous apache in black tights with the cap over his eyes, threw it at you and you caught it on your bosom. Then you whirled around the stage in a violent sarabande for ten minutes or so and the flower stuck in place. Is there glue on it?"

"There is not glue on it," she said, thoroughly out of sorts now. "Emmaline! A glass of water."

The maid brought the glass and Zoë angrily pulled the dressing gown down from her bust. Two perfect hemispheres of white appeared. They were twice as large as normal and protruded from her chest as though inflated. She set the glass of water on one of them, stuck out her chest, and reared her shoulders back. The glass stayed in place, leaning only a little to the front. The surface of the water sparkled with agitation. She got up from the chair, holding the dressing gown at her waist, and circled around the room in her long camel-like dance step. The glass clung to her. She had to bend her waist into a U and thrust her bosom upward, but the glass didn't fall. With a flick of the breast she projected it into the air and caught it. She flung it to the maid, who carried it quickly out of the room as if she had taken part in this performance many times.

Blanco applauded. She bowed with hauteur, and he put his arms onto the chairback again. "I'll take back what I said about Wagner. There's nothing like that in the *Götterdämmerung*. It's worth the trip across the Atlantic just to see it. Why don't you do that on the stage?"

"Because a flower is more artistic than a glass of water. Of course, the glass of water is much harder."

"Zoë, why don't we go out somewhere for a bite to eat? Get your clothes on; you've been sitting there twenty minutes before the mirror admiring yourself. I ought to warn you, though, that I'm still in love with my scientist. All I'm prepared to give you is supper."

"Give me? It is I who might give you something."

"You might, but I wouldn't take it."

Claire was having another recurrence of the Geographic Dream. It hadn't bothered her for months, since before her trip to America. In the dream she was wandering through the same unknown city, through streets that all resembled one another. But this time, instead of searching for something, she seemed to be trying to avoid something she was afraid of. Yet she had to keep wandering constantly through the streets, always in danger of stumbling across this place, because there was no place in the city to rest. The buildings were somehow always in the same style and yet different. Some had palm trees growing in front of them; beggars and cripples loitered in the doorways of others, or dubious women with veiled faces. Was she in a desert country, in Arabia? But the palms were artificial, she saw when she approached them more closely, made of wood and green paper. She asked one of the women which way to go, phrasing her question carefully in French, and found with surprise that she couldn't hear her own voice, so that she didn't know herself what she had said. The woman unveiled herself. She was very beautiful and young, and said nothing at all, she only smiled and pointed the way. Claire went on in the direction she indicated, even though she was full of dread.

She caught sight of a building she had seen before, a sort of temple with classical columns toward which all the streets seemed to converge. She knew the way better now, and avoided the curving streets that led toward it for a short distance and then turned away in another direction. She was approaching it from the rear, and now she saw that it wasn't a temple at all but a low modern building of rough-cut stone. It struck her that there were no people in the streets around it. This part of the city was deserted and lay in a region of perpetual twilight so that the buildings, the streets, and the sidewalk could be seen only indistinctly. The stone building had no windows. But as she walked around it she came to a gate leading into a courtyard, and beyond the courtyard was the entrance, a shadowy opening with no door to shut it. This was the place she had feared to find, even though her footsteps had drawn her to it with a kind of magnetism. Her clothing rose on her limbs and stretched toward the courtyard and the doorway beyond it, as though this same force was propelling her toward the dark opening.

She fled back down the street she had come on; it curved around and she found herself approaching the low stone building again. A man tapped her on the shoulder. He wasn't a complete man but only a pair of hands, a face, and two naked feet, all glowing whitely in the twilight. Perhaps he was wearing black clothing so that these were the only parts of him that showed in the semidarkness. He smiled evenly with his white lips and raised his hand to point the way. Following the glowing finger, she hurried over a bridge that crossed a river, not of water but of hurrying and huddled people in drab clothing. She woke up.

As usual she was perspiring and trembling, and excruciatingly thirsty. I must never go there again, she told herself, not knowing quite what she meant. Was it possible to will not to dream? This world of her dream was only in her mind. Couldn't she then think of some other world? Perhaps, but the one she thought of might be even worse. She knew quite clearly now what insanity was; you started thinking of things and found you had lost control of your mind, that it was endlessly inventing one thing after another that frightened you.

She blundered through the house, her eyes still heavy with sleep, in search of the kitchen. But she had forgotten it was the new house and she was no longer in Rue François-Villon, and she was lost and bewildered, just as she had been in her dream. Creeping stealthily in her bare feet she entered Mme Lacrosse's room and found the old woman staring at her with wide white eyes in the dark. She closed the door without a word and at last found the kitchen. There she drank two glasses of water, waited for a moment for it to drain into her body, and then filled and drank a third.

She turned and saw Mme Lacrosse behind her in the doorway, blinking sleepily like an owl, clad in a ghostly white nightgown that covered her from wrists to ankles.

"It's nothing, Mme Lacrosse. Go away. I had a bad dream and now I'm having a glass of water."

"A bad dream? Well it didn't really happen."

"This one did."

"Oh, Madame. In that case. Là, là."

Blanco had come to the end of his late supper with Zoë at the Ritz. It was after midnight, but the large dining room with its white paneling and crystal chandeliers was still half full. The other men in the room were in evening dress, and Blanco's white suit stood out like a searchlight. Zoë's costume was a long sheath of silver lamé that gathered around her bosom and hips in an astounding way when she turned her body. She carried a large ostrich-feather fan which she languidly passed before her face from time to time. Her helmet of dark curls came almost to her eyes, which were fixed on Blanco with a kind of brooding curiosity, an expression both predatory and philosophical.

The dishes had been cleared away and they were sitting over coffee and cognac. Ladies did not drink cognac, in public at least, but Zoë did. Heads turned at the other tables.

"Would it bother you if I smoked a cigar?"

"Oh, pas du tout, j'adore l'arôme. My sense of smell is very highly developed. Of fifty perfumes, I can tell which another woman is wearing. I often decide whether to like people or not according to how they smell. The olfactory organ is certainly the most delicate of the five, don't you think?"

"It's certainly the most primitive. We share it with the beasts of the forest, and they're even better at it than we are. I'd vote for taste myself. There are a lot more than fifty wines, but a man of refined palate can tell them apart without much trouble."

"You tell me which to drink, Blanco. They're all the same to me."

"Then too the eye is a rare organ. Imagine a human race without vision. We could probably get by for basic survival with the four other senses. But there would be no painting, no sculpture, no art. Life would hardly be worth living."

"And then there's clothes. If people couldn't see them, there wouldn't be any point in wearing them."

"Trust a woman to point that out. The ordinary theory about clothes is that we wear them for warmth, and for modesty. But women wear them for another purpose. You wear clothes because you're dissatisfied with your body."

"Me? You are absolutely wrong there, Blanco. I adore mine."

"But you want to have more than one. Clothes for a women are a way of having as many different bodies as she wants. Whenever she's bored she can transform herself into something different by changing her dress. She can become a different animal. She can be a different shape, if her gown is cut a certain way, or move with a different gait if her shoes have high heels. Is that dress you've got on real silver?"

"Of course. It's genuine lamé."

"It catches the sparkle from the chandeliers." It also caught the tiny flare from the match as he contemplatively lit his cigar; a mosaic of flame-colored pinpoints tremored over the silver and died out. "All these pretty baubles that distract us in our lives. It's hard for a man to bend his mind to important things when a woman is wearing a silver gown. Especially when it's that shape. The fine hourglass we've all seen in Gibson's drawings. I imagine, though, that the shape isn't really you but something you've got on under the gown."

"Oh Blanco, what important things could you possibly be interested in? I thought you were a thoroughgoing hedonist."

"I am when I'm in Paris. But if a man takes everything that Paris has to offer him, he doesn't have time to think. After I've been here a few months I begin to feel jaded with it all. Something comes over me as though I'm hollow inside, all body and no soul. Then I know it's time to go back to America. Out in the West there's plenty of time to think. The trouble is, there's nothing to think about."

"You're just like all Americans. When you're in Europe you want to be in America and when you're in America you want to be in Europe. It's a national disease. It's so boring, I hear it from all of you. I can assure you, I never want to be back in Peckham Rye where I came from."

"Do you remember, once before I told you about my Silver Lady."

"The one who used to come and stand by your bed when you were a child. You were probably playing with yourself."

"No I wasn't. I did that too, but not when she came. She inspired perfectly chaste thoughts."

"When men think of women, there's no such thing as a chaste thought."

He smiled. "It was just a childish reverie, a harmless hallucination. For years I almost forgot about her. Then one day I encountered her again. I was sitting in the ballroom of a hotel in Denver and she was standing with a magic lantern giving a lecture. It was the same woman, even to her silvery skin and her black dress."

"Ah, your lady scientist. You know, Blanco, I know perfectly well who she is. There's only one lady scientist in Paris. I read an article about her in the Petit Parisien. But I'm surprised that you're interested in her. She's supposed to be a bluestocking and a recluse, and no longer young."

"All those things are true. I can't account for my state of mind."

"How far have you got with her? If you don't mind my asking."

"Don't be crude, Zoë. Your vocabulary doesn't apply to this particular case. We're good friends. I see her once a week or so. She's very correct, a little distant perhaps. I'm hoping," he said, "to make a formal proposal of marriage."

"Then you haven't—"

"No, I haven't," he said shortly. He was genial on almost all subjects of conversation; she was surprised at his sharpness on this one. "This is not happening in your world, Zoë. I don't judge your world. It's just different from the one where I'm in love with Claire."

"According to the article in the Petit Parisien she has a daughter."

"Yes. A charming creature just eighteen. A student at the Sorbonne."

"Ah, I see your devious plan. You court the mother with distant respect, while you dally secretly with the daughter."

"I wouldn't dream of it. She's just a child. I'd love to be her father, but to do that I'd have to marry Claire."

"You are set on it, aren't you? Blanco, why don't you let me be your adviser in this matter. I know a great deal about these things. I can practically guarantee your success if you do exactly as I say."

"You know a great deal, but I don't think you've known many women like Claire."

"They're all alike. The Colonel's lady and Julie O'Grady."

"Poppycock." Still he smiled.

"First of all you must ply her with small gifts: flowers, chocolates, jewels."

"Oh Zoë. This is the woman who discovered glowstone."

"Do as I say. But consistently. Something from you should arrive at her door every day."

"I've already done that. Except for jewels. I don't think she'd accept jewels."

"Send her a diamond anonymously through the post. She won't drop it in the poubelle, I can assure you."

"I believe she might. I'm sure she wouldn't accept clothes either. Now, if you were the lady in question, I'd buy you some pretty lingerie."

"And ask me to model it. Everybody does that. With me you'd have to be more original. But we're talking about your lady scientist. When you come to the end of buying gifts, try taking her on outings in the country. Picnics by the Seine are good. Or if you have a friend in the country, get him to invite the two of you, for the weekend if possible. Bicycles are also excellent."

"Bicycles?"

"Dear Blanco, in this country, Cupid no longer has a bow and arrow, he runs a bicycle shop. They're all the rage just now. You can hire them in the Bois, or in the park at St.-Cloud. They seem innocent enough, but they stimulate a woman's soul in a place she is hardly aware of. It's the friction, you see. Of course they don't realize it themselves. Try it and you'll find it's a marvel. I know any number of men who have succeeded in this way when all else failed."

"Have you tried it yourself?"

"No, my rear is too big to fit on those little seats. Do as I say and I'll guarantee results. In the open air, things happen that don't in the salon."

It was early spring now and Claire had been coming with Boris to the Luxembourg Gardens since November. When she came home from the Institute in the afternoon, earlier than she had before her trip to America, she changed into her moiré gown and a mauve hat with a net veil and a purple artificial flower. The amethyst brooch at her throat made a striking effect against her pale silvery complexion. When Boris had done his business in the corner of the bushes, she departed in the direction of the Odéon and Rue de Tournon. She never spoke to anyone and never smiled, although Boris, as he passed people, panted brightly and pulled at his leash in the hope of being petted.

This new behavior of hers was strange even to her, when she thought about it. From a scientist in a black dress she had become a lady walking her dog in the gardens. And of course you needed a proper costume to do this, and not a dress in which you might be taken for a concièrge or somebody's aunt from the country. She had assumed a double identity; part of the time she was a scientist, and at other times she was a lady in a mauve dress walking her dog in the gardens.

It was true that Hermine had taken Boris for his walk when she was in the clinic, and could do it even now, but Boris preferred to go with her, she was sure, and wouldn't perform his duties properly for anyone else. And that would make him ill. So she reasoned, in this new part of her mind she had recently discovered that was particularly good at rationalizing her actions that began as purely irrational. In other words she first found that she wanted to do something, and then this part of her mind cleverly generated reasons why this was the proper or reasonable thing to do. She was not really shocked at this new development in her, because she recognized that this was the way most people's minds worked. She was just becoming more like other people, that was all. Occasionally she even found herself the victim of a vulgarity that she knew had lain in her soul all along and was perhaps a universal human trait. If it was, why not recognize it? When Boris hesitated in the bushes, scratching the ground and turning around to sniff at twigs and beetles, she told him affectionately, "Shit, little beast." In saying this, even softly to Boris when there was no one around to hear, she felt akin to the great mass of humanity in a way she had never felt before. She had always seen herself as special and set apart, cut off from the normal happy life of the ignorant and vulgar, privileged to a special bliss and knowledge when Paul was alive, and after his death afflicted with a private suffering that was hers alone. Now she recognized herself as a human being like the others, and felt an odd and warm sense of kinship with them. Boris generally did as she ordered, with a bright-eyed air of achievement that led him to hop up and down afterwards like a mechanical toy. At this she picked him up from the ground and hugged him. Boris was very fond of her; she was sure he liked her better than anyone else on earth and that his affection for her would never flag or tire. Of how many beings in the world could one be sure of that? Only Paul, and he was gone forever. She had to recognize that in a certain sense Boris was a surrogate for her dead husband. Even this idea didn't shock her. Of course, she was in total command of Boris and the creature had to do everything she told him. This only caused her to love him the more.

"What a lovely amethyst, Maman."

"Do you like it? It was left to me by my mother."

"But I've never seen it before."

"No, you haven't. It wasn't really left to me by my mother. I lied to you, and mothers are entitled to lie to their daughters if they see fit. It's none of your business where I got the brooch. Perhaps an admirer gave it to me."

"It was Blanco."

"No, you're too clever by half, it wasn't Blanco. Perhaps my mother did leave it to me. She was a famous beauty in Brussels, you know. She had lots of jewels, she went to balls with ambassadors and generals; she was a very grand lady. I can show you her portrait; there's a miniature in my drawer."

"I've seen it. Maman, your new dress is beautiful, but I need a new dress myself. All I have is my old polka-dot blouse and a black skirt, and my linen summer dress. And no proper coat, only the old velvet manteau I've had since I was a child. Now that we're rich—"

"What on earth do you mean by that?"

"Now that we live in Rue de Bellechasse."

"We are not rich. I felt at the time it was a mistake to move to Rue de Bellechasse, and now you see why. Because we live in the Faubourg St.-Germain you want a new dress. We're still the same people we were before, Hermine. Why do you want a new dress anyhow? Are men paying attention to you? You ought to think about your studies at the University and not about men. When I was your age I didn't even have a velvet manteau. In the winter I went about in a cape I made myself out of an old blanket."

"But if your mother in Brussels had jewels and went to balls, why did you have to go about in an old blanket?"

"I preferred it that way. I felt myself more a scientist; I was dedicated to my calling. I've paid Blanco back for the apartment. And that has left us even less rich than we were before. We are not bourgeois, Hermine, remember that. We are dedicated people, I as a scientist and you to your studies which are training you to be a scientist. We must consecrate ourselves to these things and not be distracted by the vanities of the world. Sometimes when I think of our old place in Rue François-Villon, the apartment where you were born and where Paul and I were happy, I could almost weep. The only solace is in work, Hermine."

"Why do you need a new dress, Maman?"

Toward the end of April a crew came to make a motion picture of the work of the Institute, to be shown in the newly opened Pathé projection salon in Paris and in other cities. They set up their cameras all over the laboratory, interfering with everyone's work during the week they were filming. They kept turning their klieg lights off and on, dazzling everyone when they were on and leaving them half-blinded for some time after they turned them off. They smoked cigarettes and left them burning on the workbenches, they shouted technical orders and jokes to one another over the heads of the scientists, and their director, Jules Chapin, continually interrupted Claire to ask what she was doing and whether she couldn't do it at a different angle so it would show better in the pictures. A good deal was known now about the effects of glowstone emanations on photographic film, and the magazines of the cameras were carefully shielded with lead plates. Claire lost her temper several times, Lancelot had to ask the cameramen not to make so much noise and not to bother the laboratory workers, and

Délicienne Maedl was stricken with an attack of anemia and stayed home for several days taking iron tonic until the cameramen were gone.

About two weeks after the filming the camera crew came back, to show the results to the laboratory staff and ask questions about what people were doing in the pictures they had taken so they could write captions for them. Claire, who almost never went out in the evening, had never seen a motion picture, although the shows in the projection salon in Montmartre were the talk of Paris. At one end of the laboratory the technicians hung up a screen, and at the other end they set up the projector, another goggle-eyed monster like the cameras, with cables leading to it for the arc lamp. M. Chapin asked for the shutters to be closed and the room darkened.

There was a click and an electric whir, and a few dots of light danced on the screen. Suddenly Claire found herself looking at a wavery image of Carlo Bini fastening a rat to a board, opening its abdomen with a scalpel, and inserting a tiny aluminum bead under the skin. He turned and smiled weakly at the camera, his face pallid, his eyes like black flowers. Then he jerkily turned back to his rat and pointed at something with his scalpel, his lips moving wordlessly.

"A technician inserts glowstone samples into a laboratory animal," suggested Chapin.

"A scientist," said Carlo.

"All right."

The student assistants piled bags of ore on the floor of the refining room with rapid motions, and Onyx Fabre, in the absence of Délicienne, stirred the caldrons like a sorcerer in a fairy tale. A Delvaux made out of snow and coal gesticulated toward his spectroscope, pointing out with a pencil the electrodes, the collimator, the diffraction grating, the camera which recorded the spectral lines. Chapin took down the explanations that each of them gave him.

Then abruptly an unsettling ghost appeared on the screen. Claire had seen herself in photographs and she had seen her reflection in mirrors. But the motions we follow in mirrors are our own motions, as we can verify by moving an arm or winking and seeing the reflection repeat the same gesture in reverse. Here was a Claire that was not herself and moved of its own volition, according to its own jerky and oversimplified laws. She stared at the blank white face, the inky hair, the gleam of teeth that caught a ray of light, the flash of an eye. The motions of the figure were purely mechanical; it had no soul. It jerkily held up a vial, measured the length of the precipitate that had gathered at the bottom, and replaced it in the rack. Entering the measurement in the log, it swiftly did the same with another vial, and a third. She had the impression that she was looking at a parody of herself, an animated Mme Tussaud's figure with waxen eyes and an unconvincing smile.

Chapin asked, "What is it exactly that you're doing, Madame?"

She found herself unable to answer. Another voice said, "These are samples from fractional crystallization. She's measuring the precipitate to see the degree of concentration that has been achieved."

"Too much for a caption. Madame Savarin-Decker measuring samples of glowstone."

"Claire, I didn't know you handled the samples with your fingers," said Lancelot. "You ought to be more careful. The tongs are right there on the bench."

Claire still said nothing. The scenes changed abruptly, but all these final pictures were of her. Going into the refining room, she pointed to the students to show them where to stack the bags of ore. She sat in her office working on her accounts, her glasses on the end of her nose. In the last scene the camera had caught her against a window as she examined samples of milkweed plants in the botanical room. The light, coming from behind, left her face in shadow except at the edges, where a silver line fluttered to mark her profile as she moved. Seen in this way her face had an extraordinary beauty. All the marks of the years, the lines of sorrow and fatigue, were invisible. The face limned in light might have been that of a young girl. Blanco had said that he fell in love with her in the ballroom in Denver when he saw her profile in the light of the magic lantern. His Silver Lady. The figure on the screen was jerky and mechanical; only in silhouette, rimmed with fire, did its beauty spring out like a forgotten relic of youth. She remembered something she had read in school in Brussels and forgotten for years, a fragment from a medieval saint: *If you feel yourself glow with love like an ember, I say that you are in great danger, for who can tell the glow of God from that of the Adversary?* The Sisters told her that this referred to excessive religious fervor, which in young girls is often confused with their awakening womanhood.

It was about a week later. Claire, in front of a shop at the edge of the park at St.-Cloud, was being taught by Blanco how to ride a bicycle. Cautiously she allowed herself to be put on the machine, which now seemed a very odd one, although she had seen hundreds like it before with other people riding them. The wheels were narrow and their spokes gleamed like rays of light. One's rear was held up by a seat that was exactly its shape in reverse, as though it were made from a mold of it. Down below were some platforms to put your feet on, but if you bent to look at them you were in danger of falling over.

The proprietor of the shop steadied her at one elbow and Blanco at the other. They pushed her for a short distance, then let her go. She wobbled away down the gravel path, but soon took control and mastered the thing. She had excellent coordination, and her training in physics enabled her to grasp the principle of its balance without much trouble. Of course, it is not really by grasping a principle that you learn to ride a bicycle, but by an instinct so primeval that it goes back to the ape swaying on a branch. Off she went down the path, in her mauve dress and hat with its purple flower, and turned and came back toward the shop. She even managed to stop successfully, putting down her foot at the right time. Rather belatedly, she was being introduced to the world of automatic reflexes, of unthinking and instinctively correct action, the world in which our bodies tell our minds what to do instead of the other way around.

If one thought about it, in fact, it seemed impossible for the bicycle to stay upright. The wheels were too thin, the handlebar was too wobbly, and the human body on the seat was too large to be properly balanced on the spidery machine that supported it. You might dream of riding a bicycle and having it stay upright, but it was unlikely in everyday life. This narrow machine had a consciousness of its own, it was only necessary to surrender to its design, its fine mathematical qualities, in order to soar along the path so effortlessly that it did seem like something in a dream. She also noted that the bicycle was the only machine divided into sexes. The female ones had no bar between the legs, otherwise she couldn't have got on hers in her lilac dress, and they had a netting over the rear wheel so riders wouldn't catch their skirts in the spokes. Hers had a bell operated with the thumb, and Blanco's a horn that squawked like a miniature of Roland's oliphant at Roncevalles. He demonstrated it, quite solemn, and she smiled.

They set off through the park along an avenue lined with elms with a pond in the distance. Blanco's bicycle had a basket on the back with lunch in it and two umbrellas sticking out. It was a mild still day with fluffy clouds floating overhead and a buzz of lazy bees from the grass. They turned off on a country lane through the small village of Garches, where a dog ran after them barking until Blanco yelled at it so savagely that she herself almost fell off her bicycle. The dog slunk away. From Garches the way continued along a narrow path through a meadow, past a pond called the Étang de St. Cucufa. She began laughing at that, and Blanco pedaled along behind her yelling, "Cucufa! Cucufa! Saint Cucufa, pray for us now and in the hour of our deaths!"

As they rode along the path they called to each other over the short distance that separated them; their voices echoed from the trees in the still air.

"I'm getting the hang of it."

"You're enjoying yourself."

"A bicycle is enjoyable. I'm still afraid of falling off, though."

"A friend of mine says that if you want to court a lady you should ask her to go bicycling. She says," he called from a few yards behind her, "it warms their souls. That's why I'm doing this."

"A friend of mine," she shouted back, "—it's Onyx Fabre,

the handyman at the Institute—once went on a bicycle tour of the Cévennes." She remembered how happy Onyx had been as he left, and how she had wondered why anyone would want to leave the work in the laboratory merely to go on a bicycle trip. "That would be a nice holiday, wouldn't it? After I got a great deal better. Just vagabonding through the mountains and stopping at night—" Then she blushed, realizing that she was proposing that the two of them should go off and—what?— stay overnight in inns, or camp in tents beside their bicycles.

"Watch where you're going, there's a puddle in the path."

She was anxious not to fall into the puddle in her new mauve dress. How cautious she had become of her clothes, and how vain! She scarcely recognized herself these days, and some- times felt that she must have gone benignly mad. Still, it would be a shame to spoil her new dress. She felt herself thoroughly a woman, as she seldom had before.

"Where *are* we going, Blanco?"

"We're almost there."

They passed through the small town of La-Celle-St.-Cloud and were in the country again. They came out onto an un- paved road and followed it down a hill, and ahead Claire caught a glimpse of the Seine, a long silver snake winding through a valley dotted with villages and small towns. On the hill she dropped behind and applied the brakes so she wouldn't ac- quire too much speed. Ahead she saw Blanco's hat floating down through sunlight and shadow as he passed under the shade of the trees. He stopped to wait for her in a cluster of houses at the bottom of the hill.

It was a village with two hotels on the quay facing the river, houses perched above on the green hill, and an island oppo- site where barges were loading sand. There was a café on the quay with a green front and old-fashioned diamond-paned windows, and a small terrasse enclosed by a hedge. It was a pretty little riverside town. There were no stands to hold up the bicycles and Blanco thrust them into the hedge.

She looked around with a gradual sense of recognition. "Why, this is—"

"What?"

"This is Bougival."

"Yes it is. I come here now and then to watch the artists painting the river. Some well-known pictures were done here. Corot, Meissonier, Renoir."

"I used to come here once when . . ."

"When what?"

"Never mind." There was the promenade where she and Paul had walked hand in hand, there was the inn where they had spent their honeymoon (it was called the Hôtel-Restaurant Pignon, she had forgotten the name), and this café with its white tables and wicker chairs was the one where they had come with Hermine for ice-cream. The white wicker chairs were comfortable. She felt quite fatigued and it was good just to sit. She was forty now, she reminded herself, an age when she ought to forget about things like riding bicycles and having suitors.

They ate the lunch that Blanco had brought along in the basket, and the patronne brought out tea for Claire and a glass of red wine for Blanco. Sitting at the small shabby white table scratched with knife cuts, Claire found herself feeling very odd. It was not the first time she had been here with a man; she had come here long ago with one with whom she was deeply in love. Now she was in the same place again. She looked around at the front of the café with its green sign, at the red-faced patronne in her apron, in hope of recalling these sensations that had been so vivid to her at the time. All that has happened to me is only memory, she thought. If I forget, everything in the past will not have happened. I must not forget, I must set these things up on the shelf of my memory and look at them every day, otherwise they will die.

"It would have been interesting if you could have met Paul. I wonder what you would have thought of him."

He was not at all surprised that she embarked on this subject without any preparation. "Oh, I've found out a little about him."

"You have? How?"

"There are a good many things written about him. He was a famous man, after all. In a secondhand bookstore I found a copy of the speech he made at the Royal Academy when he was awarded the Gold Medal in London. It's unbelievable. In one place he says that the glowstone he discovered is the most important invention since fire, and in another place he says that he himself is not important and that we should all humble ourselves before science."

"Oh, there's more. When we got back to Paris he compared himself to Jesus Christ."

"As a joke?"

"No. He smiled but it wasn't really a joke. He bore the Stigmata, on his hands and his side. His body was scarred from the effects of the glowstone he carried in his pocket. One might even say his death was a martyrdom. He was exhausted that day and preoccupied with the problems of his research, and this was why he didn't pay attention as he was crossing the street."

"One might say he was a martyr. Another might say that he was out of his mind."

"Do not ever say a word against Paul, my dear Blanco, if you want to be my friend."

"I wouldn't dream of it. He was a saint of science, and so are you."

"Saint Cucufa. Are you mocking me, Blanco?"

"I'm the farthest thing in the world from mocking you. How can I convince you of the enormous degree of my admiration for you? My respect? Shall I fall on my knees before you? Shall I offer you all my worldly goods?"

"Don't bother. You might ask them to bring me some more tea."

"I was about to ask you to marry me."

"You forget that I am already married, Blanco."

"He is up in Heaven looking down on you?"

"There is no Heaven. I am faithful to him. He was my whole life, and I don't ask for any other life apart from him."

"Let me tell you something, Claire. Paul Savarin was mad, and your devotion to him too is a form of madness."

"Blanco!"

"You can get up and ride off on your bicycle if you want.

Paris is that way." He pointed. "But there are some things I want to tell you, and if you stay I'm going to say them."

She remained where she was, her face warm with anger, staring at him fixedly. She was trembling in every limb.

He went on, "I've made a certain study of this man you were married to. I did so because you are very important to me, and I wanted to find out all I could about him. Madness is simply an inability to see life as a whole, in its full roundness and complexity, to see only the one small part of it that obsesses you. He led a life solely devoted to science. He made the choice to do so, and I believe he knew what he was doing. But when he did this he denied everything in himself that was human."

"I forbid you to say that! You know nothing at all about him."

"I've found that on his deathbed, instead of sending his final farewells to his child, he inquired what had been done that morning in the laboratory. He was a saint, I concede that. But saints and martyrs are mad. That's why we respect and revere them, because they have chosen their sainthood over life. The world is very full of things, Claire. It holds infinite possibilities of happiness for all of us. He chose martyrdom and self-denial."

"Paul denied himself so that the rest of mankind should be happy and free from pain." She was close to tears.

"Do you really think that's true, Claire? Suppose he had discovered in the course of his work that glowstone was of no use to mankind, or was a danger to it. Do you think he would have abandoned his research? Or would he have gone on, because it was the work itself that obsessed him, rather than any benefits it might have for mankind?"

She was silent.

"He made this choice for himself. But he didn't make it for you. You'll have to choose."

"You mean between you and Paul?"

"No. Between the ghost of Paul, and life."

The air outside the café was perfectly still. Claire was sitting facing the river and Blanco had his back to it. Through the veil of moisture that dimmed her eyes, so that the world appeared with a thin and watery clarity, she looked down the terrace to the river. Coming upstream on the Seine, along the curve to the left, was a four-man racing scull, a curious insect with eight legs that dipped into the water in even cadence, leaving each time eight dimples which spread out rapidly and dissolved, and between them a knife edge of a wake sparkling with tiny bubbles. It seemed to her that on this spring day on the Seine she had entered a striking new world in which boats were no longer boats but insects, and insects no longer insects but a kind of people with odd legs. She felt herself bewildered by this new world of the metaphor, of the transformation of the commonplace. In science, things were what they were. But in poetry, in art, things were constantly ambiguous and variable, kaleidoscopic. Bugs changed into people, girls into roses, or time into waves plashing on a beach. And it was Blanco who had injected these showy toys into her life, taking her to the Louvre, quoting Verlaine, introducing her to the bicycle which now seemed to her a metaphor of coitus so complicated that only an inventor of Satanic ingenuity could have contrived it.

Blanco saw her looking past him to something on the river. He turned his head and saw the racing scull almost disappearing now around the bend toward Chatou. When he looked at her again she had the impression that he saw into her mind and knew these odd thoughts of hers. The smile on his face was one of detached and amused sympathy, the expression of someone watching a child opening a gift. She began to wonder whether these bright distractions he held before her were real or some kind of diabolical fiction, an illusion designed to enchant her and lead her to damnation. She knew now what he offered her, and what he himself represented: the fierce desirability of the world.

She said, "It's like some strange kind of water bug."

"In America we call it a Daddy Long-Legs."

She laughed at him. "That's a good name for you."

"I don't expect to be anybody's Daddy."

VIII

The Silva e Costas. Who were the Silva e Costas exactly? Well, Blanco explained, they lived on the Île St.-Louis, that little island-enclave in the Seine where all those old Bourbons and Bonapartists hated each other so cordially, and on Sundays they were in the custom of opening their house to interesting people of various sorts, artists, intellectuals, and musicians. A curator of the Louvre came there sometimes, and a poet whose name he had forgotten.

"The name is very odd."

"They're Portuguese. Or not Portuguese exactly. They're Goans. Two quite respectable ladies, who have a good deal of money and amuse themselves by patronizing the arts."

"I'm not sure what a Goan is."

"Goa is a Portuguese colony on the coast of India. The combination of the two races produces interesting architecture, Catholic liturgy, and genetic permutations in people. Goans, at least the ones I've known, combine the spirituality of the East with the fine passions of the Mediterraneans. The Silva e

217

Costa sisters are worth cultivating, if only for the people they collect in their house. I've been wanting you and Hermine to meet them for some time. Here you are in Paris, full of interesting people, and you never go out."

"We've never cared to. How do you happen to know these people?"

"Through an artist friend of mine. He lives in the country, but when he was in town once a few years ago he took me. Once you've been taken there by somebody else, you can come yourself afterwards whenever you want."

It sounded like a high-class bordello, Claire thought, little as she knew about such things. Finally a day was fixed, a Sunday in May. Blanco insisted that Carlo should come along too—Hermine's fiancé as he called him playfully. Hermine became icy at this expression, and Carlo declined the offer to go along with them in their cab. He would come by his own means, he said. He could easily walk. It wasn't far. Probably he was still afraid they would find out about the shabby boardinghouse where he lived in Rue Monge.

Claire was uncertain whether she should buy a new dress or not. Who were these grand Silva e Costas anyhow, that they should vaunt themselves on running a salon as though they were living in the time of Voltaire? In the end she wore her lilac dress with the amethyst at the throat. Hermine put on a new midnight-blue gown with lace cuffs she had persuaded her mother to buy her, and threw over it the old black manteau she had had ever since she was a child. She discovered some scent her mother had hidden in her dressing room and applied a little to her elbows and the backs of her ears. If Claire noticed she said nothing.

Blanco came around for them in a cab, in his usual white suit and hat, which served for all purposes from bicycling to eighteenth-century salons. Claire's left hand was bandaged because of an old ulcer that refused to heal.

"I hope it isn't the same one you had to go to the clinic for?"

"No, that was the right hand and this is the left, please don't bother yourself about it, Blanco."

He helped her into the cab and she settled back into the cushions with a sigh. Probably she was still a little tired from the bicycle ride, over a week ago. And today, even though it was Sunday, she had gone to the Institute in the morning to work on her accounts and stayed until almost two, coming home just in time to take Boris for his walk.

The Silva e Costa house on the Quai d'Orléans was a queer narrow thing, five stories high but only two rooms wide, like a guillotine, and the small door at the bottom was the opening where you put your head. There was a vestibule where their coats were taken by a footman, then they went up a staircase into a room with Murano chandeliers, furniture in Louis XV style, and an old-fashioned Hammerklavier that must have dated from the time of Beethoven. Even though the salon extended from wall to wall it seemed too small for the twenty or so people who buzzed and chattered in it. The Silva e Costa sisters were a pair of old ladies the color of morocco leather: a Mme Hickman, who had this name because she had once been married to an American, and her elder sister who was simply called Ma Tante; it was not clear whose aunt she was because there was no visible niece. Mme Hickman was a dried-up little thing in a caste mark and sari, and seemed half-crazy, or frightened by something or other into total hebetude. It was impossible to tell which language she spoke, if any. As for Ma Tante, she spoke French and English in alternation, and Portuguese to her sister. She had her affliction too, some kind of nervous disease that caused her face to tremble from side to side, and gave her the air of eternally denying what the other person was saying to her. You are the famous scientist Madame Savarin-Decker? Nay nay. You are her daughter Hermine? Nay nay. And dear Blanco of course is an old friend. Nay nay.

A footman thrust a tray of champagne at them, and another came around with caviar, smoked salmon, and English biscuits. Because Claire didn't feel quite well she sipped only a little of the champagne. Carlo joined them; he had arrived early, not knowing that when an affair was announced for three one ought to come at four, and had wandered like a lost soul through the deserted salon until the other guests began to arrive.

With the bug-eyed and silent Mme Hickman beside her, Ma

Tante began to interrogate Claire. And the conversation went like this.

"We are honored to have you among us, Madame Savarin-Decker." (Nay nay). "Our little group gathers on Sundays, usually the same people. Everyone who comes is eminent in some way. What we will not tolerate is the ordinary or mediocre. Thus, after consideration, we have decided to ask you to join us."

"Usually I work on Sundays. I don't have much time for social life."

"I have read about your work. My sister and I are avid readers and we read everything that is printed. I believe that you experiment with elements."

"All scientists work with elements," said Claire, who didn't know whether to be annoyed or amused at this combination of condescension and ignorance. She decided to be amused. She attempted to conceal her bandaged hand, which seemed ugly and out of place in this gathering. Like all bandages, it had become a little soiled, probably in the cab journey across the city.

This only caused Ma Tante to stare directly at the bandaged hand. Without commenting on it she said, "Explain to me what exactly is the work that you do with elements."

Claire began to explain, while the tremor said nay to her every word. "The element we work with is glowstone. My husband and I first proved its existence, at a time when the scientific world declared there were no new elements to be discovered. Since then, we have conducted experiments on glowstone and its possible uses in medicine, agriculture, and industry."

"Does your work involve electromagnetic waves?"

"Electromagnetic waves? I wouldn't say that. The emanations given off by glowstone are similar in some ways to electromagnetic waves, but not the same."

"I ask because there was once in this house a man who declared that he could tell through electromagnetic waves what people were doing in other rooms."

Ma Tante immediately launched into the history of her niece

who had made the terrible mistake of falling in love with a scientist. A Swede he was, and a man whose specialty was performing experiments in balloons. He had taken Luisa, for that was the niece's name, off in a balloon to discover the North Pole, and that was the last that was ever heard of them. Luisa was talented, she had a lovely singing voice, and she might have become a famous opera diva. But instead she sailed off in a balloon from Dane Island, near Spitzbergen, never to be seen again. And this was why Mlle Silva e Costa, which was presumably her name, was called Ma Tante. Mme Hickman showed no emotion at this story and hardly seemed to take an interest in it, although this niece must have been her daughter. Ma Tante was not at all insane or demented, as it might have appeared. All this had really happened a dozen or so years ago. Hermine had heard of this strange story because an American had written a book about it.

"And why she went away," said Ma Tante, "with that madman of a Swede, I shall never know."

Hermine imagined the niece singing arias from *Rigoletto* while the balloon sank into the icy wastes where she and her scientist lover were to freeze to death. Carlo, who had heard of this story too, said, "It is quite feasible to reach the North Pole in a free balloon. The prevailing winds—"

"Feasible but not wise," Ma Tante interrupted him. "Who are you anyhow?"

"Monsieur Bini is an associate in our work at the Institute."

"Is he eminent?"

"He is quite eminent as a younger scientist."

"Also, he is Hermine's fiancé," said Blanco.

"He is not! He is not! I wish you would stop saying that."

"Du calme, du calme! Such vehemence is not necessary, Mademoiselle. I am not accustomed to having people raising their voices in my salon."

"How would you like it, Blanco, if I went about saying you were Maman's fiancé?"

"I'd be delighted."

"This whole conversation has taken an unseemly turn," said Claire. "Let's talk about something else."

221

At this point Mme Hickman spoke for the first time. "You have wound your finger," she told Claire in English.

"No, it isn't my finger, it is my hand, and I haven't wounded it, only burned it a little. In the laboratory we sometimes work with hazardous materials."

"Poor you."

Nay nay, said the tremor. "However," said Ma Tante in her audible person, "will you all please take something. There is plenty of champagne, and there is a small collation. Nothing elaborate. Only what we are accustomed to on our Sundays."

"So moan few may," said Mme Hickman.

After a while, Hermine was able to puzzle out that she was calling attention to the saumon fumé which the footman was offering them on a tray. Mme Hickman took several pieces of it herself on the little English crackers, stuffed one in her mouth, and cleverly arranged the others along a fold of her sari, perhaps an ethnic custom. As she chewed little fragments of crackers appeared at the corners of her mouth. Evidently her sin was gluttony, a harmless enough one under the circumstances.

"And," promised Ma Tante, "there is to be music."

Champagne was passed around freely by the footman assisted by a maid. Against her better judgment Claire took another glass from the tray. She thought it might serve as a tonic; she was a little weak and shaky. Some of the guests were unmistakably eminent. Blanco pointed out Henri Rousseau, the fashionable painter who had once been a customs inspector; one of his visionary jungles peopled with dream-tigers hung on the wall of the salon. There was Lugné-Poe the director of the Théâtre de l'Oeuvre, the first to produce Ibsen and Strindberg, and the Greek poet Jean Moréas who had been coming to the Silva e Costas for years. There was even a minor cabinet minister, who had something to do with roads and bridges and whose name was Chavaillon. Moréas, a sallow little man with a mustache, recited a poem in a shaky voice marked with the accent of his native Greek. Coming as it did through the mustache, and the accent, hardly anyone made anything out of it. The music consisted of a soprano who sang

French art songs and a trifle or two by Fauré, and a gentleman who sang Lieder in a powerful bass voice:

"Ich, ein tolles Kind, ich singe
Jetzo in der Dunkelheit;
Klingt das Lied auch nicht ergötzlich,
Hat's mich doch von Angst befreit."

The accompanist was a vigorous young man wearing the formal frock coat that was no longer quite fashionable since the turn of the century. While Hermine leaned over the old German piano and hummed to his Chopin—for he also played solos when nobody was singing—he conceived a fancy for her blue satin dress and asked her if it wasn't true that she too sang. Oh, not at all, she said. I can hardly believe that is true, he told her. And he playfully coaxed from the keys a few notes of a song that everyone knew, the one about going to the woods to cut laurels. Hermine only hummed to it at first, and then joined in as he began the verse for the second time:

"Nous n'irons plus au bois,
Les lauriers sont coupés.
La belle que voilà
Ira les ramasser.
Entrez dans la danse,
Voyez comme on danse,
Sautez, dansez,
Embrassez qui vous voudrez."

She had a small thin voice, not at all professional, but precise in pitch and not without a certain charm. When she came for the second time to the refrain, We'll to the Bois no more, she caught Carlo's eye and smiled mischievously at him; he reddened and turned the other way. She went on through the verses of the simple song, and before she had reached the end everyone in the room had stopped talking to listen to her.

As the last note died away there was a shriek like that of a wounded animal. Every eye turned from Hermine to Mme Hickman, who had seized the edge of her sari and was biting

it fiercely while tears coursed down her cheeks. She released
the cloth from her mouth and wailed again, an inarticulate
keening, not of pain but of wild and uncontrollable grief. It
might have been because this childish round leaves a little touch
of melancholy in every French heart, but she was not French;
it might have been because its author, Fabre d'Eglantine, died
tragically on the scaffold during the Terror, but it was not this
either.

"But it's idiotic," said Ma Tante. "Stop that now and get up.
It's nothing," she told the others, "it's an old song that her
daughter used to sing."

"Luisa," said Mme Hickman from the floor. She had composed herself somewhat by this time. She got up, wiped her
eyes with the edge of her sari, and came to Hermine and folded
her in her arms.

"She takes you for her daughter," said Ma Tante placidly.
"She has not been entirely right since those tragic days."

Hermine disengaged herself with difficulty. The front of her
dress was damp with tears. She patted the old lady and consoled her as best she could. Should she tell her that she was
not her daughter Luisa, the frozen singer of the arctic? Or
should she encourage her in her delusion, a harmless one which
would probably soon pass away?

But Mme Hickman, over Hermine's shoulder, caught sight
of Blanco. Still sniffing, she went to him and threaded her
arm through his. She hardly came to his elbow; she was half
as tall as he was. She led him to a kind of ottoman or footstool
and motioned that he should stand exactly next to it. When
he had done this, she climbed onto the thing, not something
easy to do in a sari, which brought her face almost to his level.
Then she wound her arms tenderly around him and kissed
him on the mouth. All this without a word. Blanco looked
around at the others and grinned. Mme Hickman came down
from the ottoman, put her arm through his elbow again, and
led him away to the orchid room, a kind of hothouse on a
balcony extending out from the house. The door closed and
they disappeared.

Ma Tante sighed. "Blanco is the first American who has been
in this house for forty years. There have been only two. The

other was her husband, that villain Hickman. He had a hat just like Blanco's, although it was not white. This is no doubt what has confused her."

"Someone should go in and bring them out," murmured Claire.

Nay nay, said the tremor. "The other one, the first one, ran off with my sister and married her without my approval. He deserted her shortly after he had planted a child in her. Probably he left because he found he would never have a penny of our money, which all belongs to me. It is as though a curse of Americans has lain across our family."

"I don't see what Americans have got to do with it."

"My poor sister is in the orchid room with another one at the moment."

It seemed to Claire that Ma Tante's concern was misplaced. This old half-Indian woman, she was sure, was not as crazy as she seemed. Blanco was by far the handsomest man in the room, and she had him alone with the door shut, in a warm place full of flowers.

"But what are they doing in there?"

"Oh, she won't do anything that any other woman wouldn't do with a man she believes to be her husband." Ma Tante seemed to take pleasure at Claire's evident discomfiture. She was certainly a malicious old woman. Nay nay, said her tremor, Blanco will come to no harm. It was her poor sister who was in peril from this confusion of Americans.

As for Hermine, she was intrigued with the whole scene. The two sisters might be mad, or malicious, but she was powerfully drawn to their pale coffee skins and their glossy raven-wing hair. She found them entrancing. The Sunday salon was the first real party, the first adult party, she had ever attended in her life. She was still floating in a daze from the attentions of the pianist in his frock coat and the applause that had greeted her song.

"Attention if you please," said Ma Tante. "The noted terpsichorean, Mademoiselle Zoë Brooking, will favor us with a sample of her art."

Claire had caught a glimpse of the red dress earlier at the other end of the room. Now the dancer came forward through the cluster of politely clapping guests. As for the dress, there was no mistake, it was the same satin gown with openwork on the bodice that the modiste had shown her in Place Vendôme. Reluctantly she took her eyes from the door of the orchid room and focused them on the wearer of the dress, a tall English-woman with abundant dark hair and hips that swelled like a cello.

The piano started up and Zoë struck a pose. The guests at first left her with only a small space for her dance. But they quickly drew back when her giraffe-like steps swung her first to one side and then to the other. Her way of dancing was not so much dancing as a way of elaborate strutting, a demonstra-tion of the varieties of sensuality. The narrowness of the skirt contributed to the effect. She bent her knees and waist and then glided across the floor with a motion that confined itself to the parts of her legs below the knees; her hips and thighs only writhed without contributing very much to the forward motion.

By this time Claire had had several glasses of champagne. An unworthy thought struck her: she was glad that Blanco wasn't present to watch this spectacle. He might be in a worse place, in the orchid room with that mad old Goan woman, but at least it saved the two of them from the embarrassment of watching this unsuitable dance together. Sipping her cham-pagne, she caught another glimpse of the dance through the rim of the goblet, which gave it a blurred and fractured, ef-fervescent quality that made it seem less real.

Blanco appeared at her elbow and said, "Your glass is empty. Allow me to refill it for you." He took it away and brought it back brimming, so full that she had to sip a little in order not to spill it. She was standing facing the dancer to whom his back was turned. She shifted around a little to keep him in this position, hoping that he wouldn't notice the gyrations which were becoming more and more orgiastic as the dance moved to its climax.

When she had drained off half the goblet she said, "I'm seriously annoyed with you, Blanco."

"Why on earth?"

"You went off into the orchid room with that crazy woman and stayed for twenty minutes."

"Now Claire, really. I was just trying to console the old lady a bit and bring her back to her senses. She's a funny old thing. She thought I was her husband. Old Wild Bill Hickman. Good heavens, he's been dead since the seventies."

"You know who he is?"

"Oh yes, everybody talked about him when I was a boy. He was always a little crazy. They said he went off to Paris and married a colored lady. I didn't know at the time it was a wealthy Goan with a town house on the Île Saint-Louis. He's a legend of the West. After he came back to America he was the last white man to be killed fighting the Indians."

"And she thinks Hermine is her daughter."

"Yes, that makes me Hermine's father. That probably accounts for at least a part of my fascination for her."

"Blanco, you have been very bad. I don't know how soon I shall forgive you."

"You know, Claire, a person would think you were jealous of me. Although that could hardly be, since I mean nothing to you whatsoever."

"It's not a question of whether you mean something to me. I wouldn't treat my little dog the way you treat me, going out and leaving him for somebody else in the middle of a crowd of strangers."

"I must say that I'm encouraged by this. Here we are having a lover's spat and we're not even lovers."

She opened her mouth to tell him with some sarcasm what she thought of this, and at that moment Zoë's dance came to an end. Amid the polite clatter of applause she bowed so deeply that her bosom seemed about to burst from the gown.

Blanco turned to applaud with the others. "I see you've been enjoying the performance of my friend Zoë. You know, she's the star of the Folies-Bergères."

"Your friend?"

"Oh yes. I've known her for years. As a matter of fact I arranged with the Silva e Costas for Zoë to come here today, because she's very anxious to meet you."

"To meet me?"

"She admires you tremendously. She wants to ask you something about costumes too. She isn't much of a dancer but she's certainly shapely, isn't she? There's a good French expression for it: Il y a du monde au balcon."

"A crowd on the balcony?"

Claire didn't know whether to be indignant or amused at this vulgarity, and at the news that she was admired by a star of the Folies-Bergères. Her head was giddy from the champagne. Everything in the room swam a little; the colored gowns of the women were a kaleidoscope amid which the black coats of the men moved like shadows. She looked around for a place to put down the goblet, which was still half full.

"Mademoiselle Brooking," said Blanco. "Madame Savarin-Decker. I imagine," he said, "that you'll soon be calling each other Zoë and Claire."

"How do you do," said Claire in English, not wishing to be rude. She felt a curious sensation as she examined the satin dress at closer range. Zoë's flesh appeared in tiny white points in the openwork of the bodice. This was a dress she had disapproved of and yet coveted in her secret heart. Oddly enough this led her to feel a sisterly link with Zoë. If she couldn't wear the red dress, then a surrogate could wear it for her. She was aware that she wouldn't be having all these thoughts if she didn't feel so giddy. She looked around again for a place to set the champagne goblet, found none, and drained off the rest of its contents.

"Enchanted," said Mlle Brooking. "Why *don't* you call me Zoë. Everyone does at the theater. When someone says Brooking I hardly know whom they're referring to."

"Your gown is charming."

"I must talk to you about gowns. You know, at the Folies I am celebrated for my lighting effects. I am called the Queen of Light. I have gowns that are illuminated from the inside, and a dance in which spotlights change my complexion from peach to violet as the mood of the music changes. I believe you are the inventor of glowstone?"

"My husband was the first to isolate glowstone. I was his

closest collaborator. Since his death I have carried on his work."

"And what is glowstone exactly, Madame? Pardon my ignorance."

"It's a previously unknown element, a member of the alkaline-earth group of metals, with an atomic weight of two hundred and twenty-six."

"Please. I understand nothing of these things. What does it *do*?"

"It has uses in medicine, it can be used to produce botanical mutations, and its study has taught us a great deal about the fundamental nature of matter."

"But it *does* glow."

"Of course."

"Here is my idea, Madame. I appear on the stage in my dance in which my complexion changes according to the mood of the music. There are yellow spotlights, peach spotlights, cherry spotlights, violet spotlights. Then all the spotlights dim, the footlights fade away, and the entire theater grows dark. Now I am seen only through the light of glowstone, which impregnates my costume so that it is visible in the dark. Around me float fairies, other dancers whose costumes have been impregnated with glowstone. Is this possible, Madame?"

"Are you very wealthy, Miss Brooking?"

"In friends and happiness I am very wealthy. In money, not."

"In that case you'd better not think about wearing a glowstone costume. It would cost as much as this house and everything in it. Besides, there's the problem of secondary emanations."

"Secondary emanations?"

"If a sample of glowstone is enclosed in a container, after a while the container too will give off a greenish glow, even after the glowstone is removed. It's a paler light but still detectable. If you wore your glowstone gown too often, you too might glow in the dark."

"How delightful. Another attraction for my audience."

"You may say so. I will admit that your idea is intriguing. But it isn't practical in the present stage of our research, first of all because glowstone is still very expensive, and second because we have no idea how to impregnate a theatrical costume with it."

Blanco had disappeared during this exchange and now he returned. This time he had comandeered a whole tray of champagne from the footman. The goblets were seized by many hands. Claire had never before in her life drunk too much wine, and she found the sensation troubling and yet in some way darkly intriguing. The perceptions of things about her were quite novel. She herself seemed to swim through the world, weightless, like a rare tropical fish or an airship. What did it matter so much if she couldn't see things clearly in the room and was uncertain of her footing when she moved? Blanco would take her home in a cab, and even if she did fall she could be set upright again. She took a goblet with the others and drained off half of it in a single long sip.

After Zoë's dance had ended everyone had begun chattering until the buzz that filled the room was deafening. You had to raise your voice to be heard above it. Ma Tante silenced everyone with a clap. "Dansez, dansez tout le monde," she commanded them.

The pianist began a Strauss waltz and a few couples moved out into the cleared space by the piano. Blanco swung Claire around for a few turns, but she was too giddy and had to be led to a chair. Hermine danced with Carlo, then with Blanco, then with Moréas the Greek poet, who held her delicately in his fingers as though she were a vase that might break. He murmured in her ear in his limpid Greek accent, "Vous chantez merveilleusement, Mademoiselle."

"Oh non, je ne chante pas du tout."

"Mais si, vous chantez à merveille."

He went on to confide softly that he had an internal complaint and his kidney hurt him, still he refused to deprive himself of the pleasure of dancing with a charming young lady. He breathed her quotations from his *Cantilènes,* which being in anapestic meter could be fitted perfectly to the Viennese waltz. Hermine broke away from him, laughing, and went to look for her mother. She found her seated on a Louis XV chair at the side of the room, looking on everything with a glazed smile. She sat down next to her and took her hand. Maman turned to her with the same smile, then broke out into a laugh. "Hermine," she said, "this is all insane."

Ma Tante appeared again and clapped to stop the dancing. She turned everything off and on in the salon like a faucet. "We now have a special treat in store for us," she announced. "Miss Brooking will perform a new dance which will soon become a part of her repertory at the Folies-Bergères. It is called—how is it called again?"

"La Pierre Ardente. The Glowstone Dance," the pianist prompted her.

He sat down at the piano and broke into a music-hall turn, a popular song which he adapted deftly to Zoë's needs. Zoë danced into the salon from a doorway at the side, wrapped in a flimsy peignoir she had found in Ma Tante's wardrobe, her face made up in a chalky white which caught the glow of the lamps. She first flung herself back and forth before the piano in the step she had made famous, the floating peignoir revealing a glimpse of drawers underneath. Then she stopped and sang in a mock-thrilling voice.

> "Oh, I am the Queen of the Light, tra la,
> If caressed I may ignite, tra la;
>   So beware of my charm
>   And flee with alarm
> If my visage should glow in the night, tra la."

She sashayed from one end of the piano to the other; the peignoir fluttered after her revealing flashes of white limbs. She raised her eyebrows, exposed a glimpse of breast, and swung around in an arc which made the peignoir float up to her thighs.

> "Don't embrace me, I beg,
>   Don't fondle my leg,
> Or you too will glow in the night, tra la."

Claire slumped back in the chair helpless with laughter. She had a stitch in her side. Zoë disappeared with a leap that showed her drawers for the last time. "I think I would like another glass of champagne," said Claire when she recovered herself.

When Claire woke up the next morning she was quite ill. She had a splitting headache and an enormous thirst. She felt lightly nauseated and her eyes were inflamed as though they had sand under the lids. She got out of bed, made her way painfully to the kitchen supporting herself on the furniture, brushed aside Mme Lacrosse, and drew herself a glass of water from the tap.

"Allow me to help you, Madame."

"I only want a glass of water. I feel wretched."

"Oh là là. I'll tell Mademoiselle."

"Don't do anything of the kind." She drank the tepid water in long swallows. Then she went back to her bed, pulled the covers over herself, and closed her eyes. Everything shimmered darkly and the pain in her head throbbed in little waves.

She heard Hermine enter the bedroom and stand looking at her for a moment, and then go away. Without a word she came back with a cold cloth and applied it to her mother's forehead. Claire groaned, but turned around in the bed so the cloth would stay on her brow. Hermine found another pillow, plumped it up, and put it behind her.

"Oh, I don't want to sit up."

"You'll feel better."

Hermine went off to the kitchen and Claire could hear her conferring in an undertone with Mme Lacrosse. Hermine would murmur something, and Mme Lacrosse would agree in her singsong voice. After ten minutes Hermine came back with some black coffee which she persuaded her mother to sip, little by little. Claire didn't think she could hold it down but it made her feel a little better. She opened her eyes and smiled weakly.

"I believe I may have a crise de foie."

"Oh Maman, a liver crisis exists only in France. Nobody has ever heard of it in England or anywhere else in the world.

There's nothing whatsoever wrong with you but a hangover. I'm surprised you don't know that. I'm the one who isn't supposed to know anything about drinking. You'll feel better when you get the coffee down and then you can have a little something to eat."

Claire thought that she wouldn't ever again want something to eat. In a weak voice she told Hermine that she was an ungrateful wretch and an unnatural child, because she showed no sympathy with her in her suffering. This tone of blame, this martyred air, she found astounding in herself and she could hardly believe that she was saying these things. Whatever it was, it was affecting her character as well as her body. "I only had a glass of champagne or two."

"It was a good deal more than that."

"And only because Blanco egged me on. Champagne had never touched my lips before I met him. It was an evil day when he introduced me to it. I don't think I care to see him again for a while."

And then, she remembered, there were the wines at Bignon's where Blanco had taken them to dinner later in the evening, and after that there were cordials. They had not got home until after midnight. "What could I have been thinking of," she groaned. Without realizing it she had totally accepted Hermine's explanation of her wretched state. They both agreed tacitly that she had a hangover, and no doubt Mme Lacrosse in the kitchen had been told of this theory and agreed with it completely. Claire groaned again.

But lying there with her head thudding and her stomach trying to come up her throat, she thought a little farther and reflected that she couldn't possibly feel this bad from drinking a little champagne. She hadn't felt well yesterday even before they went to the Silva e Costas. She remembered her sore hand, fished it out from under the covers, and looked at it. The bandage was even more soiled and had half come off. She pulled it off entirely; the abscess had almost healed and only a little sticky fluid oozed from her palm near the index finger. Hermine brought more gauze and sticking-plaster and helped her wrap it up again.

Finally after a half an hour she got out of bed and dressed

herself, with difficulty because of the bandaged hand. She felt a little better after her coffee but she was still weak and nauseated. She looked at herself in the mirror, and marveled to find that she looked much as she always did; this affliction of the soul, if that was what it was, hadn't affected her complexion or the soft luminosity of her eyes. Her pallor was the same as it had been for many months. She didn't get enough exercise and the close air of the laboratory was probably not good for the health. She pulled a comb through her hair, brushed it a few strokes, and then went to the WC at the end of the passage and shook the hand of the lion. Now she felt almost human; the headache was something she carried around with her, a small unwanted parcel, but she could ignore it by applying her will.

Nothing for breakfast. She would have a bite later in the laboratory perhaps. She pulled on her paletot over her black dress and started to leave the apartment. It was a little before nine; she would be an hour late at the Institute, a thing that had never happened to her before in her life. But in the vestibule, as she was putting her eyeglasses into her reticule, Hermine stopped her.

"Maman, there's something in the Figaro."

"I'm sure there's something in the Figaro. Please don't bother me about it now."

"But it's about glowstone."

Hermine showed her the paper that Mme Lacrosse had bought at the kiosk in Rue du Bac. Some girls in a factory in New England had died of necrosis of the jaw. At first it was thought that the disease was syphilitic, but no one could account for the fact that it affected only the girls who worked in this factory. Then it was found they all had the same job, painting the luminous dials on watch faces with paint containing glowstone.

"How could they get necrosis of the jaw from painting watch dials? They must have put the brushes in their mouths."

"Of course they did, Maman. According to the newspaper, they had to put them in their mouths. That's the way they pointed them."

Claire said angrily, "The more fools they. There are other ways to point brushes. The factory owner is negligent. He should be brought before the law. If glowstone is used properly, it's no danger to anyone."

"You needn't give me a lecture on the subject, Maman. You act as if I had invented the article in the paper."

"I'm not feeling well this morning. You know that. Nevertheless I am going to the Institute, and I shall work an hour later than usual, in order to make up for the hour I shall be late. I won't be home until eight or later. You'll have to take Boris for his walk. Hermine, we must never see any of these people again. These Silva e Costas, these Greek poets, these crazy artists and singers. Our life is in science. We have no business rubbing shoulders with music-hall dancers and drinking champagne. What would your father think of all this? If I'm unwell today, it's a punishment for doing something I knew I shouldn't have done, something which is bad for me and bad for all of us. We have more important things to do in the world than go to parties given by mad old Indian ladies." She realized that she had fallen into the stiff pompous tone she assumed with the laboratory staff when they weren't paying attention to their duties. She knew that Hermine was right that this was her lecturing voice, but she couldn't help herself. "We must go on with our research into the basic nature of matter, we must serve humanity through our work, we must remain devoted to the principles that were bequeathed to us by your father. There will be a different world because of what we have contributed to mankind, through our long struggles and our devotion to our principles. I'm fond of Blanco, but I must never see him again."

"Maman, those factory girls."

Claire smiled abstractedly, a little pained tightening of her mouth, and left the apartment without a word. Outside it was a few minutes after nine. In Rue du Bac the sidewalks were thronging with people and the shops were bustling. It was a bright spring morning and the sunlight slanted through the street. Claire turned into the boulevard and began the ten-minute walk to the Institute, past St.-Germain-des-Prés and the Carrefour de l'Odéon. She still didn't feel quite well. A kind of veil of darkness hung in the morning sunlight, obscuring it a little. She had a vision of the girls with rotted jaws, mouthing some message to her silently with the sun glinting from the raw bones of their skulls. "Leave me alone!" she cried aloud. A few spectators turned and stared at her curiously.

IX

But let's not forget that letter that Claire wrote to Lancelot from Denver, that Lancelot for some reason left in his unlocked desk at the Institute, and that Délicienne Maedl appropriated to herself on that night when she was working late in the laboratory and was so annoyed with everyone. It goes without saying that this unfortunate incident was partly the fault of Carlo Bini, because if Carlo had been kinder to Délicienne, if he had gone on offering her his virile male companionship, if he hadn't betrayed his affection to her in favor of another who might advance his career more effectively, then Délicienne might not have been in such an irrational and hostile frame of mind and wouldn't have behaved so dishonestly.

This letter in some way—we can't speculate over the exact details—found its way into the hands of a journalist, and not a very high-principled one. He was the editor of a miserable weekly tabloid called Le Cri des Boulevards, read mainly by housemaids, shopgirls, café waiters, and other people who were interested to know what shopgirls and café waiters were reading; in short it was read by thousands, especially when it uncovered the latest piece of interesting scandal in its long history of pandering to the lower forms of human curiosity. "Have you seen The Cry?" was a password among those who prided themselves on keeping up with the underside of Parisian life. This synesthetic paradox gave rise to a popular joke: "No, but I heard the stench."

This journalist, whose name was Pandore Tilsit, somehow got his hands on Claire's letter, and began his mischief by printing it verbatim in his miserable sheet. But he wasn't content with laying bare this confidential and intimate communication before the vulgar eyes of the world. Lest anyone should mistake what the letter was about, misled by its sentimental and abstract language, he provided a commentary in which he emphasized the key phrases, sometimes altering them a little for his purposes: "the total affection which this lady offers the companion of her work . . ." "this precious boon . . ." "the privacy of our companionship," and so on. He evoked the name of the deceased husband, the celebrated and respected scientist Dr. Paul Savarin, to underline the perfidy of the guilty couple. "Evidently Madame Savarin-Decker, distracted by the fumes which arise from the reagents she examines in her laboratory, has confused one Paul with another." Why then did she call her lover Lancelot in her letter? Precisely because, in her secret mind, she was shamed to address him with the name of the husband to whose memory she ought to have been faithful; and also, as M. Tilsit had reason to believe, for a more subtle and perverted reason: even though Lancelot was the gentleman's real name (l'appellation véridique de ce monsieur), it was also that of a knight of antiquity who had betrayed his monarch to engage in guilty embraces with the Queen. Thus it had become a code word, a counter in a playful amorous game, in the "total affection" which these two shared in the "privacy of their companionship." For the rest of the article, M. Tilsit referred to Claire as Guinevere. The irony was rather heavy but it suited the readers of The Cry. The article concluded, "The reason for milady Guinevere's abrupt trip to America, where these matters are handled with greater freedom, now become apparent. The child has been made to disappear, but the lovers forgot to destroy the letter." And it added, commenting on the words "this precious boon, this promise of salvation for the sufferings and ignorance of man," that the lady in question had not only confused one Paul with another but had apparently regarded the result of this Immaculate Conception (more irony for housemaids) as a new Messiah, for the moment no doubt hidden in the bull-rushes of Colorado. Probably it was M. Tilsit himself who had also written the headline: "Scandal at the Savarin Institute. Scientists dally and produce a new Messiah."

"Lancelot, how has this letter found its way into the hands of this scoundrel?"

"I have no idea, Claire. I have absolutely no idea."

"But where is it? Where is it now? The letter ought to have been in your possession. Was it you who gave it to this journalist?"

"Claire!"

"But where is the letter? I asked you a question."

"Up to now, I believed it to be in my desk here in the Institute."

"Go and see if it's there."

It was not. He came back and sat in her office, miserable and silent.

"But why did you keep it here, and in an unlocked desk?"

"At home, Claire, my housekeeper goes through everything. Nothing is safe from her. So I—"

"The letter was perfectly innocent. At least it was before it fell into the hands of this wretch who has twisted it all about and perverted everything in it."

Lancelot was unable to meet her eyes. It was a while before he replied. "The letter was precious to me, Claire. All your letters are. There are only a half-dozen of them. I couldn't leave them about in my apartment where the housekeeper might run across them."

"What you did was far worse." Claire was in despair. A kind

239

of nightmare had descended abruptly over her life, contaminating everything, filling her mind with torment and guilt, making it impossible for her to work. Nothing useful had been done in the laboratory all morning. Journalists from other newspapers knocked on the door and were turned away by Onyx Fabre, who was converted into a combination of her private guard and her jailer. In addition to being shamed before the world she was shamed in the eyes of her own staff.

"Claire . . ."

"Yes?" She hardly paid attention. She was vexed and annoyed with Lancelot, whose main quality, she saw now, was that he was gigantically and incurably boring. She had known for many years that there was something about him that made her sigh when she saw him coming, and at last she knew what it was. She put her head in her hands and closed her eyes.

"This scoundrel must be brought to account," he told her.

"That doesn't matter. The harm has been done now."

"I myself will write a letter . . ."

"For God's sake, Lancelot, don't write any letters."

"But if I explained the correct state of affairs to this editor, he would surely print it in his newspaper."

"Don't be naive."

"I don't know what else I could do."

"Ah, don't you. Well, you could go and slap his face."

"I?"

"No, *you* couldn't. But another man might in your circumstances."

"Dear Claire. For the life of me I don't see how I am guilty in this business. I find it deplorable, I would give my life for it not to have happened, but I don't see how I am responsible for what an unprincipled scoundrel has done with a letter he has stolen."

"For one thing, you might have bought a lock for your desk."

"Claire."

"So, in short, your ingenuity totally fails you in finding a way to defend me from this libel. Is that it?"

Lancelot looked even more miserable than ever. "Bring a lawsuit?"

"Well?"

"Claire, it would only draw more attention to this very unfortunate matter."

"Now as I understand it," said Blanco, "Lancelot in some way allowed this letter to get out of his desk—why in thunder did you write this letter anyhow, Claire?"

"I was lonely in Denver and his letter came. When I answered it I was in a sentimental mood, I suppose."

"Well, it's a very curious letter."

Claire had forgotten that after the debauch at the Silva e Costas' she had vowed never to see Blanco again. When he had knocked at the door and Mme Lacrosse had admitted him, she had sat down with him in the salon with a sense of relief, of succor, as an old friend to whom she could confide everything, even though she had known him only for a few months and Lancelot for years. It was about ten o'clock in the evening. Hermine, luckily, had stayed in the Latin Quarter for a student entertainment, and Mme Lacrosse was safely away in the kitchen.

She sighed. "It's a stupid thing. It was his letter to me, of course, that used the silly metaphor about our child, which was only glowstone. I repeated it in my letter because I thought it would please him."

"It pleased Monsieur Pandore Tilsit well enough. What does Lancelot propose to do about this?"

"Nothing, it seems. There's very little that can be done. As he points out, a lawsuit would only draw more attention to the affair. I'd have to appear in court. I'd be mobbed by journalists. It would make my life miserable for months."

"Your life is miserable anyhow. Clair, you can't allow your name to be sullied in this way. Your life has always been exemplary, when Paul was alive and in all the time after. You're the purest woman I know. These ugly and obscene words must not be allowed to stick to you."

"As Lancelot says, nothing can be done."

"He's lacking in imagination. What you need is a champion

and not a lawsuit. This whole affair has a medieval ring to it, starting with the ridiculous name of your associate. I will say one thing for that rascal Tilsit, it was clever of him to refer to you as Guinevere."

"Oh, Blanco, don't, I'm so miserable already."

"I didn't say it was correct of him, or that it was decent of him, simply that it was clever. Tilsit has made up a story about you. In this story, you've unwittingly reenacted one of the great myths from world literature. Your husband plays Arthur, who flung his sword into the lake and was borne off to the land of Avalon. After that the poets started writing a lot of dirt about the Queen and one of his knights."

"Oh Blanco, let's not talk about it."

"Probably the real Lancelot didn't have an affair with Guinevere either. The poets just made that up. You can see why Plato banished them from his Republic. But the rest of Tilsit's story is true. You are a queen, Claire. You're the Silver Lady. I've worshiped you from afar, like a knight keeping vigil under the window of his lady. Now at last I can do a little more."

"Blanco, what do you mean?"

"First of all I'll have to find out where this scoundrel Tilsit has his lair."

Blanco had a good many friends in Paris that Claire and Hermine knew nothing about. One of these was a Polish émigré named Bobrowski, a distant relative of the novelist Joseph Conrad. He had been exiled from Poland by the Russian authorities for political activity and made his living in France as a bookbinder and restorer of old manuscripts. Bobrowski was a colorful and somewhat improbable character who seemed to have strayed into the real world out of a novel of his relative Conrad, or out of James's *Princess Casamassima*. (I would explain that his given name was Paul, but it would strain the credulity of the reader to believe that there were three people by this name all in the same story.) He would have been a count if the Russians were chased out of Poland, but since he was for the moment an impoverished bookbinder he scorned to use the title. "Every Polish violin teacher in Paris claims to be a count," he said. Bobrowski, a distinguished-looking man in his forties with shaggy hair and the profile of a hawk, knew his way around thoroughly in matters of gallantry and gentlemanly honor, and had friends who would assist in the affair. He and Blanco met in an obscure café in Rue du Cygne behind the Halles, frequented late at night by porters and vegetable dealers from the markets. It was deserted at this time of day except for a few cab drivers at the other end of the room.

"I appreciate your help. You've gone and talked to Tilsit's people, you say?"

"Oh yes. His second is a decent enough chap. A reporter from his paper. One good thing about dealing with journalists is that they know how to keep things out of the papers as well as get them in."

"And where is the thing going to take place?"

"The customary place is the Bois de Vincennes. Just behind the fortress there's a spot called the Carrefour des Sabotiers. There's a little lake nearby. People have been fighting there since the eighteenth century. You can get there conveniently by cab from Avenue de Paris, and it's secluded with trees all around it."

"All this is illegal, I imagine."

"Oh, highly illegal. But the police won't go to a great deal of effort to chase you around the woods. Provided, of course, that the thing is done exactly according to the code. I have some friends who are perfectly familiar with how it's done."

"These things are done much simpler in Colorado. We don't bother so much about etiquette."

"As the injured party you have a choice of weapons."

"Oh, pistols. I'm not going to take up fencing at my time of life."

"You know, you can get scratched with a fencing foil. But when it's a question of pistols, somebody can get killed."

"That's the idea, as I understand it. Can you see to getting the pistols?"

"My friends will. But there's a great deal more to it than

that. You'll need witnesses to prepare the weapons, somebody to drop the white handkerchief, and so on. And a doctor."

"A doctor?"

"After all Blanco, we're not beasts in the jungle. This is an affair between gentlemen. The doctor is de rigueur. This thing is going to cost you a little."

"If Tilsit was a gentleman, the whole thing wouldn't be necessary. Expense is no object. I must say, I'm looking forward to this thing with a ferocious enthusiasm. I haven't felt this way since I was a boy and it was the day before Christmas."

"Don't forget, it may be you who needs the doctor," said Bobrowski.

Just at dawn four closed cabs gathered at the wooded spot by the Carrefour des Sabotiers. Following them came a two-wheeled gardener's cart with a pony, led by a man in a blue workman's smock. The cabs stopped and their occupants got out without a word. In the first were Blanco and Bobrowski. In the second were crowded three officers from the Vincennes cavalry barracks nearby; the third contained a young surgeon named Bonnard with his black bag of instruments; and in the last, at the end of the line as far as possible from Blanco's cab, were Tilsit and his second, a young journalist with a thin face, protruding eyes, and a small goatee. The cab drivers were told to go off and wait at the corner of the avenue. These two gentlemen were going to engage in some fisticuffs, and afterwards everyone would get into the cabs and go home.

It was a cold damp spring morning; the gray shape of the fortress not far away was barely visible in the mist. It had rained during the night and the ground was soaked. There was a clearing of bare ground a hundred paces or so long, with oak trees clustered around it like dim gray giants. The indistinct shapes of the seven men moved around in the mist. Blanco in his white clothing was almost invisible. Tilsit, a small man in a black coat and fedora, had a rounded nose and soft chin that made him look something like a rabbit. He was pale and a veil of sweat stood on his face in spite of the chill air. If he was going through with this at all it was because defending himself in duels was part of the role of a scandal-mongering editor. His only alternative would have been to resign his post, and he enjoyed his work as editor of Le Cri des Boulevards very much. Some parts of it were unpleasant, though. For one thing, he was nocturnal by habit and hated getting up early in the morning. He shivered, spoke a word to his second, and turned up the collar of his coat.

Of the three officers, the younger two were witnesses, with the duty of loading and inspecting the weapons. One of them carried the case containing the brace of dueling pistols, and the other a small musette with percussion caps, shot, and cleaning materials. Laying a clean cloth on the ground at the side of the clearing, they set about their duties. The third officer was a major in immaculate polished boots and a mustache, who in these circumstances bore the title of Président. He carried nothing whatsoever in his hands, wore gray gloves, and looked about him with an alert but composed air.

"Who are the combatants, sir?"

Blanco and Tilsit were pointed out to him.

"And the seconds? And the doctor?"

When he was satisfied who everybody was he fell silent again, gazing patiently into the oak trees, waiting for the two lieutenants to finish preparing the weapons.

When the pistols were ready they were set back onto the white cloth on the ground, and the Président stood next to them to be sure no one touched them. With the points of their sabers the two younger officers scratched two lines in the earth of the clearing twenty paces apart. Between them lay the neutral ground that neither combatant was allowed to invade. Behind these two lines, another forty paces back, were two other lines where Blanco and Tilsit were positioned. The two officers handed them their weapons.

Blanco inspected his pistol; it was the old-fashioned sort with a percussion cap and ball but it was in excellent condition. Barely visible in the mist a hundred paces from him was Tilsit, whose black form wavered slightly, perhaps through some effect of the atmosphere. At one side was the major in his horizon-blue uniform, holding a white handkerchief by the corner. Bobrowski and Tilsit's second stood off at the edge of the ground, parallel to their principals. The two lieutenants placed themselves on the other side by the trees, with Dr. Bonnard not far from them.

The major spoke with an elegant Parisian accent. "Now gentlemen," he called to them in a tone somewhere between a shout and an ordinary voice, "you will each maintain your place at the line where you are stationed. When I drop the hand-kerchief, you will advance at a steady pace toward the lines marking the neutral ground. After the handkerchief has been dropped, you may fire whenever you please. After the first shot has been fired, you will both continue to advance toward the line. The second combatant may also fire whenever he pleases. If you arrive at the line marking the neutral ground, you will stand there until the second shot has been fired. When this has happened, the honor of both parties will have been satisfied and the contest will be terminated. Do I make myself clear?"

Blanco nodded. The small black shape of Tilsit stirred slightly in the mist.

"If a pistol should misfire?" inquired Bobrowski.

"The pistols will not misfire."

"I object to the proceedings," said Tilsit's second, "on the grounds that the visibility is so poor that the combatants can't see each other clearly."

"If your principal, sir," said the Président, "will advance to the line of neutral ground, he will be only twenty paces from his antagonist and he will be able to see him perfectly." He didn't add, since it was obvious, that anyone who had the slightest skill with pistols could hardly miss a man at twenty paces.

"At this point, gentlemen," said the Président, "it is my duty to inform you that you may properly resolve your differences through an exchange of apologies. There is no need for use-less bloodshed. Since both parties have agreed to the contest, I assure you that it is perfectly honorable for the differences to be settled without the pistols being fired."

There was a silence.

"Do you wish to propose a reconciliation through apology?" Blanco shook his head.

The Président turned the other way. "And you, sir?" It was evident that he knew the name of neither principal. In this way, he could truthfully swear that he had no idea who the persons in question were.

"Once more I beseech you, gentlemen. It is honorable at this point to settle your dispute without bloodshed."

Tilsit could be seen murmuring something to his second over the distance that separated them. The second raised two white hands into the mist, and Tilsit shrugged. He turned back to the Président and shook his head. The two younger officers, standing a little apart from Dr. Bonnard, exchanged inaudible remarks.

"Very well. Are you ready, gentlemen?"

The two combatants nodded.

"Fix your eyes on the handkerchief. It is the official signal and not my voice." He looked from one to the other. "Attention! One! Two! Three! Advance!"

The white handkerchief fell to the ground. Blanco, holding the pistol loosely with his arm at his side, marched forward over the damp ground. Tilsit's small black figure advanced to meet him. At a hundred paces Tilsit could hardly be seen except as a small black spot like a mouse in a fog. At sixty, when the line of neutral ground was only twenty paces away, Blanco could see his opponent's white hand with the pistol clutched in it. At forty, ten paces from the line, the ominous round anus of the pistol pointed directly at him was visible.

Tilsit fired. The bullet sang past Blanco's ear and whirred off harmlessly into the misty air. Blanco permitted himself a trace of a smile. Still dangling his pistol at his hip, he marched steadily forward and stopped at the line scratched in the earth.

Tilsit stood rooted to the spot, still ten yards from the line. He turned wordlessly toward his second. The second mouthed something that was perhaps intelligible to Tilsit but not to the others. Dr. Bonnard, standing apart from the two officers at the edge of the trees, was watching the proceedings intently.

"Advance to the line, sir!" cried the Président in a ringing voice.

Tilsit started forward. His discharged pistol hung forgotten in his hand. His large rabbit eyes were fixed on Blanco. He trembled in every limb. Advancing one shuffle at a time, he at last reached the line and stood there staring at his opponent with a shudder.

Without any expression at all, Blanco pointed his pistol at the trees to the left and pulled the trigger. As the echo of the shot died away, there was a cry from the onlookers and Dr. Bonnard fell to the ground without a word.

The two officers rushed to his side. The Président followed after them at a more leisurely pace. Dr. Bonnard was quite dead, slain by a bullet that had struck him full in the eye and emerged from his skull at the back. He was far to the right of the point at which Blanco had fired, and at a considerable distance from the trees. There was a certain amount of confusion. Blanco stood where he was, still holding his discharged pistol, and Bobrowski came to him and whispered something in his ear. They both glanced toward the avenue where the cabs were waiting, and Bobrowski hurried off for their driver. Tilsit sat down on the ground and his second came up and took his empty pistol from him. He seemed dazed and hardly aware of what had happened.

One of the two lieutenants had gone to examine the trees. An expert judger of angles and trajectories, he had sized up the situation and now went to confirm his conjecture. It was as he had thought. Blanco's bullet, fired harmlessly to the side, or so he intended, had struck a nail hammered into an oak tree. There were plenty of nails in the oak trees, since people hung their picnic baskets on them to keep them from the ants. It had ricocheted directly into the eye of the unfortunate doctor.

"But that's prodigious," said the officer. "Imagine hitting the nail from that distance, and at exactly the right angle. It's like a feat of Natty Bumppo from your author Fenimore Cooper," he said, with what seemed an air of warm admiration.

"It was totally an accident," said Blanco.

Bobrowski came hurrying up with the cab. "Let's get out of this place. This whole thing is very unfortunate. Your honor is satisfied, however. For that, it only requires that your opponent should fire his pistol at you. Why didn't you stop after he fired?"

"Loaded pistols are dangerous. I thought I'd better fire it off."

"Come along quickly." They hurried toward the cab.

Tilsit, pale and shaken, was hustled away toward his cab by his second, who held him up by the elbow and murmured something in his ear. At the other side of the clearing, Dr. Bonnard's corpse was loaded into the gardener's cart which had been intended for his patient. A canvas was drawn over it, and the younger officers hurriedly drove it from the clearing with the assistance of the gardener in his blue smock. In the distance, another cab stopped and a pair of ghostly figures hurried toward the clearing in the mist.

An hour earlier that morning Claire was awakened by the sound of someone pounding on the door in the street below the apartment. There was an electric bell in the entrance but she hadn't heard it because she was sound asleep with the pillow over her head. Sleepily she went into the salon, opened the window, and looked down. In the light of the streetlamps she saw a man she didn't recognize, in a bowler and a coat with a fur collar, looking curiously foreshortened like a dwarf because she was seeing him from above.

"What is it?"

"Madame Savarin-Decker?"

"Yes."

"It's about your friend Mr. White."

"Who are you?"

"I'm nobody, Madame. I'm a journalist. Pardon me for disturbing you at this hour, but I have something to tell you about your friend."

"I don't care for journalists."

"I know all about that. I'm not from Le Cri des Boulevards. Your friend is in danger, Madame. If you wish to help him you must act quickly."

"My friend?"

"Mr. White," he repeated patiently.

"But who are you? What is your name?"

"My name isn't important. It's Charles Thouin. I've accidentally found out something about your friend. If you want to help him you must come with me immediately."

"Help him?"

"I'll explain to you on the way. Hurry, we don't have much time. I have a cab waiting."

After a moment's thought—she was almost awake now—Claire went to her room, dressed hurriedly, and threw on her black paletot. Checking quickly to see that Hermine and Mme Lacrosse were still asleep, she left the apartment. Dawn was beginning to break over the city; a gray murky light filled the street and dimmed the streetlamps. On the sidewalk before the door she found that M. Thouin was a quite decent-looking young man, well dressed, soft-spoken, and deferential. She entrusted herself to him with a sense of total helplessness. She had known that Blanco would do something decisive, perhaps something grim and masculine, about the matter of M. Tilsit and Le Cri des Boulevards, and now for the first time it began to dawn on her what it might be. A panic gripped her, a kind of terror that tightened her chest and made her heart pound as though it might do some damage to itself. M. Thouin helped her into the cab and it set off at a fast trot out of the Rue de Bellechasse and down the boulevard.

"But—I don't understand. How did you find out?"

"Cab drivers, Madame, are sometimes not discreet. Especially if a little extra money comes into their hands. They don't earn much, the poor wretches, and it's hard for them to make both ends meet. We're going to the Carrefour des Sabotiers, near the fortress in the Bois de Vincennes."

He said almost nothing during the trip across the city, and Claire too was silent in spite of the pounding of her heart. The moisture of their breathing soon frosted the windows of the cab and she could see nothing; formless white shapes and blobs of dirty light passed by the cab from time to time. She caught a glimpse of a stone balustrade and realized they had crossed the Seine at the Pont de Sully, which touched a corner of the Île St.-Louis before it continued on to the boulevard beyond. Never and never would she see those Silva e Costas again. But she had promised herself not to see Blanco again either. Why then was she hurrying toward him in this murky hour before daylight? She felt she had very little control over her emotions and understood them only imperfectly. She had never really had emotions until recently, and she didn't know how other people managed them.

"And so, Mr. White and M. Tilsit . . . ?"

"We're almost there, Madame."

They had passed the Bastille and were hurrying along the Avenue Daumesnil. "Please tell me. Has something already happened, or is it about to happen?"

"I hope we're in time to prevent these two gentlemen from carrying out their folly, Madame. I thoroughly disapprove of this sort of thing. My paper, L'Aurore, is a liberal one and opposed to these ritualized forms of violence. It's for that that I came to bring you to the scene, in the hope that you could prevent this unfortunate incident which may turn out badly."

"Men, men," despaired Claire. "Why must they be so violent and so intent on displaying their virility at every turn? All the harm in the world comes from that." Then she remembered that she herself had suggested that Lancelot should slap M. Tilsit's face. We are all guilty, men and women, she concluded still gripped in her terror. But it wasn't a question of faces being slapped now.

"I couldn't agree more."

"How is this sort of thing done? With swords?" Images passed before her inner vision; wounds, scars, disfigured faces.

"As for that, I have no idea, Madame."

He was most polite and solicitous. He understood the terrified anxiety that gripped her, and spoke only in response to her questions, or when it was necessary to explain something to her. The cab arrived at the fortress and Thouin called for the driver to continue, on around the fortress and past the monument marking the ghastly spot where the Duc d'Enghien had been shot by the order of Bonaparte at the foot of his open grave. From here a graveled avenue led away toward the little lake and the grove of oaks.

It was daylight now; a whitish pallor collected over the park and began to dissolve the mist. In the distance they could make out the shapes of the other cabs, like mysterious square black machines brought to the clearing for some sinister purpose. Their cab came to a halt and Thouin helped her out.

"Hurry, Madame."

The first of the other three cabs was already leaving the clearing. As it passed Claire saw that it was empty. They came to the clearing and hurried forward across a bloodstain on the ground. A small pale shaken man in a black fedora hat was stealing away toward the second cab, accompanied by a friend.

"That is Monsieur Pandore Tilsit, Madame," said Thouin, biting his lip.

Claire looked at Tilsit disappearing into the cab and then saw the body in the cart covered by canvas. She fell to the ground with a cry. Voices murmured around her, and Thouin helped her to her feet. Then she saw the white figure of Blanco appearing out of the mist. She fell into his arms.

X

Was Blanco arrested for his crime? No, but there was a good deal of fuss. Naturally this was a serious matter and Blanco had to lie low for a while until the whispers died away and there was no danger of some charge being brought against him. But the police in Paris, unique perhaps among all the police forces of the world, have a sense of irony, and they were perfectly willing to treat the incident at the Carrefour des Sabotiers as a banal firearm accident. Blanco's behavior made it clear that he had certainly not intended to kill M. Tilsit, and there was no question of his having intended to kill Dr. Bonnard. In any case, to be accused of the crime of deliberately setting out to murder a French doctor by ricocheting a bullet from a nearby tree was more of an honor than a disgrace. The two cavalry officers had no idea who it was they had prepared the pistols for on that fatal morning, and the major, at his own request, was soon afterwards posted off to the Lesser Antilles. He was a man of honor and he had agreed to preside at the duel out of honor; he did not consider himself responsible for the effects of an antiquated code of conduct on twentieth-century civilians. In later years he often wondered who the small rabbity man and the tall giant in white had been, but he didn't trouble himself much about them. In Guadeloupe he married a mulatto woman and had several lemonade-colored children.

After the duel there were some small legal details to be attended to, and Blanco's friend Bobrowski had a good deal of experience in this sort of thing. Dr. Bonnard's misfortune was diagnosed and certified by his colleagues as a tumor of the eye. He was buried without ceremony and the matter was forgotten, except for his widow and small child who lived in the unfashionable suburb of Villejuif. Blanco settled a generous pension on them, quite anonymously so they would never know where it came from. The whole incident was extremely unfortunate. Luckily, such affairs of honor were going out of fashion in the civilized world. Just as Mme Hickman's wild American husband was the last man to be killed in a full-fledged cavalry battle against the Indians, so Blanco was the last person to kill a man in the course of a duel of honor in Paris. If indeed it can be said that Blanco killed anyone. The official records contain no reference to the incident, and nobody else ever said much about it either. As for M. Pandore Tilsit, he went back to writing much the same sort of scurrilous scandal that he had before the affair, but at least he left Mme Savarin-Decker alone, and anyone connected with her. He retained both his editorial position and his notoriety and died only several years later as a result of eating tainted oysters at a restaurant in Rue Monge.

Claire never spoke of the duel or its unfortunate outcome to Lancelot. In fact there was some doubt that he knew it had taken place, since there was no mention of it in the newspapers and nobody else at the Institute knew about it. If he was a little mystified how the whole matter had been resolved, and why Le Cri des Boulevards had dropped such a fascinating and thrilling scandal so abruptly, he no doubt thought it better to let the matter lie where it lay. Claire never spoke to him again about the missing letter either. As she thought about it she began to have some idea how the letter might have come into M Tilsit's hands. Besides herself, there was only one member of the Institute staff who habitually worked late at night in the laboratory when no one else was present, and that was Délicienne Maedl. She had been surly and discontent for months; Claire had first noticed this when she came back from her American trip and Lancelot had pointed it out when he came to visit her in the clinic. No doubt the young Swiss woman thought she was underpaid, or should have more important duties at the Institute. Claire decided to have a talk with her, interrogate her gently and discreetly about the matter of the letter, and then suggest to her more interesting work or greater responsibilities in the laboratory.

But on the day she decided to do this, she came to the Institute in the morning and found that Délicienne had resigned. She left a letter to explain that her doctor had advised her that her work in the laboratory was not healthy and that she was going back to her native Canton de Vaud to be treated for anemia with plenty of sunshine, beef, and rich Swiss milk. There was nothing recriminatory in the tone of the letter, no hint that she had been unhappy in her work at the Institute, except perhaps for a remark that she chose to make at the end. "I have been honored by the privilege of working with my distinguished colleagues at the Institute and I respect and cherish them all. There is only one exception to this, Madame, which with great reluctance I feel I must bring to your attention. Monsieur Bini, whom I one time counted as a friend, I can no longer include in this category, since I have discovered serious flaws in his character. I have reason to know that he has not always behaved with honor to persons of the female sex, and I believe he is prone also to other forms of dishonesty. A number of months ago, chancing to come to the Institute at night, I surprised him in the act of removing a letter from Professor Lancelot's desk. When I interrogated him as to what he was doing, he was reticent and left the Institute without explaining. In the light of subsequent very unfortunate publicity in the press regarding your reputation, Madame, I thought it fitting to bring this incident to your attention."

Claire sighed and cut this part of the letter off with scissors. The rest of it she put away in her desk at the Institute.

If Délicienne was anemic, Claire was not feeling at her best these days either. She was still plagued by the old difficulty that cuts or burns on her hands were slow in healing and often became infected, and she was more and more prone to fatigue and a sense of weakness when it came to things like climbing stairs. If she had ridden from St.-Cloud to Bougival on a bicycle, and if she retained the fondest memories of this excursion, it left her tired for several days afterward and she came down with a bad cold that lasted for a week.

Worst of all, she was having difficulty with her vision now that she was getting older. Her eyes had always been excellent. For about ten years, from the time she was thirty, she had worn glasses for reading or close work but not for her ordinary duties in the laboratory. Until recently she could still read a newspaper without them. But since she had come back from America she had noticed a clouding of her vision, or a diminution of light, she didn't know what to call it, that made it difficult for her to see things clearly either at short range or in the distance. Her glasses didn't help with this. She was seeing things through a thin veil of milk, and not an optically asymmetrical barrier either, but one with wavers and oscillations in it. She had some idea what this was, but told no one of it and refused in her own mind to see a doctor about it.

These changes in her health had come about so gradually that she had hardly noticed them. It seemed to her that she had always had cuts that would not heal, a weakness when she climbed stairs, a lace curtain dancing delicately before her eyes. Now she was forced to face the truth: that she was not well, that she had not been for some time, and that she was gradually getting worse. She thought of cancer and of the general debilitation that sometimes comes with tuberculosis, of tumors of the brain or medulla oblongata that cause a weakness of the limbs and may affect the vision. But it was none of these. Although she was not a physician, she was a trained scientist and familiar with the basic physiology of the human body. It was not her mind but her will that refused to admit the real reason for her condition. If Onyx Fabre's film had been fogged, if old Bloch had quit his job because of pains in his joints, if the oxlike Délicienne had become anemic, this was their business and none of her own. The Institute was as safe as any other place where serious scientific work was done on unknown substances. She had told them all to wash their hands frequently, to handle active samples only with tongs, to discard soiled clothing, to leave the windows of the laboratory open as much as possible to admit fresh air. The others had sometimes not followed these rules. But she knew that she herself had not done so either.

No one knew what was wrong with any of them. They worked in a new and mysterious realm; they had invaded a territory of science that no one had ever set foot on before. Medicine had made use of the properties of glowstone they had discovered, but medicine had not considered the ailments that came from constant exposure to it; it had not been asked to. The vision of the American girls with rotted jaws came to her from time to time, but she banished it from her mind. Instead she fixed her thoughts rigidly onto the memory of Paul. He had said that glowstone was the elixir and light of the new century, that it would illuminate cities, kill bacilli, unlock the secrets of basic matter, and make possible the manufacture of new compounds that present science did not even suspect. She clung to that promise even as her hands bled and her limbs weakened on stairways. But Paul was no longer there to comfort her, to speak to her as he had in the months just after he had been taken from her. Like a photographic film, a ghost too becomes fogged in time, loses its clear outlines, fades from the inner vision, is lost in the encroaching night of the past. Paul was no longer a presence; he had become a memory. This was a consolation at least, but an ephemeral one. If her memory failed her that would be the end of herself and the universe.

Claire meditated on the relation between memory and consciousness. Imagine, she thought, that a person loses his memory little by little, beginning with the earliest memories and proceeding on to the present. In time, he may remember only what has happened in the past month, or the past week. Such symptoms have been observed in cases of senile dementia. A man may fail to recognize his own daughter, his own office, even his own wife if he has not seen them for a week. But imagine then that this darkness of memory advances further until he can remember only the events of the past day, the past hour, the past minute. Here I sit, in a room, and what I know is only what has passed in the minute before. Who am I? What is this room? Have I ever loved, or killed, or written a book? I have no way of knowing. I know only this minute trailing after me in the darkness, which now becomes thirty seconds, ten, a second, a millisecond.

With a millisecond of memory, what am I? An idiot, a mute and bewildered blob of protoplasm, a mind still perceiving but unable to make sense out of the thousandth of a second I perceive. I know nothing of language, of speech, of human communication, of the existence of others. When my memory is reduced to a billionth of a second, I am unable to comprehend, because there is nothing to comprehend. Consciousness is memory.

Perhaps I am mad, thought Claire. This idea was not new to her; it had come to her before when she was plagued with the Geographic Dream, when she had the impulse to buy a diamond, when she had fled to Blanco in the cab in the murky dawn. These speculations of hers were not healthy. Perhaps, along with the other effects of exposure to glowstone over a long period of time, it induced just such thoughts.

Claire had another and totally different secret in these days, and it was also one that she told to no one. She knew now that she loved Blanco White; her terror in the cab on the way to the Bois de Vincennes had told her, and when she had impulsively fallen into his arms on the dueling ground this had confirmed it. She could hardly believe that she had really done this; she excused it as a momentary lapse, a reflexive gesture that came out of a flood of relief in her high emotional state. And yet it was this gesture she had made and not another; it could only come from something deep and fundamental, something genuine, inside her. She had suppressed this impulse for so long that when it came it was with a violence—or a sincerity, for they were the same thing—that took her by surprise. Still she had done it. She knew what it meant and she had to admit it to herself. The evidence was unmistakable. She might conceal her inner state from others, but to lie to herself was unthinkable.

This, like the fear that she might lose her memory bit by bit and become unconscious, seemed to her another form of madness. What could it mean to say that she loved Blanco White when she was totally devoted to the memory of Paul? The whole meaning of her life came from that shadowy figure who lurked in the background of her thoughts, who offered her constant inspiration in her work in the Institute, who had set her feet on the path she knew she must follow to the end of her days, who gave her, a mere woman, the strength and resolve to guide others in the mission of glowstone research. Madness, a German doctor contended, consisted simply in the splitting of the human mind into two parts that had no contact with each other. In one of these hemispheres she was faithful to Paul. In the other she saw quite different images.

Blanco's sunny figure in his white clothing, his sauntering gait, his bantering and complicated conversation, his open grin, constantly haunted her as she lay on the edge of dream in her bed, an insistent presence that would not be banished, a presence that she, in fact, welcomed and longed for in her solitude, a private vice like touching herself in certain places that she had been warned against as a girl. But these private parts she touched were the most intimate and delicate parts of her soul, regions she had scarcely explored even at the height of her happiness with Paul. She knew now that what she had felt for Paul was tenderness, loyalty, admiration, and a deep womanly desire to please, to give pleasure through the offering of affection. What she felt for Blanco was love. It was quite a

259

different thing. For her affection and loyalty for Paul to be fulfilled, it was necessary for her to be with him at his side, collaborating in his work, taking his part in the small problems of the day, sharing with him the dinner table and the bed. For what she felt for Blanco, nothing was necessary at all. It was enough to know that he existed and that he was aware of her existence, that from time to time he might smile on her or touch her elbow in helping her from a cab. The idea of a more intimate life shared with him was something shining, distant, and remote, like the possibility of Salvation for a believer who knows himself to be imperfect.

And was it true, as she had told him at Bougival, that she couldn't accept a proposal of marriage from him because she was still married to Paul, that Paul was her whole life and she asked for no other life apart from him? But this was only an elaborate spiritual conceit, a pretty phrase as conventional as the pretense that her work in the laboratory was all she needed to make her happy in life. Paul was dead. She had never used that word before even in her own mind, she had told herself that he was passed, that he was no more, that he was taken from her, that he was a martyr who had given his life to science. Now he was dead. The atoms that had once been Paul were dispersed among the other countless swirling particles that made up the universe; in a million years one of them might appear on Mars, another in the flaming heart of the sun, another in the tilled earth of a farm in Provence. This was what she believed as a scientist and this was what Paul believed. In fact, they believed together that not even the atom was permanent and eternal, that atoms might change into other atoms, or cease to exist entirely and become mysterious fields of energy that vibrated with tremendous force in the emptiness of space. How then could she believe that Paul still existed, how could she devote herself to remaining true to his memory? For memory too was only an excitation of certain cells in the brain. If one could find a way to turn off the electricity—and this happened in certain diseases—memory too would cease to exist.

Paul had faded. She felt a pang as she thought of him, and

this pang had not diminished over the years. But it was like the pain from her scarred hands, it was always there, yet after many years it had become only an anodyne part of consciousness, of the sensation of being alive, like the water in one's own mouth which has no taste. She now had two lovers—she who had always banished the thought of love from her mind as something trivial and unimportant, necessary perhaps to the working of the world but not a thing to influence the emotions or distract her from her work. The one was a dark lover who stood obscurely in her mind, black-clad, serious, peering at her with intensity through his steel spectacles, wavering slightly as the shadow engulfed him a little more each year, causing her through his heavy absence a residue of pain rather than pleasure, like the pain of an old toothache, a tooth that one might touch with the finger now and then to see if the small twinge was still there. The other was a lover shining with light and standing strong and smiling in the sun. Was she to remain true to the night or turn to the day?

Every fiber of her being urged her now to seek the happiness of sunlight, to recapture that moment of total transcendence when she had fallen into Blanco's arms in the Bois de Vincennes. Yet in her calmer moments she knew this wasn't possible. She knew that she could never give herself to Blanco for fear of infecting him in some way with the mysterious disease that she now knew she had. She loved him totally and demanded not her own happiness but his. She would have allowed herself to be cast in a dungeon rather than put the slightest corpuscle of his body into danger. And she knew also that she would never confide this secret to him or anybody else. This knowledge made her happy in a way she had never been before.

XI

In June, when the sun came back from Australia, Blanco proposed that they should go to the country for a day to help his friend Claude pick red currants. "I mean you and I, Hermine, and Boris. The currants all ripen at once at this time of the year and I told him I'd bring some friends to pick them. He lives alone in a small country house with nobody but his wife to help him."

"Red currants?"

"It's the nicest time of the year; everything's in bloom and the countryside is a hundred different shades of green." He was filled with a boyish enthusiasm for this outing and described it in glowing terms. "It'll be like something in a picture by Fragonard. Champagne on the grass. Locals in their picturesque costumes, Claude in a big straw hat. He'll give us lunch and then we'll spend an hour or two out in the fields picking currants. Claude's wife always makes jam out of the currants. Probably they'll give us some to bring back with us, and Mme Lacrosse can make jam out of them too."

"I'm not sure Mme Lacrosse knows how to make jam. She's a city woman. She's really nothing but a concièrge. Who is Claude exactly?"

"I've told you. He's a friend of mine."

"Is he anything like those terrible sisters on the Île Saint-Louis?"

"Oh no no. He's quite different. He lives quietly and only has a few friends from time to time. He's quite an old gentleman and perfectly harmless."

"And where does he live?"

"It's on the Seine near Vernon, just a couple of hours from here. If we start at ten we ought to be there in time for lunch."

"And Hermine is to come?"

"Of course."

For a moment Claire found herself disappointed. When Blanco had first proposed the outing, she had pictured the two of them together in the country. But it would be nice to have Hermine come along, she told herself with only partial conviction. She hadn't been seeing much of her lately, she had been so preoccupied with other things. Gradually she changed her notion of the day in the country. From the picture by Fragonard, in which Blanco swung her in a long velvet swing, it became another in which the three of them picked berries in the field and chatted happily, while Claude, a countryman in a straw hat, carried off the harvest on his strong back.

When the day came it was clear that Blanco had another motive in taking them to the country: he wanted to show off his new motorcar to them. It was a Panhard of the latest model, an open tourer with seats for two in the back and one plus the driver in the front. Folded at the rear was a canvas top that could be erected over it in case of rain. Blanco explained that this was called the capote, which was a little embarrassing, because it was the same as the word for a well-known contraceptive, the kind called in English a French letter. Claire grimly ignored this but thought she caught a smile on Hermine's face. They examined the other features of the Panhard: an enormous steering wheel with brass spokes, a great handbrake that clicked like a cicada when it was pulled, and a brass horn with a rubber bulb. The rest of the knobs, pedals, and levers were mysterious; no doubt they all had some purpose.

With it came a chauffeur. Blanco introduced him as though he was a personal friend. His name was Kerjean. "It means Saint John in Breton. But you're not a saint, are you?"

"I am when I'm working for Monsieur. On my own time, I don't guarantee anything." Evidently, in Kerjean, Blanco had found a crony of his own ilk, a proletarian wag to serve as foil for his own jests and fun. Kerjean was dressed in a white cap with flaps that tied down over his ears, and there was similar gear for Blanco. Since he hadn't warned them about the motorcar, he had thoughtfully provided dusters and veils for the two women. In the trunk fastened to the rear of the tonneau, where it would no doubt get thoroughly jiggled on the trip down the Seine, was a case of Veuve Cliquot.

The two women climbed into the rear and arranged themselves. Blanco passed in Boris, who was looking around brightly at everything and too interested to bark, and he was installed on Claire's lap. Then Blanco got in himself, taking the seat in front next to the driver. Kerjean went around to the front and cranked while Blanco arranged various levers on the dash. "The mixture a bit richer, Monsieur. Retard the timing." The engine coughed, wheezed twice, and began chugging in slow pants. While Kerjean was getting back in, Blanco reached over to the chauffeur's position and squeezed the rubber bulb of the horn. It gave out a bleat like a frightened goat and several heads appeared in windows in Rue de Bellechasse. Hermine laughed out loud; Claire smiled.

Claire enjoyed the two-hour trip down the Seine in the open car. It was a beautiful June day. The sun was bright and the air a little crisp; cumulus clouds touched with gray at the bottom slid over the sky from the west. She still had not quite recovered from her illness. She felt a little shaky at times and had spots before her eyes, but all these new things were distracting and she soon forgot her physical frailties. Leaving the city at Neuilly, they crossed the river once at Chatou and once again at St.-Germain-en-Laye. After that they were in the open country. They left the Seine for a while, traveling across the gently rolling farmland of the Île-de-France, and came back to it again at Mantes. Claire had never been so far down the river. There was nothing to do in this part of France except enjoy yourself; no factories, no laboratories, no universities, no place where anyone worked or did anything useful, unless you counted farmers. In spite of her scientific training she had very little idea what farmers did; she gazed at the pastures and fields of grain with a kind of dumb and pleasant lassitude.

At Vernon, a good-sized town on the border of Normandy, they crossed the Seine and then came back five kilometers or so along the other bank. A little before noon they were in Giverny. Just outside the town, at a point where a small tributary called the Epte flowed down through marshy land to the Seine, was Claude's country house. It was more elaborate than Blanco had implied. It was a large pink-and-white structure with a tiled roof, overgrown with vines, and there were several outbuildings. Hearing the noise of the motorcar, Claude came out to greet them just as Kerjean turned off the engine.

He proved to be an old gentleman with a thick white beard, wearing a suit of checked homespun, a pleated blue shirt, and reddish leather boots. On his head was a round straw hat of the kind worn by peasants. He said, "Ah, you have got a Teuf-Teuf. Everyone has them these days. I expect I'll have to get one myself."

"I'm sure they're only a passing fad," murmured Claire.

"A Panhard Model G," said Blanco. "Twelve horsepower. Capable of sixty kilometers an hour on the open road."

"Ah, but such speeds will kill us all," said Claude genially. Finally Blanco got around to introducing the two women. Claude stared at Hermine and then bent to kiss her hand. She felt the bristly touch of the beard on her knuckles. As an afterthought he kissed Claire's hand too. He said, "It is very good of you to come and visit an old man in the country. Like Blanco, I'm very fond of the company of ladies. Until recently I was a sexagenarian. And you know what they are good at. The other day, however, I became a septuagenarian, so I am

266

not so active in such things anymore." He seemed to enjoy his joke, and so did Blanco. Claire hardly approved but she couldn't help smiling a little. As for Hermine, she thrilled with humor, the delight of nature, and the person of the bearded old man in his straw hat. The whole outing to her was a revelation, a Renaissance, a wide-opening of her soul. And she had not even met Félix yet.

With Blanco carrying Boris under his arm, Claude led them into the house. They were introduced to his wife Alice, a woman named Blanche of forty or so who was evidently a daughter, and several other guests; a young man in Parisian clothes, a pair of elderly ladies, and a Japanese gentleman who was there for a reason no one could even imagine. These were the locals in their picturesque costumes promised by Blanco.

"Alice, perhaps our visitors would like a nice glass of lemonade."

"Lemonade be damned, I've brought some champagne in the car."

"Before lunch?"

"Certainly before lunch. Why not?"

"Ah, these Parisians," said Claude.

They went outside and sat under an umbrella by a pond, and Kerjean was sent for the champagne. In addition to the cook and the servants in the house, there was a gardener working outside assisted by a boy. Boris, turned loose of his leash for the first time in his life, ran excitedly around on the grass and sniffed at what was evidently a pile of manure. The gardens were extensive: masses of flowers, enormous wisteria with branches the size of human limbs, a circular Japanese bridge, semicircular one should say, but when its reflection was added it was a perfect circle. Claire wondered why Blanco had seen fit to describe the place as a small house where Claude lived alone with his wife. She stared at the water lilies floating on the glassy surface of the pond, enormous quantities of them extending as far as she could see and continuing on under the Japanese bridge. The crinkled dark-green leaves spreading over the water, the waxy white blossoms that opened in the day and shut at night, were curiously unsettling, but in a way that somehow gave pleasure. She thought of their odd French name: nymphéas, like antique goddesses in a copse pursued by satyrs, or the plural of some delicate part of the female anatomy. She shivered a little; it was cloudier here than in Paris and because of the pond the air was cool.

The champagne came in its wooden crate chilled with ice. Far from sitting on the grass, they had it at a quite elegant white-enameled table with four white chairs around it. Kerjean pried off a board and Blanco opened a bottle. The cork came out with a loud pop and flew into the pond, and half the wine foamed out onto the ground before he could get a glass to it. They drank to art, for some reason. Perhaps Claude collected pictures. She had seen several in the house.

The old gentleman only pretended to sip a little of his and poured the glass into a rosebush. After he had greeted his guests and embraced the ladies, he had put on again the pair of smoked glasses he was wearing before. Since the hat was so large and the beard covered so much of his face, there was little to be seen except the straw hat pulled down over his forehead, the smoked glasses, and the encompassing white beard, along with a pink Santa Claus nose and two pink bulbs of cheeks. Hermine noticed that there were lace cuffs protruding from the sleeves of his rough homespun jacket. When he saw her staring, he remarked in an oracular and ironic tone, "My skin is easily irritated, particularly around the wrists."

"Have you lived here long?" inquired Claire politely.

"Oh, my goodness yes. Since far back in the previous century."

"And you've made many improvements?"

"I've worked like a navvy. I put in the pond and the garden. Before that there was nothing but weeds. The other day the curé came by and said, 'That's a beautiful garden that you and God have made.' I told him, 'Father, you should have seen it when God had it by himself.'"

"You seem to be fond of water lilies."

"I thought," he said, "that everyone knew that."

The maid came to tell them that lunch was ready. Her old-fashioned way of putting it was, "Messieurs et mesdames sont servis." On the way into the house the old gentleman broke a branch of syringa, heavy with fragrance, which he brandished for a moment like a scepter before he placed it in Hermine's arms. She carried it with her for the rest of the day.

At lunch there were ten or eleven of them at the table. Claude sat at the head and Alice at the other end, while the cook herself served the lunch with the help of a housemaid. In addition to the ones they had already met, there was a man in country garb who was a son of Claude and Alice. It was very informal and not everyone was introduced. At the end of the table the Japanese gentleman conferred earnestly with the two elderly ladies. Hermine sat across from Claire and Blanco, with the daughter Blanche at her left. On her right was the dark-haired young man in Parisian clothes, who had been introduced simply as Félix. He said little, but seemed to be examining her with a certain interest. Although she tried not to meet his glance her curiosity was aroused. He was a young man of considerable elegance, dressed impeccably in a dark suit, a white shirt with a high collar, and a necktie with tiny checks. He was thin, narrow-headed and narrow-bodied, and not as handsome as Carlo. His ears were not put on quite right, one was at a different angle from the other, and his face showed the faint crepiness of long-disappeared adolescent pimples. It made his face look like an antique statue rather than a modern work of art in marble. He sat with ease at the table with his napkin in one hand, looking around at the others with a small controlled smile. He had the air of being lightly amused at all times, with a deeper seriousness under it, just the opposite of Carlo, who was serious on the outside but trivial underneath.

For lunch there was first a hearty country soup, then pâté, cheeses, cold roast beef, and pickled onions. The bread was the tough grayish kind called pain de campagne in the Paris shops. Instead of wine there was homemade cider, which tasted of sour apples with a trace of glycerine. Hermine sipped a little and pushed the glass away with an involuntary shudder.

Félix laughed. "Claude is not a connoisseur of wine. Here

269

in the country he makes something of a fetish of living a simple life. Would you like me to ask for some wine for you?"

"Oh no. I don't usually drink it anyhow."

"Tea then. An infusion."

"Camomile. Or no, lime tea."

He caught the attention of the maid, who quickly brought her a pot of tilleul. They smiled together over this small conspiracy in which she rejected the host's beverage and demanded special privileges.

"With your tea you remind me of an English girl in a story. I know what it is—Alice, in the book about the Marvels."

"*Alice in Wonderland.*" In French it was called *Alice auz Pays des Merveilles.*

"That's it. The illustrations by Tenniel."

"And you remind me of someone in Jules Verne. Are you perhaps an explorer? Or a balloonist? Or the captain of a submarine?"

"None of those. You aren't very good at character, are you? Of course you're still very young."

"Very. That's why I can't drink wine. At least not when Maman's at the table."

"I'd be interested to know how you behave when you're not with your Maman."

"Oh, much the same." Here she fell into a slight confusion, remembering her behavior with Carlo when her mother was away in America. "Are you coming to pick red currants with us this afternoon?"

"I hadn't planned to. But if you're inviting me, it would be a pleasure."

He turned to pour her some more lime tea, a completely unnecessary courtesy, and his hand brushed lightly against hers. Something in Hermine fluttered and when it stopped it left a diffuse warm sensation inside her. Dropping her pretense of modesty, she stared openly at his thin eroded face, his subdued smile, his sparse and urban Jewish elegance. She saw that his fingers were long and narrow like those of a musician, his wrists bony and functional, his eyes set in a faint pattern of wrinkles like folded parchment. "How old are you?" she blurted.

He grinned. "I'm thirty. And you?"

"Oh, I'm just a schoolgirl."

"Madame told me you were a student at the Sorbonne."

"Madame?"

"Madame Alice."

This must have been while they were outside drinking champagne. "You're clever at ferreting out facts."

"Yes. That's because I'm not a submarine captain or a balloonist, but a journalist."

"Oh," she said, a little disappointed. "Then why are you here?"

"Because I deal with the arts, in a modest way."

This explained nothing. At least they were still talking. Hermine cast about desperately to find a way to spend the rest of the afternoon with Félix, and not all of it picking red currants with the others.

The lunch was a long one, with much conversation, and it was after three when they left the table and set out again into the garden. They would pick currants in a while, but first Claude wanted to show them about the property. They went off in a procession, first Claude with Blanco at his elbow, then Claire with Boris tripping at her heels, then Hermine followed at a little distance by Félix, a young man who seemed to Claire presumptuous in the way he had dominated Hermine's conversation at lunch and now trailed along after them without being invited. Although she was free of prejudice herself, Hermine could hardly be interested in anyone who was Jewish, and besides his complexion was not very appetizing. They inspected a grape arbor, a hothouse, a shed for pressing cider, and a carriagehouse that contained nothing but a ramshackle buggy in which the cook went to Vernon for groceries. "I myself never go anywhere," said Claude. "I am content to rest my old bones here."

"When I first knew you, you used to go to London, and to the South of France."

"Oh, I'm too old for that now. I have everything I need here. Come in here in the old barn and look at the pictures."

They entered a large brick structure with a galvanized-iron roof and whitewashed walls. In the middle of it was a dilapidated sofa splotched with oil stains and spots of dried paint. The walls were covered with paintings, all by the same hand. This old man must have some odd friends, thought Claire, because he rents out his barn to some artist who doesn't even paint very well. The canvases were all splotchy and he couldn't even draw. She looked at an attempt to paint a cloud reflected in water, at river scenes with poplars and barges, at several very large paintings of the water lilies outside on the pond. They were spotty and smeared, as though the paint had been thrown on from a distance, or as though a child had rubbed his hand over the canvas after the artist had finished. Perhaps it was her own eyesight, Claire reflected. The effect of the paintings was something like that of the watery veil that had begun to come over her vision lately. Everything was blurred into a mass of color in which blue, green, yellow, and orange worms squirmed in monotonous masses of green foliage. She paused before a large picture of the nymphéas; the waxy white flowers were smeared like clots of cream over a sheet of water that varied in color from sky-blue to violet, as though the painter had run out of color and had to use something that wasn't suitable. She bent to examine the signature in the corner, but could only make out a sprawling splash of orange as indecipherable as the painting itself. Either her eyes had suddenly got much worse or Claude's friend himself was going blind, she concluded, or was prey to some degenerative disease of the brain. She began to see Claude now as an eccentric sort of country gentleman, one who had become more confirmed in his eccentricities as he got older, as people do, and went about in a peasant hat surrendering himself to the most childish of whims, pressing apples to make sour cider, erecting Japanese bridges, renting out his barn to local daubers whose work he no doubt admired. To be sure it wasn't her own vision that was affected she fixed it on Claude and Blanco, who were at the other end of the room discussing a painting. They were clear enough and framed in their usual precise outlines. Turning around, she caught sight of Hermine and Félix disappearing out the door into the garden.

* * *

"Claude must be very rich."

"Oh, he is."

"And you say there are eight children."

"Yes. Some of them are his and some are Alice's. You see, he was married to someone else, a woman called Camille, and they had two sons. One is Jean, who was with us at lunch. Then Camille died and Claude took up with the wife of Ernest Hoschedé, a friend of his. That was Alice. She had six children of her own, and they came here and bought the house at Giverny. A few years ago one of Madame's daughters died— Suzanne, she was a favorite of Claude. It was a blow to him. So there are seven left, but they don't all live here."

"Then Claude and Alice are not married?"

"Oh yes. Claude married her a few years ago. It took him a while to get around to it."

"And where did his money come from?"

"Come from?"

"Yes, how did he become so rich."

"Why, by selling his paintings."

"Oh, so he's a painter?"

Félix stared at her. "What are you people anyhow, idiots? Have you never heard of the great Claude Monet? He's one of the best-known painters in France and a member of the Academy. He's called the Raphael of water. He founded the Impressionist school but he's gone far beyond that now."

"But I thought it was *Man*et."

"No no, Manet is an entirely different painter. Manet is dead! Long live Monet."

"And you say he is well known?"

"That gentleman Mr. Iguchi is a collector who has come all the way from Japan to look at his paintings. Didn't you notice the pictures in the house? My God. Boudin, Berthe Morisot, Renoir, Pissarro, Cézanne, Degas. Those people are all his friends."

"But how do you know all this? Are you a painter too?"

"But I told you. I'm a journalist. I'm Félix Bock. I write about pictures for Le Temps."

"And you're a friend of Claude's?"

"Oh good God no, only an humble admirer. I lay my garlands at the feet of the mighty. I wouldn't dream of criticizing Monet, any more than I would have criticized Michelangelo if I had lived in Florence at the time."

"Then some artists are above criticism?"

"Some artists are just very damned good. If Monet makes a mistake, I'll say so. Up to now I haven't noticed one."

"I'm afraid I don't know much about painting. When I was little I wasn't taken to museums. Now Blanco has taken us to the Louvre a couple of times."

"Not being dead, Monet is not yet in the Louvre. What world have you been living in anyhow?"

"I suppose it must be the world of science."

"It must be a very strange place."

"Please don't scold me. We all live in strange places. Inside our own heads."

"I wouldn't dream of scolding you." He seized her hand. "Why I—"

At that exact moment Claire appeared on the path, having gone around the garden and over the Japanese bridge several times in an effort to find where they had disappeared to. Félix abruptly let go of her hand. Hermine felt that her face was warm and smiled brilliantly.

"Oh Maman, do you know what! Claude is actually a famous painter. Mr. Iguchi has come all the way from Japan to see his pictures. Monsieur Bock says they are worth millions."

"Famous painter?"

"A member of the Academy. I'm thunderstruck that you didn't know this."

"I am familiar with the Academy, but for me it is the Academy of Sciences."

"Please don't apologize, Madame. I am sure I know nothing about your field either."

"Very likely," said Claire dryly.

"The reason we haven't heard of him, Maman, is that he isn't in the Louvre yet. He's still alive."

"That's right! You have to go to the Luxembourg."

"Or come right here," said Hermine.

"Then those are his pictures in the barn?"

"Of course."

"I see." Claire was thoughtful. "My eyes have been troubling me lately. Perhaps I need better glasses. That may be the reason that I don't quite appreciate the paintings."

"Claude has cataracts," said Félix.

When the berry-picking began, Claude provided himself with a large wooden wheelbarrow which he trundled down the path and over the bridge across the Epte, and Alice and Jean followed with a collection of baskets, all different shapes and sizes. Jean was a stout bull of a man who said little and almost never smiled. The rest of the party consisted of Blanco, Claire, Hermine, Félix, and Boris, who tagged along still happily free of his leash. Claude owned this land too on the other side of the Epte; it extended for several hundred meters and ended in a cluster of elms. It was wild and unkempt, and the foliage was dotted with tiny points of color: gooseberries, currants, and wild strawberries. They were strictly enjoined by Claude to pick only the red currants and leave the others for another time. They set to work plucking off the bright red clusters of berries that weighed down the branches. Félix was hardly dressed for this task; he had come down from Paris not to pick berries but to find out what Claude was up to in the studio. He turned back the cuffs of his coat and immaculate white shirt and handed the berries delicately, immediately getting his fingers stained. He held the hands up to Hermine and made a mock leer, like a murderer. Blanco's white suit was invulnerable. In chatting with Claude he didn't pick as many berries as the others, but the ones he did pick he handled without getting a trace of them on his clothing. Even his hands were hardly stained. He and Claude were a little distance away, talking about something they concealed from the women and occasionally guffawing. Men are such animals if they are allowed to consort together, thought Claire. She felt proud that Blanco was so masculine and shared the stout vulgarity of the rest of his sex.

They kept at this for a couple of hours. By this time Félix had grass stains on his knees and his cuffs were spotted with red juice. As they filled their baskets they carried them to the wheelbarrow and dumped in the heaps of tiny scarlet berries. The wheelbarrow was full to the top and it groaned like a cornucopia. Disobeying Claude, Hermine now and then ate a wild strawberry. They too were tiny but delicious. In the cafés of Paris a dish of them with crème Chantilly cost ten francs. She was fascinated with the gooseberries. They were about the size of strawberries and they looked like tiny melons; they were melon-colored and had light-green stripes around them like meridians of longitude; each one was a miniature world.

"Oh Claude, can't I pick a gooseberry?"

"Only one."

Hermine picked one and ate it. It was very sour. "Serves you right," said Claire. The red currants were sour too (all the Parisians tasted them in spite of Claude's injunction) but they were supposed to be; you could eat them only when they were made into jam. How long would they go on picking them? The contents of the wheelbarrow spilled over the edges and fell onto the ground.

It was a little after five o'clock. The clouds, which had been white with gray along the lower edges, were now black along the bottom and trailing ragged gray streamers. In the west the sky was dark, almost black. The air had turned a little chill.

"Well, we had better get back to the house," said Claude.

In the end the wheelbarrow wouldn't hold everything they had picked. Alice and Jean carried baskets full of berries, and Claire too took a little in her own basket even though she felt tired and everything wavered in the air around her. Claude led the procession back toward the garden, propelling the wheelbarrow not in the usual way but going ahead of it and pulling it by the shafts, like a horse hitched to a wagon. He grunted happily at the weight of the fruit behind him. Claire found herself walking next to Alice.

"And now all this jam to make. Do you do that yourself, or does the cook do it?"

"Oh, good heavens no. Claude does that himself. It's his

crotchet. He fusses endlessly with it every June, and in the autumn he presses cider. I don't have time for it myself."

"You must have quite enough to do in taking care of such a large house."

"My task, Madame, is to take care of Claude. The servants will take care of the house. If it makes him happy to make red currant jam, then I arrange things so that he will be able to do it. If he fusses around like a little child making jam, then he will paint better the next day. The only thing that is important is Claude and his work. As soon as I saw one of his paintings for the first time, many years ago, I knew that my life was changed. I left my husband, Madame, and my home to devote myself to Claude. For a long time it was very hard. We did not have very much money and we had ten mouths to feed. One of my girls died; she was Claude's favorite; he often used her as a model. Then finally the world recognized Claude and things were better for us. Now, as you see, we have plenty. But Claude must still work, and I must provide the conditions that are best for his work. I have given my life so that those paintings you see in the studio could come into being. It has all been for art. That is the only thing that is important."

The thought struck Claire that this was what she too believed, except for the changing of a single word. She wondered if there were still other things, beyond art and science, that were more important than anything in the world.

Félix, lingering at the end of the procession with Hermine, was suddenly struck with an idea. It was as though he had forgotten something.

"But you haven't seen the Île aux Orties."

"Nettle Isle?"

"It's where Claude did some of his most important paintings, before he got too old to walk so far and started painting water lilies here in the garden. The river pictures in the Luxembourg! You've got to see the place."

"But—"

"Come on. It's only—"

"Only what?"

"Only a quarter of an hour. We'll catch up to the others."

Hesitating only for a moment, she allowed herself to be led back down the path and across the bridge over the Epte. When she looked back she saw the last of the wheelbarrow procession disappearing into the garden. "I think it's going to rain. We were going to leave at five."

"I had hoped that—"

"So had I. Do you have a scrap of paper?"

"I told you I'm a journalist."

They were both fumbling, warm, and excited. He handed her a notebook and pencil. Terrified at what she was doing, she scrawled on the page, *Maman, M. Bock is going to show me the Île aux Orties. If we are not back in time, please go on without us. M. Bock has a cab and will take me back to Paris on the train.*

"You do have a cab, don't you?"

"Not now. It was going to come for me at six or a little after."

"Stay here."

Hermine tore off down the path after the others, caught sight of them going around the greenhouse, and dodged the other way. Just as she hoped, she fell in with the gardener, working with his boy by the pond. She thrust the scrap of paper into his hands and said, "Please give this to Madame Savarin-Decker." Before he could reply, she was off down the path again.

Across the bridge she rejoined Félix, who said not a word. He led her off through a meadow with wild mint. A few bees buzzed, and in the distance tiny dots of swallows plunged through the air in pursuit of the insects that rise from the grass before a rainstorm.

"I hope there aren't any nettles here in the meadow."

"If you're stung with nettles, you should press a dock leaf onto the place. There's some dock." He pointed to a plant with large glabrous leaves.

"How do you know so much?"

"I'm older than you, and as I've told you seven or eight times, I'm a journalist."

After a quarter of an hour—it was probably a little less, since they were hurrying—they came out onto the Seine at the place where it was joined by the Epte. It was marshy land, and they had to walk carefully over a path roughly paved with stones. On the bank of the river was a dilapidated boathouse with several boards missing. A punt was tied to it, half full of greenish water. Out in the river was the island, long and narrow, nothing much but a sandbar covered with nettles, with a clump of willows here and there at the water's edge. The riverbank on their side was lined with poplars, and there were more poplars on the opposite bank, half hidden by the island. Since they were only looking at half the Seine, it was quite narrow. Over the top of the island they could see a steamboat going downstream, or at least its black funnel and the tip of its flagstaff. The water before them was grayish and as smooth as glass. Here and there a little dot sprang out in it and expanded into a circle that dissolved on the mirrored surface. They could hear raindrops too in the leaves of the trees overhead.

"You see, in those days Claude used to have a péniche here."

"A péniche? Oh, a barge."

"Well, it was a long narrow thing. And he would load his easel and all his stuff on it and pole it up and down the river, to the place where he wanted to paint. You see just up there beyond the end of the island?" He moved closer to point over her shoulder for her. "That's where he did the river scenes with poplars and willows."

Instead of going on, he stopped and stared at her. She was a little breathless. "Yes. Yes. The river scenes with poplars and willows. And what more?"

"That bush with purplish flowers. I don't know what it is. Well, they're much more purple in the paintings. Claude's palette is violent."

"Very violent. Yes."

"What?"

"Go on, go on!"

"And you see this punt here. It's the same one that appears in several paintings that . . ."

"Yes. That what?"

279

"That . . . you can see in the Luxembourg."

"In the . . ."

As if moved by a common impulse that worked for both of them in the same instant, they kissed. A warm drop of rain struck her cheek and slid off onto his. She was aware of the musky odor of the clothes in which he had picked berries. His hand, as he raised it to touch her cheek, was enclosed in white linen stained with bright scarlet patches.

She whispered, "In the Luxembourg . . ."

"Shut up, you fool."

They kissed again. This time it was for a long time. The water mumbled sleepily at their feet, the old punt stirred and bumped, the swallows shrieked faintly in the distance. She thought, this is wonderful but in a while I shall strangle because I can't breathe.

She said, "You must take me to see them."

"This is downright disobedience. The little vixen. She knew we were to leave at five."

"They're just a young couple gone for a walk."

"Who is Monsieur Bock anyhow?"

"He's Félix."

"But who is he?"

"He's an art critic. And a very good one."

"She has been behaving very strangely lately, Blanco."

"So did we. So does everyone at that age."

"Someone should be sent after them."

"Now listen to me, Claire. Give the girl her head. She has better sense than you think. You're the one who is behaving irrationally. You are the victim of a very strong instinct to go on treating her as a child. But she's not a child. She knows perfectly what she is doing and probably it is the right thing."

"I don't know to what you are referring."

"Yes you do. She seems to have worked out a very good plan. She says Félix will take her back to Paris."

"Paris! He will not."

"In any case, we're going to have to leave, with her or without her."

"Stay to supper, stay to supper," urged Claude. "There will be Mr. Iguchi and those two old ladies. They are a circus all in themselves. They are English and they want to write a monograph about me, jointly."

"Do you think we ought to leave now, Kerjean?"

"I have no opinion one way or the other, Monsieur. I simply say that in a little while it is going to start raining like a cow pissing on a flat rock."

"And?"

"The road is not paved, Monsieur."

"Exactly what I think. Well, au revoir, Claude, and thank you for the privilege of being allowed to do backbreaking labor for nothing on your farm."

"Take some currants with you."

"No, Claire won't cook them and she says her housekeeper won't either."

Another couple of drops fell and they hurried toward the car. Blanco towed Claire by the elbow.

"Blanco."

"Well?"

"She is my daughter."

"Yes, isn't she a charming thing? Well, goodbye, Claude. I'll leave you the rest of the champagne."

"I won't drink it!" the old man shouted after them.

"Drink it! Drink it!"

The lovers were thoroughly drenched before they got back to the house, even though the storm had not yet reached its full strength. The cab from Vernon came a little early, thank God. They stood shivering under the porch of the house until it drew up, then got in quickly. It was really only a country buggy like Claude's out in the carriage house that the cook used to go for groceries. Under the fusty-smelling black hood there was barely room for two, jammed shoulder to shoulder, and the driver sat out unprotected in the weather. He was a country youth of twenty or so, with a coachman's hat for a uniform, and he was already soaked as they were. He slapped the reins and his white pony, steaming and reeking of sweat, started off at a brisk clop. The road to Vernon was still solid underneath but it was covered with a film of slippery mud. The buggy slid from side to side and the driver swore, pulling down his hat. By now it was raining in that copious and spectacular way that Kerjean had predicted. A hail of drops the size of marbles pelted down on the hood of the buggy.

A little over two kilometers from Giverny they came upon the Panhard tilted over at the side of the road, slumped like a wounded bird. The capote had been erected (Hermine smiled as she had at the long narrow péniche) and Kerjean was out at the side struggling with the tools to remove the tire from the wheel. The jack could not be fixed in the slippery mud. He was attempting to jam the branch of a tree under it. As they went by they caught a glimpse of Claire's white face behind the celluloid curtain on the side of the car.

"Shouldn't we stop?"

"No room in the buggy. Nothing we can do."

"I feel terrible."

"The first step in life," said Félix, "is to kill one's parents."

The buggy fled on down the muddy road. At the side of the road the poplars shook in the wind and flung off sheets of water into the air. Perhaps Claude had painted them too. *Landscape near Giverny, with Lovers Fleeing.* In a half an hour they were at the station in Vernon. There, owing to Félix's excellent planning, they had to wait only twenty minutes for a train. The carriage was one of those with a footboard along the side and narrow doors for each compartment. Once the door was shut no one could enter the compartment until they got to Paris. Félix shoved Hermine in, and then stood defiantly to block the entry of a fat peasant woman and her imbecile son into the compartment. The stationmaster came along slamming the doors and the train started.

The windows were silvered with rain and they could see almost nothing through them. The train rocked and rattled, clattered over crossings, hooted at bridges and villages. Its velocity extinguished conversation and left them with nothing to do but be bumped rhythmically together on the narrow upholstered seat with its lace antimacassars for their heads. They did very little in the compartment that they hadn't done before, except that Hermine learned to kiss without being strangled. In a little less than two hours they were at the Gare St.-Lazare. The setting sun came out just as they were reaching Paris and sent a horizontal ray of pink through the train.

Félix quickly found another cab. When they got to the hotel in Rue de Rivoli, Hermine looked at the brass plate and found it was the Hôtel d'Angleterre. Where had she heard that name before? But it was the hotel where Blanco's old beggar woman had her room! She burst into peals of laughter, to Félix's perplexity.

If the old beggar woman's room was as nice as theirs, she was lucky. The window had yellowish tulle curtains, there was a kind of Spanish shawl on the bureau and a vase with a rose in it, and there was an engraving of the Battle of Austerlitz on the wall. At last they could get out of their wet and sticky clothes. They slipped out of them as quickly as though they were peeling two overripe peaches.

And now it seemed to Hermine that she had finally entered into the magical realm whose geography she had already known, that Previous Existence she thought she had found in the poem of Baudelaire but had really been hidden inside her long before she ever heard of the poem. She and Félix wandered through this landscape of voluptuous flora hand in hand. Guided by him, she stole stealthily along from one delight to another, and to her surprise there were even some delights that he didn't know of until she indicated them with a light touch, out of a kind of instinct. The place they had entered was dark and warm and yet in some way glowing with a soft luminescence that spread into the corpuscles of their blood, cool as wine, cool as the sparkle of champagne. It was a palace in which one secret and voluptuous chamber led to another, through doors that only became visible just as they reached them. So this is what it is and it is quite wonderful, she thought. And then she discovered that what they had found up to then was only a fifth, a tenth of what there was. Everything was strange, and everything was familiar as though remembered from a dream, a childhood tale, an incarnation in ancient Egypt. Hermine found that Félix's body was a complicated machine whose supple, eroded surface concealed inner machines and engines of an unsuspected subtlety, and that her body, the one she had exposed to the weather and washed so carefully between the legs as told when a child, was the same. It was as though what they had taken for a pair of porcelain mannekins turned out to be rare and expensive Viennese clocks. Hermine's struck the hour and pealed like churches, and then his. And then it was the next hour, and the next. The church bells woke them up every hour during the night. Hermine had not thought church bells had so much stamina. Surely they would break. She would not joke again about long narrow péniches, or about capotes, which Félix had also thoughtfully provided.

Waking up after a half-hour of sleep to find herself no longer in a palace but in a quite prosaic hotel room with its yellowish tulle curtains and its battle of Austerlitz, its rose in a vase on the bureau (it was all so strange and improbable), she sat on the edge of the bed and found it was four o'clock in the morning. They had come to the hotel about eight in the evening, she thought; she had lost track of time somewhere on the train. It seemed perfectly natural to her that she had no clothes on. In fact, it seemed strange to her that people ever wore clothes. She longed to inspect Félix to see if he shared this privilege of being beautiful in the state of nature, but he had turned onto his stomach and was asleep with his head under the pillow.

She smiled to herself and meditated over the word deflower. To deflower. To be deflowered. It was an odd term because it suggested something stolen, that a thief in the night had crept into a place where he ought not to be and deprived her of something valuable and irreplaceable. As a matter of fact it was just the opposite; instead of taking a flower from her, he had made a thousand flowers grow. It put Félix in quite a different light. From a thief, he was converted into a horticulturalist. She longed to learn more about his infinity of mysterious skills. If only he would wake up.

She prodded him, elicited a groan and a slithering of limbs

284

under the bedclothes, then she pulled the bedclothes away altogether. He yawned and sat up.

"Let's go out somewhere."

"Out?"

"I'm hungry."

"You can't be hungry, it's four o'clock in the morning."

"But I didn't have any dinner."

"Would you rather have had dinner?"

"Oh, don't be difficult. You're so clever. What is that very large vein right there?"

He explained to her that sometimes men needed a copious supply of blood just at that point. "If you touch it the whole thing is going to start over again. Maybe you're right, we'd better go out."

"I'll go just like this. I'll take the rose from the vase and put it in my hair."

"But there will be nothing to eat at this hour."

"What about the Halles?"

"The Halles?"

"Yes, the farmers come in to sell their vegetables, and women sell onion soup on the corners."

"Not until around six, I think."

"We can walk around and look at things. Perhaps there are cafés open in the Halles."

"They're rather rough places. I don't know if you'd want to go to one."

They dressed, putting on their still damp clothes with little shudders, and stole out without waking the porter who snored at the desk. At this time of the morning in June it was already getting light. Of course there were no cabs or other means of transportation. She knew this part of Paris imperfectly and had only an indistinct notion of where the Halles were, even though she had been to them once in an omnibus. The single egg. She smiled again privately. Everything seemed amusing to her, and everything shining and wonderful, and innocently obscene. He led the way along Rue de Rivoli and then up Rue du Pont to the great iron sheds of the markets.

Rue de Rivoli was deserted, but when they came to the Halles there was a swarm of activity in the violet morning sunlight fresh from the rain of the night before. Porters went by wearing curious hats a yard or more across, on which were perched enormous baskets of vegetables, butter and eggs, or meat. Félix told her they were called Forts, and there was a bad and perfectly pointless joke about them: Pour être Fort, il faut être fort.

"You could be a Strong, Félix. You are very strong."

"Only in places."

The pavement was littered with broken crates and scraps of vegetables. Fishwomen cried their wares, and children unaccountably up at this hour scoured the half-empty tables for something to eat, a fragment of broken roll or the end of a sausage. A man went by who must have been the strongest of the Strongs, for he bore on his back a stack of wooden crates three times as tall as he was, so high that he couldn't have walked under a bridge. The numbers of jammed-together people were incredible. There were a thousand smells, of onions, of oysters, of expensively putrid cheese, of raw dripping beef, and for every smell there was a noise.

"Was this really where you wanted to come? You see, there's no onion soup."

"What's that?"

"Ah." He smiled. "Those men are called Bijoutiers."

"Jewelers? How do you mean?"

"And the things they are selling are called Harlequins." He drew her a little closer to show her. "After midnight, they go around to the luxury restaurants of Paris, and for a sou they buy the leftover delicacies that haven't been eaten. And the poor people, canny as poor people always are, come here to eat what you and I can't afford."

"But now we can afford it." She drew near to the table and inquired about prices. The Jeweler beamed at her, since it was rare to see such a pretty face so early in the morning in this part of Paris. In the slanting sun of the dawn, they dined off pâté de fois gras, carp with truffles, sweetbreads en croûte, mousse of salmon, Russian eggs with mayonnaise, tiny crayfish fried in batter, caviar sandwiches the size of postage stamps, boiled plovers' eggs with parsley, roasted larks, quenelle of pike, oysters au gratin, prawns grilled on skewers, broken straw-berry tarts, and fragments of meringue sticky with chocolate.

And now the time has come to cast aside all these games and pretenses, this flimsy sham of concealment, this authorial coyness, and to confess to you who I really am: haven't you already guessed? Have you, perhaps, noticed the mysterious significance of the feminine cast that this narrative has all the way through—the easy intimacy with which it deals with its female characters, the slight wall of bafflement and fascination that separates it from the male characters? Haven't you no-ticed that there is one character the narrator always puts in a favorable light, even though regarded by others with exasper-ation, with predatory concupiscence, with envy, even with hos-tility? And who could that character be but myself?

I am Hermine, different for each of the others as I assume my myriad forms in the story; Claire's only beloved and dis-obedient child, Blanco's chaste childish sweetheart, Carlo's prey which so frustratingly eluded him, the "icy little minx" of Dé-licienne Maedl, the Holy Grail that Lancelot pursued in his dream-fumbles on the train. I was not the fly on the wall, but the unnoticed child in the corner of the room, or in the next room with the door open, with excellent hearing and a pro-digious curiosity about the concerns and secrets of my el-ders—one of those, as an American novelist has put it, on whom nothing is lost. Claire is getting too sick to be the center of her own story anymore, soon her mind will be fuzzy, her stream-of-consciousness will not be easy to follow, and I must emerge to take her place.

But, if I reveal to you that I am Hermine, I must also reveal to you that I have a storytelling impulse in me which makes it impossible for me to tell something exactly as it took place; instead I must embroider on it, make it better, distort it lightly, until it becomes truly a story and not just "what happened." Dostoevsky says that the plain truth is so implausible that most people mix in a little falsehood with it; in short we are all storytellers. And the next step is that I must emerge, detach myself, and become the novelist, a separate Hermine from the Hermine in the story. Now there are two of us, and you see if you can tell us apart. I am not sure that I can.

For I am a terrible liar, and so are all novelists and storytellers. If I tell you a story which goes, "Charles felt terrible today," I cannot really know that because I am not Charles. I can only mean that Charles's brow was furrowed, that his complexion was bilious, that he only snarled when spoken to, that he ordered a laxative to be sent out from town. Yet I can say, "Charles felt terrible today," in my privilege as storyteller, and so can I tell you every detail of his emotions and physical sensations, along with anything else a person felt or thought. It is I who tell it, I am the final authority, and not even the person who is alleged to have these feelings, not even Charles himself, can gainsay or contradict me. It is my story and not Charles's. Be silent, Charles. You can tell your story to yourself, but now I am in charge.

There never could be anyone named Blanco White. Not if he wore white clothes and had a white forehead, and went about the world disseminating white ideas. And Bini is a ridiculous name and Lancelot is far too obvious for the other lover in the triangle, when his rival is a King. And even my mother. How could she, who gave to the world with the help of her husband the glow of a new and magical metal, actually be called Claire?

Reality is too banal and pointless, and not even consecutive. It needs first mythologizing and then demythologizing, and so we have novelists and critics. The novelist shows you the most ordinary things of daily life—a man dying in a hospital, another making a crêpe and selling it to a student, another trundling a wheelbarrow backwards; but he transforms these things by his art into visions that seem totally pristine, as though glimpsed at the moment of the earth's creation; he takes the tarnished old coins of our experience and polishes them until they glow like new. That is what a crêpe is! we exclaim to ourselves. That is what it is to die in a hospital! So that is what a wheelbarrow is! Then, inevitably, must come on the critic to explain how it is all done, removing the magic, displaying the stale crêpe in his museum case, allowing the coin to tarnish again as he explains the chemistry of brass polish, showing that it is not so wonderful after all, that it is all done with words, it is a trick of words and words are only accidentally, so to speak, attached to things.

A novel is only a sign. This is called semiotics. Or rather a novel is a forest, a graveyard, of signs, all pointing in different directions; until suddenly they all line up in the same direction, like molecules in a magnetized bar of iron, pointing at something in the far distance that we have not noticed before, something that we now make out for the first time, and that thing that we can discern in the distance is the Real. It is the Real of the novel, which is different from the real of the daily world. So the critic explains to us.

And yet, it all really happened.

XII

My mother's health deteriorated in the summer after the visit to Giverny. By August it was clear that she was seriously ill and would have to go back to the clinic at Fontenay-aux-Roses. She was soon installed there in her old room, and that same Dr. Simon who had treated her before now took charge of the management of this far more serious illness. She was so weak now that she could scarcely get out of bed without assistance. Her small cuts and burns would still not heal, and she had a persistent pain in her left side which was finally traced to the spleen. To locate the spleen, pass your right hand around the left side of the body as far as you can reach. That was where it hurt. And there was a new symptom: when she combed her hair it came out in handfuls, which she dropped into the wastebasket with a thoughtful and vacant expression, feeling her skull afterwards to see if patches of bare skin were left behind.

What was wrong with her? Dr. Simon spoke of anemia, which is not a disease but only a term meaning that there were not enough red blood cells in her veins. It explained nothing. The failure of lesions to heal was caused by low-level sepsis. What caused the low-level sepsis? Many things might. If her hair fell out this happened to many women her age. As for her vision, she had the beginnings of cataracts. She could still see well enough, and even read fine print with the aid of a lens, but at dusk it was difficult for her to make out things, and sometimes she saw things that were not there.

"Maman, are you comfortable here?"

"Oh, yes."

"Dr. Simon is an excellent physician."

"He is very capable. He only has two faults: he doesn't know what is wrong with me, and he doesn't know how to treat it."

"You need a rest. You're run-down and you've been working too hard."

"Yes. Picking red currants. Riding bicycles."

She seemed to blame herself for every moment of relaxation, every indulgence, every small pleasure she had taken in her life. The bicycle ride to Bougival had taken place over three months ago. I waited day after day for her to blame me for the episode at Giverny, when I had gone off in the buggy with Félix and left her in a disabled motorcar in the rain, but she never spoke a word of this. When I came home the next morning, after the Feast of Harlequins, she had nothing much to say and only remarked dryly, "Do not write that journalist any letters, or he will put them in his paper." I don't know why she was so forgiving about this escapade of mine, or why she chose to ignore it; perhaps it was something that Blanco had told her, or perhaps she herself in her own mind, in her own sick and tormented mind, had come to a different set of conclusions about human destinies and the part that love and spontaneity play in our lives.

"Then you don't lack for anything, Maman? Can I bring you something to read?"

"Yes. Newton's *Principia*, in English."

"Are you joking?"

"Not at all. He writes with great clarity, and it is a pleasure to see him unfolding his ideas one by one."

GLOWSTONE

Instead I brought her some popular magazines, a book about travel in America, and a novel of Jules Verne, which she enjoyed although she wouldn't admit it.

She lay in bed night and day in half-reclining position with pillows behind her because of the pain in her side. Both her hands were bandaged, the old scars broke out and suppurated, and she turned the pages clumsily as though she were wearing boxing gloves. When she had to hold the lens in one hand, it was even more difficult. The Sisters provided her with a bright electric lamp to focus on the page. She remembered the time when she and Paul had predicted that the light of the world would be provided by glowstone.

The nights were the worst: not for the physical suffering, which diminished a little when the lights were turned down and the clinic became silent and shadowy, but because of the dreams; or rather, since she never slept for more than a few moments at a time, for the visions that appeared in the region that lay just between her waking hours and the moments of fitful sleep. At times she found herself wandering again in that strangely familiar city of the Geographical Dream, although it was not a dream, she really saw and went to these places, if only for instants that left behind them recollections of vivid clarity. It was as though a tiny fragment of cinema film were run rapidly through the projector, and then the screen turned white again. She caught sight of the mysterious temple, then she entered it and found it was only the laboratory in Rue de l'École-de-Médecine. The transparent rats staggered over the floor, stopped before her, and stared at her with their eyes like fish eggs. The pygmies, the alchemists, the necromancers and wizards appeared suddenly and held out to her their retorts and alembics which exuded a glowing steam. Or, as she turned to call the Sister to come and turn her light on so she could read, there was another fluttering episode that went on a little longer than the others. The alchemists and necromancers busied themselves with their flasks, gesticulating, smiling fiendishly and setting their fingers on their lips, and a flare of light broke from one flask and illuminated the room brilliantly. They nodded to one another with glee; they laughed silently. Taking a pair of tongs, a wizard in a pointed hat and a gown covered with stars reached into the blazing flask and extracted a small cube of glowing metal. This he threw to the pygmies who were waiting at one side in their costumes of medieval jongleurs. They caught it with glee, throwing it from one to another, laughing and crying out silently Ow, Ow, Ow, at its scorching heat. Finally one of them flung it high into the air, pressing his burnt hands to his armpits and seething at the pain while he laughed. It drifted slowly in an arc across the room and when it struck the floor it exploded, quite silently but with a blinding flash that made everything disappear. Claire screamed.

"What is it, Madame?"

"Please bring a light."

"Are you in pain?"

"No. I want to read."

"Here is the life of Saint Ursula."

"Bring me Jules Verne."

"Madame, Dr. Simon says your life is in peril. Have you thought of Eternity?"

"Damn Dr. Simon."

"Oh, Madame."

The Sister, her white habit floating behind her like heron's wings, hurried off in search of the book and the lamp. She came back with the Matron, who told Claire she should come to her senses and not bother the other patients in the middle of the night. The Matron had been awakened from her own sleep and had only flung on the habit over her coarse nightgown. She glanced at the book; it was *Le Château des Carpathes*. "What nonsense." Hermine had chosen it because it had nothing whatsoever in it about science.

On another occasion—perhaps it was the same night, since time had become a fluid substance that seeped around and under her life, confusing one day with another—she was visited by a succession of veiled girls, who wore identical white dresses and passed before her one by one. As each one passed she drew back her veil to show the rotted jaw, the black serum of necrosis that dripped from the bone, the cataract-eyes that were like the eyes of fish boiled with their heads on, opaque and unseeing. They smiled hideously and their jaws glowed with luminescence. Paul, she cried. Paul! quite silently. He came at once, but he was no longer her beloved, no longer her companion of work, the solemn and serious Paul who explained the world to her. Instead he was the master of the factory who had led the girls on their pilgrimage to her bedside. The girls disappeared and he came toward her bed, smiling cryptically. She sensed his cold fell hand falling across her, drawing her to him in the dark offing. He held up his hands to show her, then he began taking off his clothes. It was because he wished to show her the third of the Stigmata, the one on his side caused by the vial of glowstone he had carried from London to Paris in his vest. When he was naked he pointed, still smiling, to the place. He had no genitals; they had rotted off and left only a little black stub. She called the Sister again.

"I want a sleeping potion. I want a very strong one. Twenty grains of chloral. I wish to sleep so soundly that I will not dream."

"I would have to ask Dr. Simon."

"No. You will not ask Dr. Simon. You will bring it to me, or I will tell the doctor you are a religious hysteric who threatened me with death and forced me to read the lives of the Saints."

She hurried away, frightened.

"So you have come, Paul."

From her position on the heaped-up pillow, a white emaciated figure in the white bedclothes, she stared at him wide-eyed and glinting, with a fixed smile. The rest of us exchanged glances. We had all come out from Paris, brought by Blanco in his Panhard, for the occasion of her birthday, the twenty-sixth of August. Blanco was at the far end of the room, saying little. Carlo Bini and I stood at the foot of the bed, and Lancelot at the bedside next to her. She looked directly at him so there could be no mistaking whom she meant. It was not clear whether, after all these years, she had at last reached this final intimacy of calling him by his given name, or whether she mistook him for her dead husband. She had shown no other signs of mental confusion and her mind seemed clear, although restless. As we hesitated, waiting to see what Lancelot would respond, she clarified the situation herself. "It's ridiculous that I've gone on all these years calling you Lancelot. We talked about it once—queer, it was in this very room, and at that time I said . . ." A slightly glazed manner came over her and she quickly went on. "I don't know what I said, but we've been old friends for so long I feel we might have been twins in the cradle." Thus, effectively casting the taboo of incest over any possible sentimental relation between them, she ended the matter. She went on, however, to raise a new confusion, one that left us even more baffled and embarrassed than before. She was very talkative today and not in good spirits exactly, but vigorous and clear-minded, except on certain points.

"It's so good of you all to have come. I get so bored here and the Sisters are a nuisance. The twenty-sixth of August. Paul and I would have been married twenty-one years today. We were married in the Mairie of the Sixth Arrondissement and we went to Bougival on our honeymoon. We went on bicycles. Paul was all in white."

I looked straight ahead at the blank wall behind the bed. Carlo and Lancelot had their eyes cast down at their feet. I couldn't turn around to look at Blanco. Finally it was Lancelot, bless him, who made some effort to clear up the confusion. "It's your birthday also," he said with his eyes still on the floor.

"Yes, of course. Did you think I didn't know that? But on that day when Paul and I were married, the Claire who lived before ceased to exist. I was reborn into a different existence. On that day, I became nothing in the world but Paul's wife, his companion, and his assistant in the work of the laboratory. The twenty-sixth of August will always be for me not my birthday but the beginning of a new life."

She looked around with a smile. "So it's to celebrate this that you've all come out from Paris and brought cordial, and dragées, and little cakes—"

"Dr. Simon said absolutely no champagne," said Blanco.

"I know, and I'm sure he's right. It's bad for me. If you've brought me cordial and little cakes, we can have a little party and drink to the years. Paul, you're so lugubrious, why don't you cheer up."

"I'm perfectly cheerful, Claire. It's good to see you looking so well."

"Oh Paul, don't be such a dreadful hypocrite. My hair is awful. The Sisters won't even let me brush it. They insist on doing it for me and you can imagine what their idea of brushing hair is. None of them have had any for years. The poor things, they don't know what to do with a beautiful woman when they've got one." This playful vanity was another new turn in her manner. Something had changed in her. I was pleased but bewildered by this. I was glad to find her so cheerful, but this wandering of her mind—a mind which at the same time seemed perfectly clear—was disquieting. If the Sisters brushed her hair for her, I thought, it was probably to keep her from seeing how much of it came off on the brush.

"At least they've let you put on your own nightgown for your birthday, Maman."

"Oh, that linen thing they wanted me to wear is dreadful. It isn't just because you've come. I wear this gown all the time now. When it's being washed, there's another one that Matron fished up from somewhere. I'm sure it isn't hers; it has rosebuds on the neck. Probably it belonged to somebody who died."

She was still quite cheerful. The Sister brought tiny little glasses no bigger than thimbles and we drank apricot cordial out of them. The sugar-coated almonds, served ordinarily at christenings and first communions, had always been a favorite of mine; I kept dipping into the box and ate far more than was necessary for ceremonial purposes. Maman's good spirits had cheered me up too, although I felt that the cheerfulness was hollow and forced, kept alive only by her slightly demented playfulness.

Then something else happened and the tone of the occasion

changed abruptly. The Sister came in to change the bandages on her hands. It was an inappropriate moment for it, we were still sipping our cordial and eating little cakes, but it was done twice a day and in the imbecile and mechanical way of hospitals and clinics they did it always at the same time. The Sister smiled and motioned for us to go on talking. "Give me your hands, Madame."

Instead of talking we watched while the long streamers of gauze were unwound from her hands. At the bottom of each there was a pad of gauze stained with serum pressed against the palms. Maman too watched complacently as the Sister went about her work. It was as though the hands might have belonged to someone else. But, as the Sister reached for the gauze and scissors to make new pads for the palms, she turned away from her to us. Holding up her hands, she exposed the palms to us with a little smile. They were covered with the ropy scars of old burns, and there were several open ulcers on each. I realized now that for years she had concealed the insides of her hands from me and from everyone. I remembered a curious way she had of going about the apartment with her fingers curled into her palms and her thumbs holding them down. When she took something into her hand, a hairbrush or the handle of a saucepan, it was with a grimace of pain which she converted into a kind of frozen-faced smile. Now she showed us her secret. For some time she lay propped in the bed holding out to us these eloquent and disturbing emblems of her illness.

"They aren't pretty, are they? I have done this to myself. We have all been too careless—you, Paul, and you Carlo. I can see you all now only as though I am looking through a lace curtain. That too I have done to myself. That is our business if we want to do it. But what we have no right to do is to do such things to others."

She dropped her hands to the bed but still would not let the Sister touch them. "I have been thinking a great deal lately about our responsibilities, the responsibilities of scientists. Who will call us to account for what we do? No, go away, you tiresome creature, I won't be bandaged yet, have a little cordial or eat a dragée. Who will call us to account? For years we have worked together in the Institute. We have discovered new facts about the basic nature of matter, we have demonstrated that the atom is not the last finite particle in the plan of the universe, that it can change itself into other atoms or even into pure energy. Once science had advanced a step, it can never be taken back. And we have advanced that step."

"The credit is due to you and Dr. Savarin," murmured Lancelot.

"Paul, don't be a fool. I am not speaking of credit. Those factory girls in New England with necrosis of the jaw. Who shall take the credit for them? Are you ready to do so, Paul? It is you who urged that we should be more practical, that we should find ways of applying the results of our research in industry, in medicine, in the military. But even if we had not done this—even if we had not found out how to make paint glow in the dark, even if we had not tinkered with putting little glowstone capsules in rats, even if we had confined our research to the realm of pure science—we would still be guilty if we allowed this knowledge to pass into the hands of others. We must not give our secrets to pygmies! It means death, Paul. We hold the power of death over the human race. We have become half-gods; we cannot confer life but we can confer death. It is a terrible thing to be a half-god. When I am gone, Paul, the Institute must be closed down. It is called the Savarin Institute and after me there will be no more Savarins."

"That day will be a long time from now, we can be sure," said Lancelot in his low voice. "And there will be Hermine."

"The Institute is to be closed, Paul. I am firm on that point. This is why I have called you today to come to me here. To tell you this."

At this point Lancelot couldn't contain himself. He was full of respect for Maman, he was on the point of tears, he would have allowed himself to be cut into bits for her, but he could not admit the thought of the Institute being destroyed on her funeral pyre in a kind of Indian suttee. And his way of objecting to this was to say, "You are mistaken, Claire. You haven't called us here today. We came to congratulate you on your birthday. It was Blanco's idea."

"I called you here," she repeated firmly. She seemed amused

at Lancelot's confusion and alarm. Finally she allowed the Sister to rebandage her hands. "Look at this simple creature," she told us. "She has devoted her life to God, and she spends her days alleviating the pain of her fellow human beings. Can we say as much? Can we say that we are as good as this obscure and humble Sister of God?"

"The emanations from glowstone," said Lancelot, "can be used to find bullets in wounded soldiers."

"Oh Paul, this is so tiresome. We found that out years ago. Nowadays it can be done much better with X rays." She leaned back and pointed to the bottle of cordial. The Sister began to object, but Blanco came forward and filled her tiny glass again.

She sipped it, holding it in the bandaged hand, but her verve and clarity were gone and she became thoughtful, distant, almost as though we weren't there. "We must not give our secrets to pygmies," she said once again.

This mysterious utterance baffled everyone, but I was eventually able to piece out what it meant, after talking to her about her dreams and the matter of the chloral which neither the Sisters nor Dr. Simon would let her have. As for the confusion over her wedding and whether she and my father had gone on their honeymoon on bicycles, my own opinion is that this mistake was deliberate, a way of laying the ghost of her husband on this day that was dedicated to her marriage with him. Blanco had been created, perhaps, to fill the gap left in her life by the loss of Papa, a spotless and living embodiment of the vision she had devoted herself to since the tragedy had struck her. So she reasoned, or so her emotions welled and told her. At first she had mistaken Blanco for a lover, even though an unwanted one, and this notion had caused her guilt. Finding that she loved him in return, and even longed for his embrace, she concealed this feeling, and destroyed any chance of her own happiness, because of the fear that she might contaminate him in some way with her illness. She and Blanco would never embrace. But Blanco was Paul, the one was the shadow, the other was a play of light. She had gone with her lover to Bougival and been happy. When had this happened? Was it twenty-one years ago or only this spring? She had gone with her lover to Bougival and been happy, and the shadow and the play of light had merged into one, extinguishing each other and leaving her chaste and untouched, in a different kind of happiness. This was the playful, detached, distant gaiety she displayed in the room of the clinic, just before she transfixed us with her Delphic pronouncement about pygmies and secrets, and her sentence of destruction on the Institute to which she had devoted her life.

There were two other visits to the clinic that I remember from that time. When Félix and I came to tell her we were married, in September, she drew us to her with a weak smile and embraced us both. She had been reading when we came, and she laid the book down on the bedclothes. Her eyes got a little better from time to time and she enjoyed reading; she had never had time for it before.

I took the book from her and looked at it. It was *The Ambassadors*. I had no idea where she had got it. Perhaps it was from the library of the clinic, brought by some patient who left it behind when he died.

She took it back from me. "When I began this book I thought that Henry James was a silly old maid who wrote in a way that was far too complicated. But he knows something. Strether has failed. He was sent to bring Chad back to America and he did not. But see what he tells to Little Bilham in Gloriani's garden."

She began reading in a strained and painful voice from the place where she had left the book open. " 'Live all you can; it's a mistake not to.' " I tried to take the book away from her so I could read it myself, but she went on, squinting at the words through the clouds on her eyes. " 'It doesn't matter so much what you do in particular as long as you have had your life. If you haven't had that what have you had? . . . I'm too old— too old at any rate for what I see. . . . It's too late. . . . What one loses one loses; make no mistake about that. . . . Still, one has the illusion of freedom; therefore don't, like me, be without the memory of that illusion. I was either, at the right time, too stupid or too intelligent to have it, and now I'm a case of reaction against the mistake. . . . Do what you like so long as you don't make my mistake. For it was a mistake. Live, live!' " She set the book down and smiled at us. "Like Strether, I didn't know the simplest thing there is to know, that the point of life is to live. And I found out too late."

"You've lived, Maman."

"Love each other, my darlings, and find out all the different ways there are to live."

I left her a poem I had written about my own love for Félix; it was called "The Feast of Harlequins," and I wasn't sure she would be able to understand it, but it was skillfully written and showed talent, even she could see that. She never mentioned it to me afterwards. The next time I saw it, a number of months later, it had been folded and reopened until its wrinkles had become a part of its substance like the face of an old person. I have it here with me among my effects, where I am now.

A couple of weeks later, when I had come out alone to spend the afternoon with her, a strange wrinkled brown creature in a sari arrived at the clinic, slipped in past the Sisters, and stood at the foot of the bed, staring owlishly at her out of two syrup-eyes with the red dot of a caste mark between them. After a moment of bewilderment I identified her as Mme Hickman, the crazy old lady of our Sunday at the salon on the Île St.-Louis. Maman recognized her immediately and smiled without saying a word.

Mme Hickman clutched in her hand a pitiful spray of marigolds, one of them broken and fallen over her hand. With a ceremonial gesture she laid it on the bed.

"Sorry," she said. "Sorry." She meant that she had come to offer her sympathies. Maman nodded and encouraged her. How on earth she heard that Maman was ill I have no idea. And then she made quite a speech, for her.

"I am Deena. Please call me Deena. I have a name but for

years no one has called me by it. They all call me Madame Hickman and my sister calls me you. I have come here to bring flowers and to tell you to call me Deena."

"Thank you, Deena."

"You must marry Blanco. He is a good and handsome man." And then she turned and fled.

Maman and I talked about her afterwards. She said, "It was not really so important that we call her Deena. She wanted to tell me that everyone is a person, not just somebody else's sister or mother. She wanted to tell me to be myself and not to please anyone else. That's why she told me to marry Blanco."

After a moment I said, "She did that once when she ran away with the American cowboy."

"That's right. And the rest of her life she has suffered from it."

It was about this time too that the news came that Délicienne Maedl had died in Switzerland. Maman showed no emotion at all when I told her this. I wasn't even sure that she understood, but I didn't explain any further.

Toward the end of September another doctor, Professor Mansard, came out from Paris to serve as consultant in my mother's case, at the suggestion of Blanco. He was a member of the Faculty of Medicine and a specialist in wasting diseases. He examined Maman and questioned Dr. Simon thoroughly. Then he and I went out and walked together down a country lane in Fontenay, along hedges heavy with the roses that Lancelot had promised Maman long ago in the winter. Professor Mansard was a portly man in his sixties with a shock of white hair, in a light gray suit and panama hat. It was a sunny mild day, unusually warm for the autumn. He took off his hat and wiped his brow with an immaculate folded handkerchief, and then he put the hat back on again.

"Such a case may seem strange to you. It often does to a layman. But I can assure you that, in my work in the Medical School, every day I come upon new unaccountable things, often grotesque and unendurable, that can go wrong with the human body. I won't lie to you. You seem to be a very clever young woman, and you also seem to have your emotions under control. I don't know exactly what's wrong with your mother. I haven't seen a case exactly like this before. But I have some idea what caused the symptoms she's suffering from."

"What do you mean?"

"How long has your mother been exposed to these materials in the laboratory?"

"For more than twenty years."

"And what precautions did she take?"

"She washed her outer clothing frequently. She kept the laboratory well ventilated. And she—always handled the active material with tongs."

He noticed the hesitation as I told him this. "Considering the scars on her hands, I can hardly believe that."

"Dr. Simon has diagnosed myeloid leukemia. It might happen to anyone, he says."

"The symptoms are identical to those caused by excessive exposure to X rays. A good deal is known about this now. That Simon is a fool."

"If she had been treated earlier?"

"It would have made no difference."

"Surely something can be done at least about her eyes. Can't cataracts be removed by surgery?"

He stopped and turned, looking at me intently with a sympathy quite free from sentimentalism. "We don't need to worry about those cataracts, Madame Bock. I will speak to you frankly. It will be four or five years before those cataracts are ripe to operate. And your mother does not have four or five years to live."

I had known this was true, but it gave me a little cold shock to hear it. No one had yet spoken the words aloud.

"Then how long does she have?"

"No one can say. Four or five weeks. Or four or five days."

"Can't something be done for her suffering?"

"She isn't suffering much in her body. She complains of nightmares, or hallucinations in the half-waking state. I've ordered a sleeping draught of chloral. Twenty grains. It isn't good for people in the long run, it tends to be habit-forming, but in her case it makes no difference."

"Professor, how is it that you in speaking frankly to me have removed a dread that the others couldn't remove by telling lies?"

"You are a sensible young woman. To others I would tell lies. I often do."

"Professor, is it true that glowstone is useful in medicine?"

"No doubt. It's said to burn away tumors. To the rest of the body, I imagine it does much what it has done to your mother."

"So there's no progress in medicine then?"

"Oh yes. We learn to put new names to the various human sufferings. And we learn to alleviate pain. Twenty grains of chloral. It will allow her to sleep peacefully."

She died in my arms. People often say that as a figure of speech but in this case it was quite literally true. Professor Mansard's prognosis was accurate; the end came only five days after his visit. She had had difficulty breathing all day, and I had spent the afternoon with her, supporting her with an arm behind her back when she tried to cough even though she hardly had the strength. From time to time a Sister came and gave her a teaspoon of expectorate or a sip of hot water with menthol, and Dr. Simon looked in once to comment that it was only a little bronchitis and the fever would subside of itself in a couple of days. Around four o'clock she was seized with a particularly violent fit of coughing. With one hand I supported her and with the other I held the basin. She managed to bring up a half a cupful or so of foul green sputum. I set the basin aside and came back to enfold her in my arms, and for five minutes or so she was quiet. She said nothing of course; the coughing had left her weak. She looked straight at me with a secret smile, as she had years ago when I was a little girl and she had some special surprise to offer me, a walk in the park or something good for dinner. Then she closed her eyes and simply stopped breathing. I stayed with her for a minute or two to be sure, then I went for the Sister.

A few moments later the room was full of hurrying and whispering Sisters, a flurry of white heron-wings. The Matron came and surveyed the scene with a calm detachment. I believe she was a good woman and managed the clinic as best she could. Sometimes it was necessary to be severe with the patients. She had seen many people die. The sheet was drawn over Maman's face and the mirror was covered with a cloth; the Sisters were very superstitious. As I turned to leave, I saw Blanco standing in the shadows at the end of the room, motionless amid the hurrying Sisters who fluttered past him and paid him no attention. I don't know how he came without my noticing him; he hadn't been there earlier in the afternoon. Tears filled his eyes. We stood looking at each other for a moment or two, then he turned without a word and left the room. In a little while I heard the sound of his Panhard starting up in the street, a chuffing that gradually diminished as he drove away. I afterwards heard that he went back to America and never visited Europe again.

So ends the story of my mother. What happens after that must be my own story and there is not much to tell. For the storyteller has no story of her own, except insofar as she puts herself into the story she tells about others. No, I didn't have children. I think perhaps it's better that I didn't, considering this world I would have brought them into, the world of Paris in 1943. If I had had a son when I married Félix, he would be in his thirties now, of military age. And I didn't become a scientist, I became a novelist. Hermine Bock-Savarin, winner of the Prix Fémina, short-listed for the Prix Goncourt but outmaneuvered by more astute literary politicians. . . . I had a satisfactory career in every way, both in acclaim and in money, and that is not even taking into consideration the pleasure of writing, the heady and joyous power of sitting down every day to create artificial worlds more colorful and complex than the mundane everyday world we all live in. My books are there on the shelf. You can look at them if you want. Some of them are quite good.

GLOWSTONE

Happy is the nation that has no history, and if that were done into Latin, it would begin with the word Félix. I have had that joy too, the joy of a love that continues undiminished through the years and grows greater in spirit as the capabilities of the body weaken and pass away. I am a gray-haired woman now, hiding in a cellar in Paris from the Germans. They wish to arrest me because Félix, even though he was in his sixties, worked for the Resistance. They have already captured him and shot him; this happened a few days ago. He was a good art critic and probably a better writer than I am, he enjoyed his work and he enjoyed every minute of his life, and he was happy until the day they shot him. Now that he is gone, now that his ordeal is over, I am happy too because I have my work and I can lose myself in that, and I hope the Germans don't discover me. They will probably find me sooner or later. Other people have been taken, and if pushed to the point, if it becomes dreadful enough, they will surely tell all they know. So would I if I were in their place. So that I can only wait, there is no other place for me to go.

The reason I am able to be happy even though these things are happening all around me is that I live, now, mainly in my thoughts and remembrances of that Belle Époque, so long ago, when there were horse cabs and omnibuses, when it was improper for a young girl to go to a café on the Boulevards, when skirts were long but came off just as easily as they do now, when a meal for two with wine was five francs at the Bouillon Duval, when we drank champagne in the country and Félix and I kissed on the boggy bank of the river. I don't like the present day as much. Perhaps I am old-fashioned, but I have my reasons. You already know some of them.

A mother, according to Félix's Resistance friends, was asked by a German officer to choose which of her two sons would be shot, otherwise they both would be. There is no limit to the unspeakable things that human beings do to one another. Only a week or so ago, before I came here to this cellar, I was with some scientists from the University. They told me that a Jewish mathematician has thought of a bomb so powerful that it would destroy an entire city. Rumors of this have been passed secretly in the scientific community although it is not known publicly. It is feared that the Germans may learn how to make this bomb; they are already importing a special kind of water from Norway for their experiments. And so the Americans must make it too, in order to have it before they do. I hope this doesn't happen. If it does happen, if the wizards give their secrets to the pygmies, then they too will be blown up when the pygmies throw their glowing cube into the world. Those who have thought of this terrible weapon will not be able to blame it on the politicians. It was not the politicians who thought of the formulae, but they, clever fools like Lancelot, dreaming of mathematical figures behind their pale and lofty foreheads.

If they are not careful, there will be no foreheads, no formulae, no universities and no cities. There will be only silence and forgetfulness, oblivion. I believe that is what is going to happen to me soon, and I am not too sorry for it. What is important to me is this pile of typewritten papers, which I am just adding the last sheet to now. When I am finished, I will wrap it in brown paper and tie it with a string, and a brave boy will come and take it to a place in another part of the city, where no one will find it until after the war, or not perhaps for many years. Then you, reader, will know what has happened, what I have done and what I have dreamed, what all of us have seen and felt. You can laugh if you want at Blanco or poor old Lancelot (I have made him funnier than he was), but you must weep too, for even ridiculous people suffer and have regrets, are denied the joys they long for, love in vain, and die in despair. Hypocrite reader, my double, my brother! Old Baudelaire understood well enough; he knew how to make his sins seem more interesting than they were, and at the same time involve his reader in the common guilt. That Previous Existence in his poem is the one I have lived myself, not in another life but in this one. It is a life I have imagined for myself, just as we imagine our other incarnations. But the mind tricks, we believe these things have really happened, and because we believe they have really happened, they have.

And so I am here, amid these piles of paper, old Baedekers with passages underlined in spidery red, maps, notes, fragments of paper with a scrap of dialogue on them or an image about which I cannot make up my mind; shall I say a penetrating intelligence, or a questioning intelligence; and so I leave both on the page. Old broken mirrors, mirrors covered with gray splotches like forgotten continents. Can anyone be interested in that? Yet if I am clever enough, if I work to the point of exhaustion, perhaps I can paste together all these scraps of paper, glue together the broken mirrors, transcribe the address of a café from the Baedeker, trace out the route on the map, and this city, these people, these anguishes and joys, will erect themselves magically like a house of cards, a world of paper events even solider and more vivid than the prosaic world we are all condemned to inhabit. There is very little food left in this place, but I have left my hungers behind, along with my passions and my regrets. A very little will suffice me, a cup of coffee with chicory because it is wartime, a Black Market cigarette, a memory of a hotel room with yellow tulle curtains. Farewell now! I must wrap up this package. Where is a bit of string?

Childhood
Social, Legal and Health Studies

Dedication

To my son, Ultan.
E.Z.O'B.

To my mother, Mary Shanahan, my husband, Chris, and my daughter, Rebecca.
M.P.

Acknowledgements

I wish to thank my son, Ultan, my friends and colleagues for their support and encouragement.
E.Z.O'B.

Thank you to Chris Prangnell and Aisling Davenport for their support and meticulous feedback.
M.P.

Thanks to Jane Rogers for her considered and diligent editing of this book and to all involved in its development and production.

Contents

Introduction to Policy in the ECCE Sector

ORIGINS AND DEVELOPMENTS

CHAPTER OUTLINE

- Introduction
- International influence: United Nations Convention on the Rights of the Child (1989)
- What is policy and how is it relevant to childcare practitioners?
- Factors in and influences on the development of childcare policies in Ireland
- Early policy developments up to 2000
- In Focus: The National Childminding Initiative Guidelines
- In Focus: Our Children – Their Lives: National Children's Strategy (2000), including the Whole Child Perspective

INTRODUCTION

Our concept of what childhood is, how childcare is defined and thought of, is influenced by many different strands. According to Hayes (2002, p. 21), 'Childhood is both a biological reality and a social construct. It is defined not only by biology, but also by a particular society at a particular time in a particular way which represents the view that society has of childhood.'

This quote illustrates that the society we live in influences how we think of, define and behave in relation to a given topic. For instance, in Victorian times children were thought of as 'mini-adults', a view which doesn't recognise that childhood and children have unique characteristics, separate and distinct from the characteristics of adulthood. Nowadays we understand that there are distinct differences between how children and adults feel and think; we recognise childhood as an important time which shapes the adult we become. The importance of supporting children and childhood is seen as fundamental, which is reflected in the numerous policy documents on how best this can be achieved.

Yet is this attitude a relatively new one? In looking back at Ireland's history and attitudes, and the policies and legislation that encapsulated them, we will see that before the ratification of the United Nations Convention on the Rights of the Child (UNCRC) the prevailing view did not see children and childhood as we do now. We will track the development of childcare policy and legislation from the early 1990s onwards and the different influences and factors that came to shape it. This will help us to make sense of what can be an overwhelming volume of policies and legislative developments. First let's look at the UNCRC, which Ireland signed up to in 1990 and ratified in 1992, marking a watershed in Ireland's approach to children and the development of relevant legislation and policy.

International Influence: the UNCRC

It can be hard for us to imagine a time when children's 'rights' weren't recognised. Even the idea that a child should be respected and bestowed individual rights would have seemed unbelievable to those who either saw children's rights as part of, and not separate from, those of their parents or family. Indeed it is only very recently, with the outcome of the Referendum on Children's Rights (2012), that our Constitution (Bunreacht na hEireann) conferred upon children individual standing and rights. Before then a child did not have separate rights as a citizen of Ireland; instead, their rights were contained within the 'family' unit. This anomaly was highlighted in the case of 'Baby Ann', in which the rights of the baby's birth and adoptive parents were considered by the Supreme Court. No consideration of the best interests of the child could be given at that time, as under the Constitution such rights did not exist for the child.

When examining the history of childhood we see children considered as mini-adults in Victorian times, and children thought of as property, a phenomenon still all too common. It is against this backdrop in Ireland, a landscape where the idea of children's 'rights' was virtually non-existent, where the vulnerable (such as those in poverty or with disabilities) were treated with a charity-based approach. It is this backdrop that makes the UNCRC all the more remarkable.

The seeds of the UNCRC were sown by the work of Janusz Korczak, a doctor and pioneer of children's rights. We can see his influence in the Convention on the Rights of the Child (CRC), which is **rights**-based rather than charity-based. This means recognising the inherent dignity of a person and treating them with respect, not out of charity or kindness but as a right.

The UNCRC is the most widely ratified treaty: in 2010 it had been ratified by every state in the world with the exception of Somalia and the USA. In signing up to the UNCRC, countries agree and are bound to meet its provisions and obligations. The treaty represents a commitment to uphold the rights of the child in all spheres – cultural, political, social and economic. It is a manifesto demanding that governments act in 'the best interests of the child', an aim reflected in its 41 articles. The articles themselves, the product of ten years of negotiation, are wide-ranging and all-encompassing. While the articles are not weighted in terms of importance, recognising the inter-relatedness of each article to the other, four general principles emerge as paramount, and it is these principles around which all other articles revolve.

Four General Principles

- *Article 2:* All the rights guaranteed by the Convention must be available to all children without discrimination of any kind.
- *Article 3:* The best interests of the child must be a primary consideration in all actions concerning the child.
- *Article 6:* Every child has the right to life, survival and development.
- *Article 12:* The child's views must be considered and taken into account in all matters affecting him or her.

Ireland and the UNCRC

How well has Ireland engaged with and implemented the Convention? Ireland signed up to the UNCRC on 30 September 1990 and ratified it on 28 September 1992, in doing so committing itself to protecting and advancing the rights of the child. The UNCRC was a product of ten years of negotiation and consensus-seeking, and its mutuality is arguably where its strength lies. This shared approach is witnessed in its monitoring mechanism, which assesses how well – or badly – the states that signed up to the Convention are implementing it.

1998 UNCRC Assessment

In its first assessment, in 1998, the UNCRC monitoring committee found a 'fragmented' approach to the adoption of the UNCRC in Ireland. The committee recommended that Ireland remove all constitutional barriers to the implementation of the Convention; and that it put in place a range of measures to promote children's rights and to put the Convention into practice, including appointing an ombudsman for children and establishing an inspectorate for residential units.

2006 UNCRC Assessment

In 2006 Ireland's performance was reviewed again by the monitoring committee. According to Emily Logan, Ombudsman for Children, 'The general principles about which the UN Committee raised most concerns with Ireland at that time were: **discrimination**; **the best interests**; and **the right to hear their views**' (Logan 2012, pp. 3–4).

One of the criticisms made by the UN Committee on the Rights of the Child in 2006 was that these general principles had been imperfectly integrated into Irish law. In particular, the UN Committee expressed concern that the 'best interests' principle was not fully integrated into all legislation relevant to children and that insufficient provision was made for children to be heard in judicial or administrative proceedings affecting them. 'Although these principles are clearly not absent from the Irish statute book, implementation of these principles will need to be improved if Ireland is to comply in full with its international obligations' (Logan 2012, pp. 3–4).

Policy Document	Rights	Needs
National Childcare Strategy	58	119
'Ready to Learn'	5	125
National Children's Strategy	50	125
Commission on the Family	120	160

Source: Kiersey & Hayes 2010, p. 7

As we can see, in ratifying the UNCRC Ireland agreed to implement the Convention's articles and to follow the UNCRC's rights-based approach. Up to this point Ireland had very little legislation and very few polices pertinent to children; in adopting the UNCRC the government was forced to adopt strategies and policies that reflected the goals of the UNCRC, which is why we have seen an explosion of developments in the area of child policy, including childcare. (For more information on the UNCRC, please see Appendix A.)

We will examine legislative developments in greater depth in Chapter 2, but it is worth noting here that the Child Care Act 1991 was enacted a year after Ireland signed up to the UNCRC. The title of the Act can be deceptive – it covers the care of children in general, not just childcare (part VII refers to this) – but its concern is the welfare of children, and it places a duty on the HSE to identify children who are not receiving adequate care and protection. In addition, the Act also allows for the provision of family support services.

Before we go any further, now is a good time to examine how legislation and policy are defined before we look at them in relation to childcare.

POLICY
What is Policy?

Every day our lives, personal and work, are impacted upon by policy, even if it is not obvious to us. Whereas the impact of legislation is clearly in our minds – for example, if I drive through a red light I am breaking the law and am liable to be prosecuted by the State – policy does not necessarily have the same observable impact. While legislation is created and mandated by the government and is enforceable, policy at its simplest can be thought of as an agenda or ideas informed by research and best practice to improve outcomes or lives.

What Does 'Policy' Mean?

According to Hogwood and Gunn (1984), cited in Jones and Norton (2010), policy can be described as any, or all, of the following:

- a field of activity (e.g. economic or childcare policy)
- a general intent (e.g. a drive to make the world a healthier place)
- a specific proposal
- something that requires formal authorisation or legislation
- implementing a programme of action.

These definitions are broad, highlighting the relationship between a 'problem' and the strategies needed to solve it. If we take this approach and apply it to childcare as the 'problem', we might decide that the 'problem' is that childcare is fragmented, under-resourced and unregulated. Having identified childcare as the problem, we might then develop strategies and policies to improve childcare by looking at best practice in other countries and by research. As we will see later in the book, in Ireland this approach led to a number of 'policies' being developed to address this issue. Throughout the book we will see how research continues to inform policies, as does the evaluation of how policies are being implemented.

FIGURE 1.1 POLICY FORMULATION

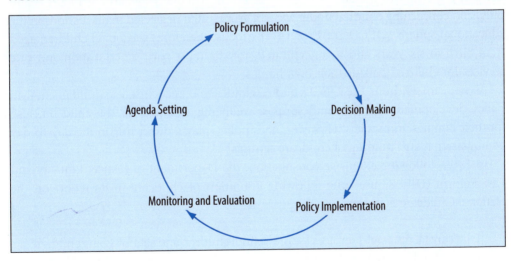

Who Develops Policies?

As with legislation, the government can create policies, and it often invites other stakeholders into the process of policy development (e.g. the National Children's Strategy). Groups other than the government can also develop policies, for example charities or advocacy groups such as the Children's Rights Alliance, Barnardos, hospitals, crèches and schools (e.g. anti-bullying policies). Policies can be informed by legislation;

for example, anti-discriminatory and equality and diversity policies that were developed in response to equality legislation (Equal Status Act 2000 and 2004). Conversely, policy can also influence and encourage the establishment or improvement of legislation. Fundamentally the policy process is best understood as an interplay of institutions, ideas and interests (John 1998).

Policymakers and their Role in ECCE settings

> Policy makers have recognised that access to quality early childhood education and care strengthens the foundations of lifelong learning for all children, contributes to equality of opportunity for women, and supports the broad educational and social needs of families. Research shows too that families operate best in a framework of security supported by services, and that young children develop well within quality early childhood services. (OECD 2004)

Definition of Childcare

The OECD definition describes early childhood care and education (ECCE) as 'all arrangements providing care and education of children under compulsory school age, regardless of setting, funding, opening hours or programme content. ... It was deemed important to include policies – including parental leave arrangements – and provision concerning children under age 3, a group often neglected in discussions in the educational sphere' (OECD 2001, p. 14). Its focus, therefore, was on all children aged from birth to six years and it concentrated, for the most part, on education and care services for children outside their own homes.

As we can see from the OECD quote, childcare is recognised as fundamental in policy development to create and support wellbeing, not just for the child but also for their families and society. However, does policy play a direct role in the day-to-day administration and running of childcare settings?

In 1999, following extensive consultation, the Department of Justice, Equality and Law Reform (DJELR) used the following definition of childcare in its report on the National Childcare Strategy:

> [D]aycare facilities and services for pre-school children and school-going children out of school hours. It includes services offering care, education and socialisation opportunities for children to the benefit of children, parents, employers and the wider community. Thus, services such as pre-schools, naíonraí [Irish language pre-schools], day care services, crèches, play groups, childminding and after-school groups are included, but schools (primary, secondary and special) and residential centres for children are excluded. (DJELR 1999)

POLICY AND CHILDCARE PRACTITIONERS AND SERVICES

As we will see, here and in Chapter 3, policy plays an integral role in the day-to-day running of childcare services; it shapes how practitioners interact with children and supports children's development. In Chapter 3 we will look at specific policies and their impact on ECCE. For now let's consider why policy is important in general.

In order to give the best quality care possible, childcare practitioners must be guided by and implement standards, best practice and legislation. To help achieve this, childcare settings are required to maintain information in the form of their own policies and procedures to demonstrate that their services meet the required standards.

According to Willoughby (2008), 'policy' and 'procedure' can be defined as follows:

> A **policy** is a statement of principles, values or intent that guides, or usually determines, decisions and actions to achieve an organisation's goals. Policies help to ensure that a consistent approach in line with the service's values is adopted throughout the service. They provide the basis for agreed, consistent and well thought through decisions.
>
> **Procedures** spell out precisely what action is to be taken in line with the relevant policy and outline the steps to be followed or the way that a task is to be performed. Procedures can reduce the need to make decisions under pressure or to have to wait for a decision, they provide consistency and they allow everyone to know what is likely to happen in a given situation.

So how do we see policies at work in childcare services? The following is a range of policies that might be seen in childcare services:

- Intake/Admission Policy
- Positive Behaviour Management Policy
- Child Protection and Welfare Policy
- Personnel/Human Resources Policy
- Outdoor Play Policy
- Parental/Guardian Involvement Policy
- Accident/Incident Policy
- Out of School Care Policy
- Anti-Bias/Anti-Discrimination Policy
- Cleaning and Prevention of Spread of Disease Policy
- Food Safety Policy
- Confidentiality Policy.

Reviewing Your Existing Policies

It is essential that your service regularly reviews and monitors all its policies and procedures. This helps you to learn from experience, as your service grows and evolves.

As you strive to meet your clients' changing needs, your policies and procedures should change too. As policies and procedures are used daily you need to review them continuously.

Some issues that may require you to change your policies and procedures are:
- Changes in legislation relevant to childcare
- Other mandatory updates/amendments (ECCE, CCS Scheme, etc.)
- Requests from parents or staff
- Service developments that involve a change in structure and therefore have an impact on current policies
- Child Protection Policy
- Behaviour management
- Curriculum planning.

In addition, you should:
- Review your policies and procedures annually
- Analyse the appropriateness of your policies and procedures for the service you are providing. It is the responsibility of the manager/committee members to ensure that policies and procedures are reviewed and are amended/updated
- Regularly include a review of policies and procedures on the agenda for staff meetings
- Agree a process for informing all staff and parents of any new policies and procedures and any updates to existing ones. (Adapted from Willoughby (2008).)

In Practice

Where do we get the information to formulate these policies?
From legislation, policies and best practice guides. We will examine legislation and policies in depth in Chapters 2 and 3 and look at how they shape the policies seen in crèches and the work of childcare practitioners. As you read these chapters, take notes on what you as a childcare practitioner believe to be the most important policies and legislation.

So how did childcare policy develop in Ireland and what were the influences on it?

THE DEVELOPMENT OF CHILDCARE POLICIES IN IRELAND

According to the White Paper *Ready to Learn* (DES 1999), 'The inextricable linkage between education and care means that early education comprises just one element in an all-encompassing policy concerning the rights and needs of young children.' It also outlines a number of factors that combined to bring early childhood issues to the top of the policy agenda in recent years:

1. There is growing recognition of the benefits for all children of good-quality early childhood education.
2. The importance of early education in addressing socio-economic disadvantage and the contribution of education to economic development have given rise to demands for improved early education for all children.
3. The needs of employers for greater numbers of workers, as well as increased participation in the labour force, have simultaneously increased the demand for and reduced the supply of childcare places.

These factors certainly provide an insight into why childcare policies developed, but other influences were also involved, including:
- international influences
- the changing role of women
- economic influences.

International Influences

The Children's Act 1908 was a landmark document for the care of children in Ireland. It focused on the treatment, as opposed to the punishment, of children and bestowed a separate legal status on children. This Act was replaced by the Child Care Act 1991. The UN Declaration on the Rights of the Child (1958), the UN International Year of the Child (1979) and the UN Convention on the Rights of the Child (1989), ratified by Ireland in 1992, raised the profile and prominence of children as citizens in society. (Walsh & Kiernan 2004, p. 4)

In addition to the ratification of the UNCRC, discussed earlier, another international influence was Ireland's entry to the European Economic Community (EEC), now the European Union (EU). In joining the European community, Ireland began the process of bringing our laws, policies and, arguably, societal attitudes more in line with those of our European neighbours. This had a positive impact, particularly on women, those with disabilities and children, as legislation and policy began to reflect a more rights-based and egalitarian approach.

Taking the case of women, we can clearly see the impact that joining the EEC had on Ireland as it began to implement European directives. Previously in Ireland women who married were prevented from working in some areas (e.g. banks and the civil service), but the enactment of the Civil Service (Employment of Married Women) Act 1973 and the Employment Equality Act 1977 secured women's right to employment after marriage. In the arena of children, the influence of the UNCRC on the development of policy on children's rights and on early education and care cannot be overestimated. In light of the criticisms made in the UNCRC assessment (1998) the state undertook to implement some of the measures suggested, including the development of a **National Children's Strategy** (2000), which paved the way for the establishment of the **National**

Children's Office in 2001. We will look at both, along with other policy initiatives, in greater detail later in the chapter, but here we'll look at other influences that shaped the development of policy in relation to children and to childcare.

The Changing Role of Women

As we have seen, Ireland's participation in the EU prompted changes to legislation in an effort to become more compliant with EU directives and standards, and we saw that legislation was introduced to ensure women's right to employment after marriage. This change gives us an insight into how women were perceived and treated in Ireland. Traditionally a women's role was seen as homemaker and mother, reflecting the strong relationship between Roman Catholic Church and the State. Further, the Constitution – which encapsulates the guiding principles on which the State was founded – offered particular protection to families and the woman's role in the home. The following articles in the Constitution refer specifically to women:

> 41.2.1 In particular, the State recognises that by her life within the home, woman gives to the State a support without which the common good cannot be achieved.
>
> 41.2.2 The State shall, therefore, endeavour to ensure that mothers shall not be obliged by economic necessity to engage in labour to the neglect of their duties in the home.
>
> 45.4.2 The State shall endeavour to ensure that the strength and health of workers, men, women, and the tender age of children shall not be abused and that citizens shall not be forced by economic necessity to enter avocations unsuited to their sex, age or strength.

Note: The first draft of Article 45.4.2 of the Constitution included the words 'inadequate strength of women'. Women's organisations and many individual women considered the phrase very offensive. They wrote to Mr de Valera and met him by appointment. The wording was changed to read as it does above (Scoilnet).

    As we can see, women's place in society reflected a particular perspective rooted in the idea of a woman as a wife and mother whose principal role in life was in the home. In such a society there was little need for childcare arrangements. That's not to say that women didn't work outside the home, rather that the number of working women was relatively small, especially when compared to other European countries.

> Married female labour force participation had been notoriously low in the 1960s and '70s, by Western standards. Only 5.2% of married women were employed in 1961 and this had only increased to 7.5% by 1971. However, from 1971 to 1981 the rate more than doubled to 16.7%. This created the impetus for

convening the first Government Working Party on Childcare Facilities for Working Parents in 1981. (Fine-Davis 2007, p. 3)

Ireland's entry into the EU and the subsequent legislation relating to women's right to work, as discussed earlier, marked a shift in the role of women in Ireland and opened up greater opportunities for women to work and particularly to continue working after the birth of children. This was facilitated through the increasing secularisation (moving away from the control or influence of religion) of Irish society and gender equality reforms. Another major impact on female participation in the workforce was the 'Celtic Tiger', which saw the economy grow rapidly, resulting in increasing numbers of workers needed to fuel it. Below is a table which highlights the significant upsurge in married women's participation in the workplace.

MARRIED WOMEN'S LABOUR FORCE PARTICIPATION IN IRELAND, 1961–2001 (%)

	1961	1971	1977	1981	1989	1994	1997	1999	2001	2004
All ages	5.2	7.5	14.4	16.7	23.7	32.4	37.3	45.3	46.4	49.4
Ages 25–34	4.8	8.8	16.7	21.6	39.0	54.5	58.2	66.3	64.7	65.5

Figures from Fine-Davis 2007, p. 4.

Economic Growth and Changing Employment Patterns

It is important to recognise the impact of economic growth on early childhood education and care. The rapid and significant economic changes that occurred in Ireland from the mid-1990s – the Celtic Tiger – had a profound effect on the country and both demanded and facilitated changes in family life. The 1980s and early 1990s had been marked by a period of recession with high unemployment. Taking the perspective that the role of childcare is to meet the needs of working parents, high unemployment will clearly have an impact on the need for childcare. Of course, we know that the purpose of childcare is more diverse than that. Nonetheless, the economic situation did play a role in the development and proliferation of childcare policies. The substantial growth that the Celtic Tiger brought in its wake thrust into the spotlight the need for structured and supported childcare services to meet the needs of working parents.

As alluded to earlier, the White Paper *Ready to Learn* acknowledged the growing recognition of the positive impact of ECCE on children's outcomes, this forming a further rationale for policy developments tackling the lack of childcare provision. According to Fine-Davis (2007, p. 3), childcare has increasingly become a subject of political and social debate. Between 1983 and 1999, seven reports deliberated on the issue of childcare, yet no significant government initiatives were forthcoming until in 2000 the government finally created a childcare policy – the Equal Opportunities Childcare Programme (EOCP) (DJELR 2000).

Let's take a look at some early developments in policies to support children's needs.

EARLY POLICY DEVELOPMENTS

The Child Care Act 1991 and the ratification of the UNCRC in 1992 marked the beginning of a period of focus on children's wellbeing, including childcare. In 1999, as part of its commitment 'to put the family at the centre of all its policies', the government launched the Families Research Programme in recognition of the lack of research available and with the hope of informing future policy directions. In this section we will explore the development of policies and structures put in place to develop initiatives aimed at supporting and improving children's development.

- **1998:** *Strengthening Families for Life: Final Report of the Commission on the Family* (Department of Social, Community and Family Affairs (DSCFA))
- **1998:** *Report on the National Forum for Early Childhood Education* (Department of Education and Science (DES))
- **1999:** *Ready to Learn*: White Paper on Early Childhood Education (DES)
- **1999:** *National Childcare Strategy: Report of the Partnership 2000 Expert Working Group on Childcare* (DJELR)
- **2000:** Equal Opportunities Childcare Programme (EOCP)
- **2000:** *Our Children – Their Lives: National Children's Strategy* (Department of Health and Children)
- **2001:** National Children's Office (NCO)

Strengthening Families for Life (1998)

The first initiative we will examine is *Strengthening Families for Life: Final Report of the Commission on the Family*, published in 1998. Its scope was wide, incorporating original research, including a national survey of over 1,300 families with children aged 12 or under on childcare arrangements made by families. Research also included an overview of family policy and examined fathers and their role in the family. Analysis of issues affecting families was outlined and some forty recommendations made across several different policy areas.

Core Themes

The Commission's main findings and recommendations are presented in terms of desirable outcomes for families. These outcomes form the core themes of the report. They relate to:
- Building strengths in families (Part 2)
- Supporting families in carrying out their functions – the caring and nurturing of children (Part 3)

- Promoting continuity and stability in family life (Part 4)
- Protecting and enhancing the position of children and vulnerable dependent family members (Part 5).

Strengthening Families for Life marked an important development as research and, especially, policy became more geared to considering the needs of families and children. This can be seen in its conclusion:

> [T]he institutional framework which is recommended must aim to **put families centre stage** at political, executive and administrative levels. In this context, the Commission recommends that 'family well-being' should be singled out as an area of critical importance for Government in the years ahead.

The Commission further suggested the establishment of a Family Affairs Unit whose purpose would be to 'co-ordinate family policy, pursue the findings in the Commission's final report and undertake research and promote awareness about family issues'. We will see how this unfolded through the following policies, which reflect the growing importance given to families, children and childcare.

Report on the National Forum for Early Childhood Education (1998)

The National Forum for Early Childhood Education, held in 1998, was a week-long consultation process which took place as part of the process of preparing *Ready to Learn* (DES 1999). It is particularly noteworthy that this was the first national forum on early childhood education to be held in this country. The aim of the forum was 'to provide an opportunity for all interested groups to engage in a full exchange of views, to put forward their own particular concerns and objectives while, at the same time, taking account of the objectives and concerns of the other partners in the process' (Daly & Forster 2009). Issues raised included concerns over the lack of a national curriculum for young children outside the primary school sector, including those aged under 3. From this forum sprang *Ready to Learn* and the seeds of **Aistear** (the early childhood curriculum framework for children from 0 to 6 years). We will look at Aistear in depth in Chapter 3, but in the meantime let's look at the result of the consultation process that led to Aistear, *Ready to Learn*.

Ready to Learn White Paper (1999)

Ready to Learn was the result of a consultation process aimed at developing a White Paper on early education. It addressed in particular concerns about the absence of a curriculum for children aged under 6. Its aim was to ensure that early childhood provision would be structured, developmental and of high quality. Further, the White

Paper drew attention to target groups such as 'the disadvantaged and those with special needs', proposing that early support should be provided to families of children with special needs.

Its guiding principles were:
- Quality will underpin all aspects of early education provision.
- The State will build on existing provision and use the existing regulatory framework, where possible.
- Implementation will be undertaken on a gradual, phased basis to allow all the participants in the system to prepare adequately for the challenges that lie ahead.
- Progress will be achieved through a process of consultation, dialogue and partnership. (Citizens Information)

The focus of the White Paper on Early Childhood Education was not only supporting the needs and development of the under-6s in childcare settings, whether private providers or community groups; supporting parents to help their children learn and a strategy for improving the quality of infant education in primary schools were also included. **Quality** of provision was emphasised and a strategy set out to increase standards in terms of professional competencies, curricula and methodologies. The need for inspection and evaluation to support providers achieve high standards was recognised and structures to facilitate the effective co-ordination of provision, regulation and improvements in quality were outlined.

One of the clearest ramifications of the *Ready to Learn* paper was the establishment of the Centre for Early Childhood Development and Education (CECDE) and, in the long term, **Síolta**. One of the objectives of *Ready to Learn* was the establishment of a body to advise the Department of Education and Science on policy issues relating to early education and care. To this end, in 2002 the Minister for Education and Science appointed Dublin IT and St Patrick's College, Drumcondra to jointly establish CECDE.

Centre for Early Childhood Development and Education (CECDE) (2002)
The scope of CECDE was extensive, focusing on all care and education settings for children aged from birth to 6 years of age. It attempted to bridge many of the traditional divides between education and care and between early years settings and the formal education system.

Within this broad framework, the objectives of the CECDE included:
- Developing a National Framework for Quality (NFQ) for early childhood education
- Developing targeted interventions on a pilot basis for children who are educationally disadvantaged and children with special needs
- Preparing the groundwork for the establishment of an Early Childhood Education Agency as envisaged by *Ready to Learn*.

CECDE was instrumental in informing policy and initiatives aimed at improving early childhood education. The National Framework for Quality for early childhood education is better known to us as **Síolta**, which was published in 2006. We will explore Síolta in depth in Chapter 3 and throughout the book consider its prominent and guiding influence in ECCE. We will also discuss the concept of **quality**, which is integral to the development and delivery of childcare in Ireland.

The government ceased funding CECDE and it closed at the end of 2008, marking a retrograde step in the development and promotion of early education and care.

National Childcare Strategy: Report of the Partnership 2000 Expert Working Group on Childcare (1999)

The Expert Working Group on Childcare was set up in 1999, in light of what it referred to as the 'crisis' in childcare, under the wing of the Department of Justice, Equality and Law Reform. You may wonder why a group looking at childcare came under the aegis of the Department of Justice: it's because Partnership 2000 was interested in the topic of equality and it looked at the provision of childcare from this perspective. According to the Partnership 2000 agreement, 'child care is clearly an important issue in promoting equality for women and especially in promoting equal opportunities in employment'. The establishment of the Expert Working Group on Childcare was arguably a response to economic demand to provide for mothers entering the workforce and the increase in productivity that would result. Regardless of why the group was established, the resulting *National Childcare Strategy 2000* marked an important step forward in childcare policy and the development of a structured, supported and regulated childcare system.

Members of the Expert Working Group were drawn from many bodies, including government departments, statutory organisations, non-governmental bodies and parents, to develop a strategy for the delivery of childcare and early education services. In developing a national childcare strategy the group was guided by the following principles:

- the needs and rights of the child
- equality of access and participation
- diversity
- partnership
- quality.

(Chapter 6 will explore in depth the theme of equality and diversity in childcare.)

The government saw the National Childcare Strategy as the third prong of childcare policy, along with the report of the Commission on the Family (*Strengthening Families for Life*) and the report of the Forum for Early Childhood Education. These three policy developments reflected government recognition of the necessity for childcare provision. The National Childcare Strategy was initially implemented through EOCP.

Equal Opportunities Childcare Programme (EOCP) 2000–2006

We have seen that the emerging need for childcare services was identified as a key policy issue in the late 1990s, resulting in the development of the *National Childcare Strategy*. EOCP evolved in response to the strategy and provided the financial impetus to support it. EOCP was an EU/exchequer co-funded investment programme with a total allocation of €499.3 million over its seven-year span; of this sum, just over €180 million came from the EU.

The objectives of EOCP were:

- to improve the quality of childcare in Ireland
- to increase the supply of childcare places by 50 per cent (or about 28,000 additional centre-based places) to enable parents to remain in or return to employment, education or training
- to introduce a more co-ordinated approach to the delivery of childcare.

EOCP proposed three key elements to meet these needs:

1. The provision of capital grant assistance to community-based not-for-profit groups and, in a more limited way, to private childcare providers to support the creation of new and enhanced childcare facilities;
2. The provision of grant assistance towards the staffing costs of community-based groups which are located in areas of significant disadvantage, and finally;
3. The provision of supports for quality enhancement. The funding stream set aside for each of these elements is €155 million; €195 million and €83 million respectively, while about €18 million will be required over the seven years of the Programme to meet the elaborate administrative arrangements necessitated in delivering an EU Programme of this magnitude. (Moreau 2004)

The €83 million invested in quality enhancement supported a number of initiatives, including the creation and support of the **City and County Childcare Committees** (CCCs). Under EOCP, the primary focus of County Childcare Committees is to facilitate parents in availing of training, education and employment opportunities through the provision of quality childcare supports.

In Chapter 3 we will examine the subsequent investment programme financed by the State, the **National Childcare Investment Programme 2006–2010**.

Before continuing, let's pause and take a look at one childcare initiative that focuses on the care of children in the home by childminders.

In Focus: National Childminding Initiative and Guidelines

According to the National Childminding Initiative (NCMI), childminders represent the largest type of childcare for families of pre-school children in Ireland today, with over 73,000 families around the country using childminders as their favoured mode of childcare.

Following the report of the *National Childcare Strategy*, a number of initiatives were implemented, including the establishment of the NCMI, to provide supports for childminders and for people interested in becoming childminders. The NCMI is administered locally by the CCCs, which are responsible for supporting the implementation of the NCMI at local level.

The NCMI is made up of a number of different elements, including:

1. *National Guidelines for Childminders* (OMC 2008)
2. Childminding Development Grant (CMDG)
3. Quality Awareness Programme (QAP)
4. Information, training and networking opportunities for childminders
5. Voluntary notification of childminders.

In relation to the last element, Daly (2010, p. 8) says in her evaluation of the NCMI that the report of the Expert Working Group (DJELR 1999) noted that 'childminding is the most common (childcare) arrangement among women with paid jobs and the second most common overall', taking place largely outside the formal economy. Though it was recommended that 'All those providing childcare services for one or more children, in addition to their own, including persons employed by the parent/s of the child, either in the child's home or in the childminder's home, should be required to register', this recommendation has yet to be implemented. Over a decade later, several other recommendations of the group have also not been implemented, illustrating that while those producing policy and strategies may make recommendations, these recommendations don't legally have to be implemented.

In relation to legislation and notification relating to childminders, the NCMI outlines the following:

What legislation governs childminding?
- Childminding is governed by the Childcare (1991) Act and the Pre-School Regulations (2006). Childminding is regulated only where four or more children – unrelated to you or each other – under the age of six are minded.
- A single handed Childminder can mind up to five pre-school children.
- A Childminder can mind no more than two children under the age of 15 months (except in the case of siblings).

- Childminders must notify their local Health Service Executive if they mind four or more children (excluding their own) pre-school children.
- Childminders who are not required to notify the HSE may voluntarily notify their city or county childcare committee and sign up to a voluntary code of good practice, including insurance and training.
- There is no regulation at present of school age childcare services. However, the Report 'School Aged Childcare in Ireland' published by the National Co-ordinating Childcare Committee, recommends a ratio of one adult to eight children. (www.childminding.ie)

National Guidelines for Childminders

As mentioned earlier, one of the strands of the NCMI is the *National Guidelines for Childminders* (OMC 2008), which assist childminders by providing guidance for good practice in the area. They include details on:
- Nationally agreed guidelines for good childminding practice
- Detailed information on Statutory Notification to the Health Service Executive (HSE) and Voluntary Notification
- Services provided to childminders by the CCCs, the childminder advisory officers and Childminding Ireland.

Core Requirements for Childminders

There are four nationally recognised core areas in which childminders should meet certain requirements:

1. *Suitability of the Person*
   The Childminder must be a person aged 18 or over who is genuinely interested in caring for children and is of suitable character to do so.
2. *Wellbeing of the Child*
   The Childminder must have a commitment to providing quality childcare which ensures that the wellbeing and development of child is paramount.
3. *Physical Environment*
   The Childminder's home should provide a secure and happy environment in which the health, safety and welfare of the child is assured and in which the developmental needs of the child are met.
4. *Health & Safety*
   The Childminder must provide evidence that adequate health and safety procedures are in place. (OMC 2008)

THE DEPARTMENT OF CHILDREN AND YOUTH AFFAIRS

We shall conclude this chapter with an examination of the early days of the Department of Children and Youth Affairs (DCYA), which is the government's child and youth policy wing. It was established as a dedicated department in 2011 to oversee issues that had formerly been dealt with by a number of other government departments.

Our Children – Their Lives: National Children's Strategy (2000)

The National Children's Strategy is a ten-year plan with a vision of:

An Ireland where children are respected as young citizens with a valued contribution to make and a voice of their own; where all children are cherished and supported by family and the wider society; where they enjoy a fulfilling childhood and realise their potential. (DoHC 2000)

The national goals of the strategy are:
- Goal 1: Children will have a voice in matters which affect them and their views will be given due weight in accordance with their age and maturity.
- Goal 2: Children's lives will be better understood; their lives will benefit from evaluation, research and information on their needs, rights and the effectiveness of services.
- Goal 3: Children will receive quality supports and services to promote all aspects of their development.

It includes a range of actions across a number of areas, such as giving children a voice so that their views are considered in relation to matters that affect them; eliminating child poverty; ensuring that children have access to play and recreation facilities; and improving research on children's lives in Ireland. The strategy is the first comprehensive national policy document for the full range of statutory and non-statutory providers in the development of services for children and is underpinned by the UNCRC.

National Children's Office (NCO)

The National Children's Office (NCO) was set up in 2001 to drive implementation of the National Children's Strategy. It is the only government agency that aims to improve all aspects of children's lives, as set out in the strategy. It now comes under the umbrella of the Department of Children and Youth Affairs.

The role of the NCO is to encourage co-ordination of policies and services for children at national and local level; it supports and monitors the work of different government departments in implementing the National Children's Strategy; and it liaises with state agencies, voluntary organisations, youth organisations, children and young people. In addition the NCO is responsible for commissioning research to gain further understanding of children and young people.

The NCO has lead responsibility for: increasing children's and young people's participation; research; and priority issues identified by the Cabinet Committee on Children. It works in the following areas:

- Children and young people's participation
- Research on children and young people
- Driving and monitoring implementation of the National Children's Strategy
- Supporting implementation of the Youth Homelessness Strategy
- Supporting Ireland's international obligations in children's policy
- Play and recreation policies
- Co-ordinating implementation of the Children Act, 2001. (NCO 2004)

In 2005 the National Children's Office became part of the Office of the Minister for Children and Youth Affairs (OMYCA).

Before we leave the NCO/OMYCA, let's take a look at the 'whole child perspective', which underpins policies in relation to meeting the needs of children.

In Focus: What is the Whole Child Perspective?

The whole child perspective, adopted by the National Children's Strategy, recognises the multidimensional nature of all aspects of children's lives. The recognition that all parts of children's lives are interlinked has, in turn, implications for public policymaking and the integration of services relating to children.

What is interesting about the 'whole child perspective' is that it takes an ecological approach (looking at the environment or context) in attempting to understand children's lives. This approach recognises that systems (or layers) of influence exist in a child's life, from close layers – the immediate family – to more distant influences, such as government policy. Looking at the illustration of the whole child perspective developed by the NCO, we can see that many and varied influences are included to gain an understanding of the child and the context of the child.

Think about it!
Can you see the whole child perspective in ECCE settings? How would you apply the illustration to the children in your care to help meet their needs? As we continue to examine policies, standards and guidelines in Chapters 2 and 3, see if you can recognise the influence of the whole child perspective at work.

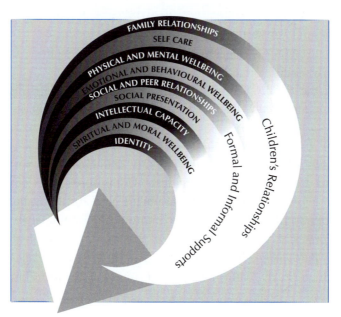

FIGURE 1.2 ALL PARTS OF CHILDREN'S LIVES ARE INTERLINKED

CONCLUSION

As we have seen in this chapter, many influences shape and guide not just the development but also the implementation of policy. We have explored how childcare became an important issue for government, which developed childcare policies not just to meet economic and employment needs but also as an instrument to support families and vulnerable or disadvantaged children. A plethora of reports and policies were devised, which illustrates how lacking Ireland was in developing and supporting childcare within the State. Of course, this can at times be overwhelming for the reader as there seem to be so many reports and policies, but we hope that the journey through policy from the early 1990s has illustrated the flow of policies at that time and the influences that sparked them.

We will use the National Children's Strategy as a timely marker to leave policy for a while and concentrate in the following chapter on legislation. We will consider the Child Care Act 1991 and particularly the Child Care (Pre-School Services) (No. 2) Regulations and (Amendment) Regulations 2006, which had a direct impact on those working in ECCE settings. Once we have explored legislation and its implications for childcare, in Chapter 3 we will return to policy from 2000 onwards.

References

Citizens Information (website), 'Early Childhood Education', http://www.citizensinformation.ie/en/education/pre_school_education_and_childcare/early_childhood_education.html

Commission on the Family (1998) *Strengthening Families for Life: Final Report of the Commission on the Family*. Dublin: Department of Social, Community and Family Affairs

Daly, M. (2010) *An Evaluation of the Impact of the National Childminding Initiative on the Quality of Childminding in Waterford City and County*, Report commissioned by Waterford City and County Childcare Committees and HSE South, http://omepireland.ie/presentations/Dr%20Mary%20Daly%20-%20Evaluation%20of%20Impact%20of%20the%20National%20Childminding%20Initiative.pdf

Daly, M. and Forster, A. (2009) *The Story of Aistear: the Early Childhood Curriculum Framework: Partnership in Action*. NCCA, http://www.ncca.ie/en/Curriculum_and_Assessment/Early_Childhood_and_Primary_Education/Early_Childhood_Education/How_Aistear_was_developed/Consultation/Aistear_Partnership_in_Action.pdf

DES (Department of Education and Science) (1999) *Ready to Learn*: White Paper on Early Childhood Education, http://www.education.ie/en/Publications/Policy-Reports/Ready-to-Learn-White-Paper-on-Early-Childhood-Education.pdf

DoHC (Department of Health and Children) (2000) *Our Children – Their Lives: National Children's Strategy*. Dublin: Stationery Office, http://www.dcya.gov.ie/documents/Aboutus/stratfullenglishversion.pdf

DJELR (Department of Justice, Equality and Law Reform) (1999) *National Childcare Strategy: Report of the Partnership 2000 Expert Working Group on Childcare*. Dublin: Stationery Office, http://www.justice.ie/en/JELR/Childcare1.pdf/Files/Childcare1.pdf

DJELR (2000) *Equal Opportunities Childcare Programme 2000–2006: General Guidelines for Funding*. Dublin: DJELR, http://www.justice.ie/en/JELR/Pages/Childcare_programme_funding_guidelines

Fine-Davis, M. (2007) *Childcare in Ireland Today*, briefing paper to the Irish Congress of Trade Unions, http://www.ictu.ie/download/pdf/briefing_paper_on_childcare_final_draft_14_june_2007_mfd.pdf

Hayes, N. (2002) *Children's Rights – Whose Right? A Review of Child Policy Development in Ireland*, https://www.tcd.ie/policy-institute/assets/pdf/BP9_Children_Hayes.pdf

John, P. (1998) *Analysing Public Policy*. London: Cassell

Jones, B. and Norton, P. (2010) *Politics UK* (7th edn). London: Pearson

Kiersey, R. and Hayes, N. (2010) 'The Discursive Construction of "Children" and "Rights" in Irish Early Childhood Policy'. Paper presented at the 20th EECERA Conference, Knowledge and Voice in Early Childhood, Birmingham, UK, 6 September, http://arrow.dit.ie/cgi/viewcontent.cgi?article=1009&context=csercon

Logan, E. (2012) 'Check Against Delivery'. Address to the Medico-Legal Society of Ireland, 21 January, http://www.oco.ie/wp-content/uploads/2014/03/OCOMedico-LegalSpeech.pdf

Moreau, P. (2004) *Supporting Quality through the Equal Opportunities Childcare Programme (EOCP) 2000 – 2006*. Dublin: CECDE, http://www.cecde.ie/english/pdf/Questions%20of%20Quality/Moreau.pdf

NCO (National Children's Office) (2004) *Making a Difference for Children and Young People*, http://dcya.gov.ie/documents/publications/NCO-MakeDifference_DL.pdf

OECD (2001) *Starting Strong I: Early Childhood Education and Care*. Paris: OECD

OECD (2004) *Thematic Review of Early Childhood Education and Care Policy in Ireland*. Dublin: Department of Education and Science, http://dccc.purposemakers.net/wp-content/uploads/2009/12/OECD-Thematic-Review-Early-Childhood.pdf

OMC (Office of the Minister for Children) (2008) *National Guidelines for Childminders*, http://www.dcya.gov.ie/documents/childcare/guidelines_for_childminders.pdf

Scoilnet (website), 'Women and the Constitution of Ireland', http://womeninhistory.scoilnet.ie/content/unit6/opposition.html

Walsh, T. and Kiernan, G. (2004) 'When Two are One: The Changing Nature of Early Childhood Care and Education in Ireland', ESAI presentation, April. Dublin: CECDE, http://www.cecde.ie/english/pdf/conference_papers/When%20Two%20Are%20One.pdf

Willoughby, M. (2008) *Practical Guide to Developing Childcare Policies*. Dublin: Barnardos

CHAPTER 2

Legislation

INTRODUCTION

In this chapter we will examine legislation and its role in ECCE settings. In considering pivotal pieces of legislation related to childcare, it is not possible to cover every piece of legislation, so all pieces of legislation relevant to ECCE settings are listed in Appendix B. Also see *Operating a Childcare Service: A Guide to Legal Requirements*, a comprehensive guide available online from Clare County Childcare Committee.

Chapter 4 will review legislation pertinent to child protection, including the **Children First Bill 2014** and its implications for practice. In examining central legislation in childcare we will also consider how legislation impacts on childcare settings, including the relationship between regulations (particularly regulation 5) and Síolta.

IMPORTANT LEGISLATION

The major pieces of legislation pertinent to childcare settings are:

1. **Child Care Act 1991 (Part VII)**
2. **Child Care (Pre-School Services) Regulations 1996**
3. **Child Care (Pre-School Services) (No. 2) Regulations 2006** and **Child Care (Pre-School Services) (No. 2) (Amendment) Regulations 2006**: came into effect in September 2007 and provide the regulatory framework for pre-school services in the State. The aim of these regulations is to improve childcare standards and to

ensure the health, safety and welfare of pre-school children, as well as promoting their development while attending pre-school services.

4. **National Standards for Pre-School Services:** informed and developed in response to the Childcare (Pre-School) Services Regulations; contains 20 standards, under four headings, developed by ECCE stakeholders, which ECCE practitioners should strive towards.

5. **Childcare (Amendment) Act 2007:** providers of services for school-age children must also notify the HSE.

6. **Child and Family Agency Act 2013:** the law in Ireland provides for the regulation and inspection of pre-school childcare services. Under the Child Care Act 1991, as amended by the Child and Family Agency Act 2013, Tusla (the Child and Family Agency) is charged with ensuring the health, safety and welfare of pre-school children attending services.

7. **Children First Bill 2014:** this Bill will put the Children First National Guidelines on a statutory basis to implement the Programme for Government commitment.

How are Laws Made?

Before we continue any further, let's overview the Oireachtas, the law-making body of the State.

As we saw in Chapter 1, policy is different from legislation or law. Unlike policy, legislation is enforceable and people who break the law can be punished. In Ireland, legislation is generated by the Oireachtas and generally passed into effect through the Dáil.

THE OIREACHTAS

President	Dáil	Seanad
Signs legislation, but may refer legislation to the Supreme Court May convene Oireachtas for message of national importance	Elects or dismisses Taoiseach and government Debates, passes legislation Makes ministers accountable Approves budget Debates issues of concern	Debates, passes legislation Makes ministers accountable Debates issues of current concern

Source: Harvey (2008, p. 13)

In this chapter we shall focus on regulations governing ECCE settings. Let's start with the Child Care Act 1991.

CHILD CARE ACT 1991 (PART VII)

The title of this piece of legislation can be a little misleading, as it does not refer to childcare alone. 'Child care', as opposed to 'childcare', refers to all aspects of the care, welfare and protection of a child. This piece of legislation recognises the State's responsibility to promote children's welfare; for example, it includes care orders for the removal of a child. The legislation previously responsible for child welfare was the Children Act 1908 – which suggests that in the intervening 80-odd years the issue of children's welfare was not ranked highly. Part VII of the Child Care Act 1991 is the section that is pertinent to 'childcare', and it covers the regulation and supervision of pre-school services. The following (in Section 58) outlines the exemptions to Part VII of the Act:

> For the avoidance of doubt it is hereby declared that the provisions of this part shall not apply to–
> (a) the care of one or more pre-school children undertaken by a relative of the child or children of the spouse of such relative,
> (b) a person taking care of one or more pre-school children of same family and no other such children (other than that person's own such children) in that person's home,
> (c) a person taking care of not more than 3 pre-school children of different families (other than that person's own such children) in that person's home.
> (Child Care Act 1991, Section 58)

Part VII of the Child Care Act 1991 facilitated the introduction of the Child Care (Pre-school Services) Regulations 1996.

CHILD CARE (PRE-SCHOOL SERVICES) REGULATIONS 1996

O'Kane (2005) states that Child Care (Pre-School Services) Regulations 1996 represents the first legislative control over early education services in Ireland.
The regulations focus on:
• the development of children
• the physical environment of children's services
• safety and emergency aspects
• appropriate record-keeping.

The primary goal of the regulations was to put in place structures to support the development of the ECCE sector and to take the first step on the path of regulation, including establishing minimum standards throughout the sector. While this was a first step in introducing statutory standards, the 1996 Regulations were criticised for omitting training standards for those employed in childcare.

In 2006 the Minister for Children introduced new regulations which superseded the 1996 Regulations. Before we look at the 2006 Regulations, it's a good time to explain the difference between regulation and policy.

- **Regulation** is documentation that can be enforced by law.
- **Policy** is documentation outlining guidelines and recommendations for practitioners to follow.

CHILD CARE (PRE-SCHOOL SERVICES) (NO. 2) REGULATIONS 2006 AND (AMENDMENT) REGULATIONS 2006

These regulations, which came into effect in September 2007, provide the regulatory framework for pre-school services in the State. The Pre-School Inspectorate of the Health Service Executive (HSE) was given the legal responsibility for enforcing the regulations; since 2013 the responsibility now rests with Tusla (the Child and Family Agency), which we shall examine later in this chapter.

How different are the 2006 Regulations from the 1996 Regulations? The standards laid out in the 1996 Regulations represent a mere starting point in safeguarding the safety, health and welfare of young children. The 2006 Regulations contained amendments which, though welcome, were considered too limited. According to the Office of the Minister for Children, the main adjustments to the 2006 Regulations included:

- An expansion of the Regulation on Child Development, which requires the service provider to ensure that each child's learning, development and well-being is facilitated within the daily life of the service.
- The inclusion of a requirement that all staff, students and volunteers in the service will be appropriately vetted once the relevant procedures to facilitate this are in place. (Office of the Minister for Children (2005), cited in Síolta (n.d.))

The main areas of change between the 1996 and 2006 standards are shown on the next page.

The aim of the 2006 Regulations was to improve childcare standards and to ensure the health, safety and welfare of pre-school children, as well as promoting their development while attending pre-school services. Its purpose is not just to regulate but to encourage and ensure good practice. This emphasis on good practice and quality can be seen in the changes recently made to the way inspectors report on Regulation 5 (see 'In Practice', p. 35). Certainly a greater emphasis on linking practice to Síolta (Quality Framework) and Aistear (Early Years Curriculum Framework) will become apparent.

MAIN CHANGES IN THE REGULATIONS

CATEGORIES OF PRE-SCHOOL SERVICE

- Sessional Services: No change.

- Full Day Care: No change.

- Part-Time Day Care: New type of service offering a structured day care service for pre-school children for more than 3.5 hours and less than 5 hours a day. This service will be required to meet the same rest and play facilities as Full Day Care Services. This service does not have to provide a hot meal but will be required to have adequate food storage and food heating facilities if required.

- Overnight Services: These are services that are provided for more than 2 hours between 7:00p.m. and 6:00a.m. If a service is providing this facility it will be inspected to ensure the service is suitable for over-night care and supervision is adequate.

- Drop-In Services: These services must notify the HSE at least 14 days before the commencement of the service (it is 28 days for all other services). (For childminders see below.)

ADULT CHILD RATIOS (Explanatory Guide – Regulation 8)

Full Day Care & Part Time Services

- 0–1 year 1:3 (no change)
- 1–2 years 1:5 (changed from 1:6)
- 2–3 years 1:6 (new age range)
- 3–6 years 1:8 (no change)

Sessional Services

- 0–1 year 1:3 (changed from 1:10)
- 1–2½ years 1:5 (changed from 1:10)
- 2½–6 years 1:10 (no change)

The interaction of siblings attending the Pre-School Service is promoted in the new Regulations.

Childminders

In the Child Care (Pre-School Services) Regulations, 2006, childminders are required to care for no more than five children at any one time (some exemptions apply). This is a reduction from six children at any one time. The childminder will not be required to reduce the number cared for to five until the first child from that group leaves to start school or leaves voluntarily.

SPACE RATIOS (Explanatory Guide Regulation 18)

Space requirements refer to the recommended clear floor space. This has changed for day care services.

Full Day Care & Part-Time Services

- 0–1 year $3.5m^2$ from $3.7m^2$
- 1–2 years $2.8m^2$ (no change)
- 2–3 years $2.35m^2$ from $2.32m^2$
- 3–6 years $2.3m^2$ from $2.32m^2$

HEALTH WELFARE & DEVELOPMENT OF THE CHILD (Regulation 5)

The revised inspection tool allows the inspection to assess compliance of the care provided with regard to the age, stage of development and child's cultural context. This holistic approach provides a detailed assessment of the following:

a   The basic physical needs of the child.

b   The emotional well being and social development of the child.

c   That learning and development opportunities are adequately provided.

d   That learning experiences and cognitive development for children is facilitated within the daily life of the service.

e   The service is responsive to the children's learning, development and well-being on an individual basis.

This assessment is in accordance with the 'Whole Child Perspective' as outlined in the National Children's Strategy. The article supports the value of play as part of the child's development. As Inspectors, we are delighted to note the increased focus on the quality of the child's experience with the service and the increased emphasis on care that is age appropriate and child centred.

REFERENCES & GARDA VETTING (Regulation 8)

It is now required that pre-school providers obtain Garda vetting of their staff, students and volunteers. Three national organisations – Barnardos, the National Children's Nurseries Association (NCNA) and the Irish Pre-school Playgroups Association (IPPA) – have arrangements in place to assist with this process. Garda vetting in the Pre-School Section is still at an early implementation stage. Regulation 14 requires a written record of Garda clearance to be kept on the premises.

BEHAVIOUR MANAGEMENT (Regulation 9)

In the 1996 Regulations this was referred to as Corporal Punishment. This has been broadened to specify that the service must ensure that there are no harmful practices that are disrespectful, degrading, exploitive, intimidating, emotionally or physically harmful or neglectful to the children attending the service. Written policies must be in place to manage children's behaviour appropriate to their age and stage of development.

RECORDS (Regulation 14)

There is now a requirement that all services keep a record in writing of references for all staff, students and volunteers working the service. Pre-school providers should have written policies on the management, recruitment and training policies with the service. These records must be available for inspection.

FEES (Regulation 31)

The annual fees have been changed as follows:
- Sessional Service €40 (was €32)
- Childminder €40 (was €63)
- All other services €80 (was €63)

(Barnardos 2007)

Below is a table outlining most of the regulations. The regulations are grouped together by theme (for example regulations 5 and 9 relate to the label 'Health, Welfare & Development of the Child'). This approach to grouping can be seen in the Pre-Inspectorate Reports and offers a useful perspective in examining the regulations. All ECCE settings must comply with the 2006 Regulations.

2006 REGULATIONS

Regulation	Description
	INFORMATION ON PRE-SCHOOL SETTING
32	Inspection
10	Notice to be Given by a Person Proposing to Carry on a Pre-school Service
11	Notice of Change in Circumstances
31	Annual Fees
	INFORMATION ON MANAGEMENT AND STAFFING
8	Management and Staffing
12	Number of Pre-School Children who may be catered for
	INFORMATION ON HEALTH, WELFARE & DEVELOPMENT OF THE CHILD
5	Health, Welfare & Development of the Child
9	Behaviour Management
	INFORMATION ON PREMISES AND FACILITIES
18	Premises and Facilities
19	Heating
20	Ventilation
21	Lighting
22	Sanitary Accommodation
23	Drainage and Sewage Disposal
24	Waste Storage and Disposal
25	Equipment and Materials
28	Facilities for Rest and Play
	INFORMATION ON SAFETY MEASURES
6	First Aid
7	Medical Assistance
16	Fire Safety Measures
27	Safety Measures
	INFORMATION ON FOOD & DRINK
26	Food & Drink
	INFORMATION ON RECORDS
13	Register of Pre-School Children

14	Records
15	Information for Parents
17	Copy of Act and Regulations
30	Insurance
	GENERAL INFORMATION
29	Furnishing of Information to HSE

In Practice

Prepare a short overview of the areas identified in the table above, which could be used as a resource for less experienced staff in your setting to raise their awareness of the regulations.

As we can see, there are many regulations that need to be considered when working in and running an ECCE setting in order to comply with the regulations. While it can be tempting to see these regulations as something alien to day-to-day- practice in ECCE settings, we strongly believe that it is essential to understand how these regulations 'fit' into daily practice. To this end, in this chapter and throughout the book an emphasis is placed on demonstrating just this. Later in this chapter we will consider how regulation and practice can be seen in how 'observations' and record-keeping allow practitioners to demonstrate compliance with the regulations.

While it's not possible to give a detailed overview of all the regulations, useful web links providing additional information on the regulations can be found at the end of this chapter. In this chapter we will concentrate on Regulation 8 (Management and Staffing) and Regulation 5 (Health, Welfare and Development of the Child) to illustrate how the regulations function and fit within ECCE practice.

To begin with, let's take a look at Regulation 8, which covers ratios and staffing.

Regulation 8: Management and Staffing

Full-/Part-time Day Care	Drop-in Centres	Sessional Services	Childminding	Overnight
Age 0–1 year 1:3 Age 1–2 years 1:5 Age 2–3 years 1:6 Age 3–6 years 1:8	Age 0–6 years 1:4 1–4 children (no more than 2 children under 15 months) Max. group size 24	Age 0–1 year 1:3 Age 1–2.5 years 1:5 Age 2.5–6 years 1:10	5 in total	Age 0–1 year 1:3 Age 1–6 years 1:5

Notes:
1 When a full day care service also takes children not on a full-day basis, sessional service adult numbers apply.
2 These ratios may not apply if the service is participating in the Early Childhood Care and Education Scheme (free pre-school year), which we will look at in Chapter 3)

There are five main types of pre-school childcare service in Ireland:

1. **Sessional services:** Playgroups, crèches, Montessori groups, playschools, High/ Scope groups, naíonraí (pre-school through Irish) and Steiner groups throughout Ireland offer sessional pre-school services. Services normally offered are planned programmes, consisting of up to 3.5 hours per session (usually a morning or an afternoon). Generally these services are provided for children aged 3–5 years.
2. **Full day care:** Nurseries, crèches, etc. This is a structured day care service for more than 5 hours per day.
3. **Childminders:** Children cared for in the childminder's own home.* Throughout the year, childminders offer this service for the full working day or for different periods during the day. Parents and childminders negotiate their own terms (hours, rates, duties, etc.).
4. **Drop-in centres:** A pre-school service in a drop-in centre is a service where care is provided for pre-school children for not more than 2 hours while the parent/ guardian is availing of a service or attending an event, for example in shopping centres, leisure centres or other establishments, as part of customer service.
5. **Part-time day care:** A pre-school service offering a structured day care service for pre-school children for a total of between 3.5 hours and 5 hours a day.

*   Only childminders caring for more than three children (other than their own) are covered by the Child Care Act 1991, so those with fewer children are not covered by the Pre-School Regulations. (Willoughby 2007, pp. 9–11)

In addition, the Pre-School Regulations also make specific provisions for **overnight childcare services**, which are provided either by a crèche-type service or a childminder. These are services that are provided for more than 2 hours between 7p.m. and 6a.m.

In terms of staffing, a criticism levelled at the 2006 Regulations was the lack of specificity regarding training and qualifications. What does this mean?

Training: A Criticism of the 2006 Regulations

As we saw earlier, a criticism of the 1996 Regulations was the omission of training standards for the sector. While training was addressed in the 2006 Regulations, training was still not placed on a statutory footing. The 2006 Regulations specify staff qualifications as follows:

> A suitable and competent adult is a person (over 18 years) who has appropriate experience in caring for children under six years of age and/or who has an appropriate qualification in childcare. ... It is acknowledged that many childcare staff have a qualification or are working towards achieving one. In centre-based services, it is considered that the person in charge should aim to have

at least fifty percent of childcare staff with a qualification appropriate to the care and development of children. The qualified staff should rotate between age groupings. Induction training should be provided by the service. (HSE 2006, cited in Barry & Sherlock 2008, p. 11).

Barry and Sherlock comment, 'In 2006 the OMC distributed guidelines for childminders which included professional requirements for childminders, environmental guidelines including health and safety, and statutory/voluntary notification requirements. The guidelines are slightly more specific in language than that of the Childcare Regulation policy documents, but still fall short of measurable requirements' (2008, p. 11).

This criticism has been more recently addressed through the creation of a **Learner Fund** of €3 million to increase staff qualifications and bring the sector in line with international standards. The Level 5 requirement will now be a regulatory necessity, while a Level 6 requirement will be a condition of the ECCE contract related to pre-school leaders.

The next regulation we shall focus on is Regulation 5, which looks at the importance of child development in ECCE practice. We are going to take an in-depth approach to exploring this regulation, to illustrate the many strands that influence its practice and assessment.

Regulation 5: Health, Welfare and Development of the Child

A person carrying on a Pre-School Service shall ensure that each child's learning, development, and well-being is facilitated within the daily life of the service through the provision of the appropriate opportunities, experiences, activities, interaction, materials and equipment, having regard to the age and stage of development of the child and the child's cultural context.

The health, welfare and development of a child are the cornerstone of ECCE practice. We shall touch on this central and fundamental issue throughout the book. Chapter 7 explores factors and policies relating to child wellbeing; and Chapters 4 and 5, on child protection, discuss issues of child welfare.

Regulation 5 reflects a '**whole child perspective**', as developed by the Department of Children and Youth Affairs (DCYA) and discussed in Chapter 1.

As we've seen, Regulation 5 is concerned with the health, welfare and development of the child, so how is this measured or assessed? The best place to look for that answer is the assessment approach used by pre-school inspectors.

As part of the inspection process for Regulation 5, assessment is divided into four sections:

1. The extent to which personal care provided meets the basic needs of the infants and children.
2. The extent to which relationships around the children are supported.
3. The extent to which the physical and material environment supports the development of children
4. The extent to which the programme of activities and its implementation support children's development. (HSE 2011)

The *Child Health, Welfare and Development Assessment Guide* (HSE 2011) further expands on these four sections, offering guidance on what areas are considered as part of the assessment process. Let's look at some of the guidance offered.

Section 3 Physical and Material Environment

The guidance states that 'Both the physical and material environment should be supportive of children's development.' The indoor or outdoor environment provides a wide range of developmentally appropriate experiences for children, incorporating a cultural context.

> (b) The indoor environment provides a range of developmentally appropriate, challenging, diverse, creative and enriching experiences for all children (e.g. a range of toys to offer stimulation of all senses ... including paint, play-dough, sand, water and finger paint, toys and materials that support all areas of development) ...
>
> (e) The outdoor environment provides a range of developmentally appropriate, challenging, diverse, creative and enriching experiences (e.g. ... opportunities for challenge and safe risk). (HSE 2011)

Section 4 Programme of Activities and its Implementation

(a) **Play** (creative, manipulative, imaginative, physical)
(b) **Language development** (singing, rhymes, reading stories, story-telling)
(c) Each child is enabled to **participate actively ... in activities, in conversations and in all other appropriate situations, and is considered as a partner by the adult**
(d) Each child has opportunities to **make choices, is enabled to make decisions, and has her/his choices and decisions respected**
(e) Each child has opportunities and is enabled to **take the lead, initiate activity, be appropriately independent and is supported to solve problems**
(f) Opportunities for play ... **give the child the freedom to achieve mastery and success, and challenge the child to make the transition to new learning and development**

(g) Planning ... is based on the child's individual profile, which is established through systematic observation and assessment for learning. (Adapted from French 2008)

In Practice

How well do you implement and support these different elements of child development in your own practice and setting? Can you identify examples of how you meet each of these guidelines? Are there obstacles that prevent you from fully developing these guidelines (e.g. time, resources, staffing)? Remember to keep a note of these in your reflective journal, which is useful for modules that include work experience, supervision, and personal and professional development.

'Relationship' in Regulation 5

Earlier we saw that 'relationship' is a central part of Regulation 5 for fostering healthy child development and wellbeing. How do we achieve such positive interactions? The following are some guidelines on how best to support positive adult–child interactions, illustrating a practical approach to supporting those relationships and ensuring compliance.

In Practice: How to Support Positive Adult–Child Interactions

Interaction Strategy	Examples
Assisting children to identify and express their feelings	• Identifying and validating children's feelings • Asking open-ended questions, e.g. how, why, when
Modelling social skills	• Creating a balance between child-initiated and adult-initiated conversations and activities • Promoting positive behaviour • Encouraging respect for each other • Urging children to interact with each other
Encouraging problem solving	• Identifying what they are doing and talking to them about it • Encouraging children to persevere with difficult tasks • Creating a safe environment for children to think and problem solve new situations • Supporting children's understanding of the world around them
Helping children to become more independent	• Taking their opinions into account • Offering choices and respecting those choices

Acknowledging children in a positive way	• Recognising children as individuals • Using the child's name • Talking with children, not at them • Talking with them at their level, physical and verbal • Ensuring that each child is positively attended to each day
Enjoying and appreciating the children	• Smiling, laughing and sharing their discoveries and milestones • Being involved in children's play • Building on children's interests

Adapted from Kildare CCC, 'Guide to Interactions', http://www.kildarechildcare.ie/wp-content/uploads/What-why-and-how-interactions-.pdf

As we have just seen, 'relationships' are of central importance, not just as part of the inspection assessment of Regulation 5 but in the process of becoming a childcare practitioner. So how can we incorporate in our daily practice approaches that will enable us to become expert practitioners?

In Practice: Reflective Practice

How can we best connect and build partnership with the children in our care, their parents and families and our colleagues? Through reflective function. This can be seen as part of the evaluation process that is both a key principle in statutory requirements and a standard in Síolta. Reflective function, or reflective practice, plays a pivotal role in relationship building and intra-personal awareness and skills. These concepts of emotional intelligence and reflective practice (or function) are integral to the acquisition of skills needed by care workers to engage and communicate with themselves, clients and other professionals.

So how can we use reflection as part of our practice? The following are some questions you can ask yourself, perhaps keeping a diary and recording your responses.

Reflection:
• What happened?
• How did it compare with previous experience?
• What did I do?

Critical reflection:
• How well did I do?
• What could I have done better?
• What could I have done differently?

The concept of reflective practice is further explored and discussed in Chapter 8, which looks at how to improve personal and professional development and how development is linked to work experience.

We have seen some of the areas examined in the assessment process used to determine compliance with the regulations, but how can we demonstrate compliance? The next section focuses on how to achieve compliance through planning and assessment.

Assessment and Planning

A process of assessment and planning should: be at the core of practice elements; be an opportunity for reflective practice; and be considered part of a continual process. That planning and assessment are core functions of childcare practice can be seen by their inclusion in both Síolta and Aistear.

In Focus: Regulations and Aistear – Planning and Assessment

One of Aistear's four Guidelines for Good Practice is 'Supporting Learning and Development through Assessment'. From this guideline a research paper was developed (Dunphy 2008) that outlines the following six key features of assessment:

1. **Characteristics and complexities of early learning:** Early learning is highly complex and finding ways to assess that complexity is challenging.
2. **Centrality of relationships:** Relationships are central to the assessment process. The practitioner develops increased understanding of what and how children are learning by interacting with them. Parents, because of their unique relationship with their children, have a very important contribution to make to the assessment process.
3. **Interactive processes:** Assessments of early learning are interactive, informal and often embedded in everyday activities. Watching, listening, talking to, and empathising with children are central. Children's engagement with peers is also important for illuminating the learning processes.
4. **Assessing what is valued:** Good assessments are holistic in nature, cover all aspects of a child's development and are concerned with dispositions, skills, attitudes and values, knowledge and understandings. Assessment focuses on strengths and also on aspects of learning that need further development.
5. **Authentic assessment:** Assessment of early learning and development is informal, carried out over time and is embedded in tasks and play-based activities that children see as significant, meaningful and worthwhile.
6. **Professional development for assessment:** Practitioners need extensive education and support in the area of assessment in order to be equipped to carry out assessments that adhere to the principles of good practice, are conducted in a skilled and informed way, and do justice to children.

In Practice

Reflect on the six key aspects of assessment and consider how they relate to your daily practice. Remember that this reflection can be an entry in your 'Work Experience' reflective diary and that it also ties in with the learner log in 'Supervision in Childcare'.

How do we go about 'assessing'? Aistear suggests the following methods; and to best capture a child's development and learning it is advised to use a combination of these methods. Aistear describes five methods of assessment, from child-led to adult-led:

1. Self-assessment
2. Conversations
3. Observation
4. Setting tasks
5. Testing.

We have seen how self-assessment can be achieved through reflective practice and keeping a journal (see Chapter 8 for more on this); but here we will focus on observation as an assessment tool.

Observation

Observations can and should be used to demonstrate a child's development and wellbeing and to comply with the regulations, including Regulation 5. So what are observations and how can we best plan and record them?

According to the HSE (2011): 'Observations should capture the progress of the child in a service in a holistic manner which reflects the overall philosophy of the service. Observation should be used to inform the planning of activities to enhance the learning and development of each child.'

What is Observation?

Observation involves watching and listening to the children and recording what we see and hear to help develop the children's learning and development. Observations can be used with babies, toddlers and young children and are particularly helpful with non-verbal and pre-verbal children.

Like conversations, observations can be planned or can happen spontaneously. There are different methods of undertaking observations, including:

- **Time sampling:** Observing a child, group or activity over a period of time at pre-specified intervals and recording what happens.
- **Frequency observation:** Identifying an aspect of behaviour of a child or group and recording every time this behaviour occurs.

- **Duration observation:** Recording how long a child or group spends at an activity or exhibiting certain behaviour.
- **Focused observation:** Choosing a specific child or group to observe (because more information is needed) and making detailed notes.
- **Target child observation:** Focuses on a particular child. Observation is recorded at pre-set intervals throughout a session or sessions so that a full picture can be built up over time on the child's interactions, learning and development.
- **Anecdotal observation:** A written narrative on examples of work, such as photos of constructions, dances, outdoor activities, etc., or paintings and drawings. These are recorded after the event with another staff member, child or parent.

Once we have observed the behaviour or learning it is important that we create a record to demonstrate not just the learning but also compliance with the regulations. **Written documents required for inspection of Regulation 5** include records, policies, procedures, logs, registers, etc.

- Written curriculum or programme being implemented, which is based on the child's individual profile (ensure that special needs children are incorporated into an appropriate programme to meet their needs).
- Written evidence of a partnership approach with a lead professional for children attending who have special requirements.
- Evidence of review at end of each period; daily, weekly, monthly or school term.
- Evidence of sharing information with parents.

For more information on assessment and regulation in ECCE settings, see Kildare CCC, 'Guide to Assessment and Curriculum Planning in Practice', www.kildarechildcare.ie/wp-content/uploads/What-Why-How-Guide-to-Assessment-Curriculum-Planning-in-Practice1.pdf.

> Additional Information
> Written documents required for other 2006 Regulations can be found at: www.tusla.ie/uploads/content/Pre_School_Documents_for_Inspections.pdf

Finally, observations build and strengthen relationships with parents/guardians, a key element of partnership:

> Regular recorded observations on each child which captures their time and progress while in the service. Observations can consist of written records or books, and photographs. It may be useful to use the observation records as a communication book between the childminder and home setting for sharing key information on care routines; fun and learning experiences from during the

day; interests shown by child; and other observations or relevant information. Notes on individual children's interests can be used to forward plan activities that link into their areas of interest. Consideration could be given to the visual attractiveness of the observations/communication records, as these will become treasured keepsakes for many parents. (HSE 2011, p. 4)

We have seen that planning and assessment are fundamental in complying with Regulation 5. More than that, they are essential in supporting children's development and learning, which is at the heart of ECCE practice. The following piece discusses the role of Síolta and how it complements and integrates with the regulations, illustrating the intertwining of legislation, policy and practice in ECCE settings and also the centrality of Síolta to childcare good practice.

Síolta and the Childcare Regulations

There is a direct relationship between legislation and childcare practice. Síolta was developed to complement the existing regulatory and curricular frameworks specific to the ECCE sector in Ireland, including the Child Care (Pre-School Services) (No. 2) Regulations 2006. Our discussion here will centre on Síolta Standards 9 and 15 and how best they can be implemented in childcare settings.

Connecting with Síolta and the 2006 Regulations

Underpinned by similar principles, Síolta (the National Quality Framework for Early Childhood Education) and the Framework for Early Learning both support adults in improving the quality of their work with children from birth to six years. The Framework for Early Learning, as its title suggests, concentrates on extending and enriching children's early learning and development by giving adults information and examples to help them work towards improving their practice in areas such as curriculum, partnership with parents and families, interactions, and play. By doing this, the Framework will help practitioners and childminders work towards meeting a number of standards as set out in Síolta.

Article 5 of the Revised Pre-School Regulations 2006 places a strong emphasis on children's development and states that:

A person carrying on a pre-school service shall ensure that each child's learning, development and well-being is facilitated within the daily life of the service through the provision of appropriate opportunities, experiences, activities, interaction, materials and equipment, having regard to the age and stage of development of the child and the child's cultural context.

Since children's learning and de[v]   for
Early Learning, using the Frame   [to]
provide children with appropriate   [able]
experiences as set out in the regul[a]

One example of the direct lin[k]   [be]
found in Síolta Standard 9, which   [with]
the Childcare (Pre-School Services

- ensuring that your service com   [t] by
  the HSE
- ensuring that all policies and p   [ions]
- ensuring that all staff are awa[re]   and
  comply with them at all times
- acting immediately on any issues arising from pre-school inspections
- keeping up to date with any changes or revisions to the regulations and adapting
  practice as appropriate.

> ### In Practice
>
> Referring to both this chapter and Chapter 3, in which there is an overview of Síolta Standards, identify what other Standards in Síolta can be applied to the 2006 Regulations. For example, Standard 8 on Planning and Evaluation could incorporate observation, as a tool demonstrating compliance to Regulation 5, or keeping a reflective diary. Regulation 26 covers 'Food and Drink', and guidelines on nutrition in ECCE settings are outlined in Chapter 7.

Another important regulation, which is linked into legislation and child protection issues, is Regulation 9 – Behaviour Management. Regulation 9 highlights the importance of being knowledgeable about child protection issues, and further information on this can be found in Chapters 4 and 5. Let's take a look at the regulation itself.

Regulation 9: Behaviour Management

(1) A person carrying on a pre-school service shall ensure that no corporal punishment is inflicted on a pre-school child attending the service.

(2) A person carrying on a pre-school service shall ensure that no practices that are disrespectful, degrading, exploitative, intimidating, emotionally or physical harmful or neglectful are carried out in respect of any child.

(3) A person carrying on a pre-school service shall ensure that written policies and procedures are in place to deal with and to manage a child's challenging behaviour and to assist the child to manage his or her behaviour as appropriate to the age and stage of development of the child.

Standards 9 and 15 and how they best can be implemented in Childcare settings.

Child Protection

Following the framework of *Children First* (DCYA 2011), a pre-school service should develop clear written guidelines on identifying and reporting child abuse. Article 2.2 of the UN Convention on the Rights of the Child states:

> All child care services and providers should consider the child's welfare to be of paramount concern.
>
> All children should be respected and treated with dignity at all times.
>
> Children's rights should be acknowledged and respected at all times.
>
> Children should never be subjected to any degrading or abusive behaviour.

Positive behaviour management should be included in the written policy and procedures document of the service.

> For a comprehensive overview of the 2006 Regulations the following link is particularly useful: www.wexfordchildcarenetwork.com/Publications/PreSchool.pdf

Policy Development

The final element we will consider in discussing the 2006 Regulations is the development of policies in childcare settings. Below is a sample policy for Regulation 9 Behaviour Management, which we looked at earlier.

Sample Behaviour Management Policy

The management and staff of _____ Childcare Service believe that children should be encouraged to grow and develop to their full potential in a suitably planned environment, where they know what is expected of them, and where clear limits are set, appropriate to their age and stage of development and any special needs they may have.

Procedures
- Children's efforts, achievements and feelings will always be acknowledged so as to promote the growth of self-esteem and self-discipline.
- The service will strive to manage behaviour consistently in order that children have the security of knowing what to expect and can build up good patterns of self-discipline.
- Adults working in the service must be good role models by following codes of behaviour and showing respect for each other and the children. Rules that apply to children and adults in the group will be discussed and agreed. These rules

will be made known to all adults, staff, parents and children. Rules will be kept to a minimum.

- It is recognised that the key to behaviour management is good observation skills in the adults.
- Ongoing discussion, training and practice will be availed of to train staff in the skills of behaviour management.

Positive Strategies for Behaviour Management
- One-to-one adult support will be offered to the child who has misbehaved to help the child to see what went wrong and offer possible solutions.
- Comfort and support will be offered where another child has been hurt in an incident.
- Explanations for challenging unwanted behaviours and attitudes will be made clear immediately to the child/children.
- It will always be made clear to the child in question that it is the behaviour that is unacceptable – not the child.
- Staff will use simple language, speaking calmly and quietly to the children when dealing with these situations. Staff will demonstrate respect and empathy by listening and being interested.
- By offering alternatives, positive behaviour is encouraged and helps to teach children about the value of compromise.
- Recurring problems will be dealt with in an inclusive manner following observations and involving the child's parents and other appropriate adults.
- Books and activities will be available to help the children explore and name their feelings, where appropriate, in conjunction with an adult.

You can find more sample policies and procedures at:
www.galwaychildcare.com/uploadedfiles/Sample%20Policies&Procedures Manual %20updated_March2011.pdf

When drawing up policy documents for use in ECCE settings, some or all of the following topics need to be considered:
- Area to be covered (e.g. play) and the rationale for including it (why it is important)
- Relevant legislation/policy
- National guidelines
- Aistear and Síolta standards involved
- How to meet the needs:
  ◆ of the child or children
  ◆ of parents/guardians

♦   of fellow practitioners and stakeholders.

A substantial portion of this chapter has been devoted to exploring the 2006 Regulations and capturing their central importance in ECCE settings. Next we are going to consider the National Standards for Pre-School Services.

NATIONAL STANDARDS FOR PRE-SCHOOL SERVICES 2010

The National Standards for Pre-School Services were informed by and developed in response to the Childcare (Pre-School) Services Act and 2006 Regulations. They comprise 20 standards, developed by ECCE stakeholders, for the sector to strive towards. As you will see from the standards, which are grouped under four headings, they closely mirror the 2006 Regulations, and the 2010 Standards and 2006 Regulations should be viewed together. It is hoped that the Standards will encourage providers to deliver a higher level of quality than is strictly required under the 2006 Regulations.

NATIONAL STANDARDS

Choosing a Service	Management and Staffing	Quality of Care	Premises and Safety

1. Information
2. Contract
3. Working in Partnership
    with Parents/Guardians
	4. Records
	5. Organisation and
	    Management
	6. Evaluation
	7. Complaints
		8. Care, Play and Learning
		9. Nurture and Well-being
		10. Behaviour
		11. Child Protection
		12. Health Care
		13. Food and Drink
		14. Sleep
		15. Children with Disabilities
		16. Equal Opportunities
			17. Premises
			18. Facilities
			19. Equipment and
			    Materials
			20. Safety

Source: DCYA (2010a)

Of these Standards:
- **Choosing a Service:** Aimed at parents who are choosing a facility for their children, and contains the information they will need to come to an informed decision.
- **Management and Staffing:** Aimed primarily at service providers, and contain information relating to the running and ongoing evaluation of the service.
- **Quality of Care:** Relate to the way in which the children in the service are cared for, and cover both the physical and the mental wellbeing of the children.
- **Premises and Safety:** Relate to the physical environment of the childcare facility.

According to the DCYA, each Standard describes a particular quality outcome, and is accompanied by a set of supporting criteria designed to provide information as to how the outcome can be achieved. Some of the criteria refer to requirements under the Child

Care (Pre-School Services) (No. 2) Regulations 2006 and service providers are obliged by law to meet these requirements. Other criteria are more flexible, and the service provider may choose to take a different route from that stated, in order to achieve the same outcome (DCYA 2010b).

In Practice

Review the policies and procedures in your setting in relation to the relevant National Standards:
1. Does your setting address all areas clearly?
2. Would a new member of staff or a parent understand the layout and content?
3. Does the presentation of each policy and its content make it a usable document in terms of guiding daily practice?

This review would tie in with both the 'Work Experience' and 'Supervision in Childcare' modules.

The last pieces of legislation we will look at in this chapter are explored in more depth in Chapters 4 and 5 on child protection.

CHILD AND FAMILY AGENCY ACT 2013

This piece of legislation, which established the Child and Family Agency (Tusla), came into effect in January 2014. The Act amalgamated several bodies into a single agency:
- HSE Child and Family Services
- Family Support Agency
- National Education Welfare Board
- other services relating to the psychological welfare of children and to domestic, sexual and gender-based violence.

The Act is particularly relevant to childcare settings and practitioners because:
- The Early Years Inspectorate (previously the Pre-School Inspectorate) will move from the HSE to the Child and Family Agency.
- The Minister will now have authority to set minimum qualification requirements for staff in early childhood care and education services.
- Legislation has been amended to allow for the regulation of school-age childcare.
- The sector will move from a system of 'notification' to a system of 'registration'.

The creation of Tusla arguably marks a new stage in how we approach supporting and caring for children and their families. Tusla integrates several different bodies into one agency to improve the co-ordination of policies and services and ensure better outcomes. Let's take a closer look at this new agency.

In Practice: Tusla (the Child and Family Agency)

On its establishment in January 2014, Tulsa was heralded as the most comprehensive ever reform of child protection, early intervention and family support services in Ireland. This new agency will have responsibility for improving wellbeing and outcomes for children across the country and aims to provide a better, more effective service.

Under the Child and Family Act 2013, Tusla is charged with:

- supporting and promoting the development, welfare and protection of children, and the effective functioning of families;
- offering care and protection for children in circumstances where their parents have not been able to, or are unlikely to, provide the care that a child needs. In order to discharge these responsibilities, the Agency is required to maintain and develop the services needed in order to deliver these supports to children and families, and provide certain services for the psychological welfare of children and their families;
- responsibility for ensuring that every child in the State attends school or otherwise receives an education, and for providing education welfare services to support and monitor children's attendance, participation and retention in education;
- ensuring that the best interests of the child guides all decisions affecting individual children;
- consulting children and families so that they help to shape the agency's policies and services;
- strengthening interagency co-operation to ensure seamless services responsive to needs;
- undertaking research relating to its functions, and providing information and advice to the Minister regarding those functions; and
- commissioning services relating to the provision of child and family services.

Tusla is responsible for a range of universal and targeted services:

- Child protection and welfare services
- Educational welfare services
- Psychological services
- Alternative care
- Family and locally based community supports
- Early years services
- Domestic, sexual and gender-based violence services

(www.tusla.ie/about)

Tusla has a wide remit, which covers several different areas of child wellbeing issues, such as child protection and welfare issues, which will be discussed later in the book. For now, let's take a look at the impact Tusla will have on early years services.

One impact Tusla will have on early years services is the change from notification to registration. This is enabled by Part 12 of the Act, which makes an amendment to Part VII of the Child Care Act 1991; but what will this mean for ECCE services?

The change to statutory registration means that it will be illegal for an early years service to operate if it has not registered. It is also planned to eventually move towards the development of a standards-based inspection model that will aim to enhance both the quality of service provision and the care and welfare outcomes for children who attend early years services. We will have to wait and see what format this will take and what it will mean for the National Standards and the 2006 Regulations.

> ### *In Practice*
>
> Prepare an overview of Tusla to share with staff in your setting. It is vital that all staff keep up to date on current events that impact on their practice.

CHILDREN FIRST BILL 2014

The Children First Bill 2014 aims to put child protection and welfare guidelines on a statutory footing. Three main areas have been identified:
1. A requirement for organisations providing services to children to keep children safe and to produce a Child Safeguarding Statement
2. A requirement for defined categories of persons (mandated persons) to report child protection concerns over a defined threshold to Tusla
3. A requirement for mandated persons to assist Tusla in the assessment of a child protection risk, if requested to do so by the agency.

(At the time of writing the Bill is still going through the legislative process, so it is not yet law.)

That ends our overview of legislation pertinent to ECCE settings. As you have seen, the legislation is wide in scope and depth; and there is an emphasis on developing and co-ordinating legislation and practice to ensure the best outcomes for children. In the next chapter we will explore more recent policy developments, including Síolta and Aistear.

2006 REGULATIONS: USEFUL LINKS

Tusla: http://www.tusla.ie/services/preschool-services/early-years-pre-school-inspection
-services/questions-asked-to-the-hse-from-the-early-years-sector

DCYA: Child Care (Pre-School Services) (No. 2) Regulations 2006 and Child Care (Pre-
School Services) (No. 2) (Amendment) Regulations 2006: http://www.dcya.gov.ie/
documents/publications/Child_Care_Pre-_School_Services_Regs_2006.pdf

Barnardos: *A Parent's Guide to the Child Care (Pre-School) Regulations 2006*: http://www.
barnardos.ie/assets/files/publications/free/preschoolregsweb.pdf

References

Barnardos (2007) 'Childcare in Transition', *ChildLinks*, Issue 3, http://www.barnardos.ie/
assets/files/publications/free/childlinks_body15.pdf

Barry, U. and Sherlock, L. (2008) *Provision of Childcare Services in Ireland*. UCD School
of Social Justice Working Papers 8(1): 1–31, http://researchrepository.ucd.ie/
handle/10197/2037

Clare County Childcare Committee (n.d.) *Operating a Childcare Service: A Guide to
Legal Requirements*. Clare CCC, http://www.clarechildcare.ie/zdocs%5CLegal%20
Booklet%20%282%29.pdf

DCYA (Department of Children and Youth Affairs) (2010a) *National Standards for
Pre-School Services*. Dublin: DCYA, http://www.dcya.gov.ie/documents/childcare/
National_Standards_for_Pre-School_Services.pdf

DCYA (2010b) Foreword to the *National Standards for Pre-School Services*. Dublin:
DCYA, http://www.dcya.gov.ie/docs/Foreword_to_the_National_Standards_for_
PreSchool_Services/1941.htm

DCYA (2011) *Children First: National Guidance for the Protection and Welfare of Children*.
Dublin: DCYA, http://www.dcya.gov.ie/documents/Publications/ChildrenFirst.pdf

Dunphy, E. (2008) 'Supporting Early Learning and Development through Formative
Assessment', Aistear: Early Childhood Curriculum Framework research paper.
Dublin: NCCA, http://www.ncca.ie/en/Curriculum_and_Assessment/Early_
Childhood_and_Primary_Education/Early_Childhood_Education/How_Aistear_
was_developed/Research_Papers/Formative_assessment_full_paper.pdf

French, G. (2008) *Supporting Quality Book 2: Guidelines for Professional Practice in Early
Childhood Services – Enhancing Children's Learning and Development* (3rd edn). Dublin:
Barnardos

Harvey, B. (2008) *Working for Change: A Guide to Influencing Policy in Ireland*.
Dublin: Combat Poverty Agency, http://www.combatpoverty.ie/publications/
WorkingForChange_2008.pdf

HSE (Health Service Executive) (2011) *Child Health, Welfare and Development Assessment
Guide – Regulation 5*. Dublin: HSE

O'Kane, M. (2005) *Quality and Regulation in Early Childhood Care and Education: A Study of the Impact of the Child Care (Pre-School Services) Regulations (1996) on the Quality of Early Childhood Services in Ireland*. Dublin: CECDE, http://www.cecde.ie/english/pdf/Questions%20of%20Quality/Kane.pdf

Síolta (n.d.) *Research Digest: Standard 15 Legislation and Regulation*, http://www.siolta.ie/media/pdfs/Research%20Digest%20-%20Legislation%20and%20Regulation.pdf

Willoughby, M. (2007) *A Parent's Guide to the Child Care (Pre-School Services) Regulations 2006*. Barnardos, http://www.barnardos.ie/assets/files/publications/free/preschoolregsweb.pdf

Policies since 2000

INTRODUCTION

As we saw in Chapter 1, policy is instrumental in shaping and informing childcare practice. Also evident was the dramatic increase in interest and the subsequent proliferation of policies on aspects of children's lives, including early childcare and education. In this chapter we continue to focus on policy developments, looking at the period from 2006 onwards, though a brief recap of the National Children's Strategy 2000–2010 will be included here. The main emphasis in this chapter will be on policy specifically directed at ECCE settings and practice and will include both **Síolta** and **Aistear**, frameworks which promote quality in childcare and offer a curriculum to support children's learning and development. Before discussing Síolta and Aistear we will first look at the development of the **National Children's Strategy** and the **National Childcare Investment Programme**.

OUR CHILDREN – THEIR LIVES: NATIONAL CHILDREN'S STRATEGY 2000–2010

The National Children's Strategy marked a watershed representing not just a commitment but a strategy to enhance children's lives through the development of integrated services underpinned by a programme of research to better understand children's lives and those of their families. The National Children's Strategy is an expression of commitment to, and integration of, the UN Convention on the Rights of the Child (UNCRC), as can be seen in the goals of the strategy.

Three central goals of the National Children's Strategy are:

1. Children will have a voice.
2. Children's lives will be better understood.
3. Children will receive quality support and services to promote all aspects of their development.

In the first chapter we considered what policy is and what influences or informs it. Outcomes often guide policy development and implementation, which focus on what we hope to achieve or see. Outcomes can focus on what's happening *now* in children's lives or what *will* happen in the future. As the strategy spans a ten-year period, it plans not just for immediate goals but also longer-term ones. Before looking at those goals or outcomes, let's consider the six operational principles that underpin the strategy.

Operational Principles	Explanation
Child Centred	The best interests of the child shall be a primary consideration and children's viewpoints shall be given due regard
Family Oriented	The family generally affords the best environment for raising children and external intervention should be to support and empower families within the community
Equitable	All children should have equal opportunity in relation to access, participation in and derive benefit from the services delivered and support to achieve this
Inclusive	The diversity of children's experiences, cultures and lifestyles must be recognised and given expression
Action Oriented	Service delivery needs to be focused on achieving specified results to achieve standards in a targeted and cost effective manner
Integrated	Measures should be taken in partnerships, within and between relevant players in the state, voluntary/community sector and families

Source: DoHC (2000)

As we saw in Chapter 1, many factors, including the economy, the role of women in the workforce and the recognition of the importance of early years supports in child development and learning, led to an urgency to address childcare provision in the State. We can see this drive in the proliferation of policies and strategies to meet this demand. To address this further, the Department of Justice, Equality and Law Reform (DJELR) established an **Expert Working Group on Childcare** to develop the National Childcare Strategy. One of the most important findings of this expert group was the need for greater standardisation of training and qualifications for the industry. A set of occupational profiles and qualification levels for childcare services was agreed upon.

Another feature of the strategy, which was introduced later, was greater support for parents of children under six, such as:

- A new **Early Childcare Supplement** payment to parents, amounting to €1000 in a full year
- Improved **maternity and adoptive leave**
- Increased **Maternity Benefit**
- A new programme of **educational opportunities** for children and adults in areas of disadvantage.

Further, Delivering Equality of Opportunity in Schools (DEIS) was established under the auspices of the Department of Education but linked with the National Childcare Strategy. The key objective of DEIS was to support the educational needs of children and young people from disadvantaged communities. For pre-school children this was achieved with the **Early Start** programme, which targeted 1650 children in 40 centres. An associated programme is the Rutland Street Project in Dublin's inner city, which acted as a pilot to approaches that were then integrated with Early Start. Guidelines for childminders were also published.

In Practice

The six principles of the National Children's Strategy clearly mirror aspects of the UNCRC. Which can you identify? When we come to look at Síolta and Aistear you will see that there are connections between the principles and the policies, for example the 'Integrated' principle ties to Síolta Standard 3, Parents and Families. How many more can you spot?

While the principles outline the thinking behind the strategy, **outcomes** offer more real and tangible goals to be attained. The *Agenda for Children's Services 2007* identified seven outcomes as important.

National Service Outcomes for Children in Ireland

- Healthy, both physically and mentally
- Supported in active learning
- Safe from accidental and intentional harm
- Economically secure
- Secure in the immediate and wider physical environment
- Part of positive networks of family, friends, neighbours and the community
- Included and participating in society

(OMC 2007, p. 12)

You can find more information on the *Agenda for Children's Services*, including a range of policy documents introduced to reinforce the Strategy over the years, via this link: www.dcya.gov.ie/documents/publications/CS_handbook[ENGLISH]lowres.pdf

The Children's Rights Alliance's report on the implementation of the National Children's Strategy can be accessed at: http://childrensrights.ie/resources/ten-years-did-national-children%E2%80%99s- strategy-deliver-its-promises.

As we shall see later in this chapter, *Better Outcomes Brighter Futures* (2014–2020) is the second phase of the National Children's Strategy and builds on the work of its predecessor, *Our Children – Their Lives*. The launch of the National Children's Strategy led to the development of several important policy documents and initiatives. First we'll look at the launch in 2004 of the first ever national policy on play.

READY, STEADY, PLAY! A NATIONAL PLAY POLICY (2004–2008)

When Ireland launched *Ready, Steady, Play! A National Play Policy* in March 2004, it became one of the first countries in the world to produce a detailed national policy on play. The reason for the development of such a policy by the government was to honour commitments made in the UNCRC (1989), the National Children's Strategy (2000) and the Programme for Government (2002). The publication of the National Play Policy was an acknowledgement that in the past children's play had not been given the priority or attention it deserved; the policy also aimed to raise awareness of the importance of play and to contribute to the expansion of public play facilities over the implementation period.

The objectives of the National Play Policy were:
- To give children a voice in the design and implementation of play policies and facilities.
- To raise awareness of the importance of play.
- To ensure that children's play needs are met through the development of a child-friendly environment.
- To maximise the range of public play opportunities available to all children, particularly children who are marginalised, disadvantaged or who have a disability.
- To improve the quality and safety of playgrounds and play areas.
- To ensure that the relevant training and qualifications are available to people offering play and related services to children.
- To develop a partnership approach to funding and developing play opportunities.
- To improve on, and evaluation and monitoring of, play provision for children in Ireland. (National Children's Office 2004)

Ireland's National Play Policy is included in this chapter because play is central in the frameworks of both Síolta and Aistear, as will become clear when we explore them. Here we can see how policy is visible and influences later policy developments and strategies.

In Practice

Piaget said that play is the work of childhood. What do you think he meant by this? Can you see it in your observations of the children you support? Identify the different types of play children engage in and how you, as a practitioner, can support them.

GROWING UP IN IRELAND: NATIONAL LONGITUDINAL STUDY OF CHILDREN

Another important initiative was the development of a longitudinal study to examine the lives of children in Ireland. *Growing Up in Ireland* (ESRI and TCD, www.growingup. ie) has a dual purpose: to gain a better understanding of children's lives; and to improve the planning and delivery of policy and services.

Growing Up in Ireland is a government-funded study of children which takes place over seven years and follows the progress of two groups of children: eight thousand 9-year-olds and ten thousand 9-month-olds. Longitudinal studies aim to examine a topic, group or individuals over a long period; this approach gives a better understanding of, and insight into, changing patterns.

Child Wellbeing Indicators

Growing Up in Ireland has over 40 measures or 'indicators' of children's wellbeing and development. The development of the child wellbeing indicators can be viewed against the backdrop of increasing interest in this area internationally since the ratification of the UNCRC. The indicators form an integral element of the National Children's Strategy, as they allow not just for the measurement and evaluation of children's well-being but are used to inform policies and practice. We will discuss in more detail concepts of child wellbeing and indicators in Chapter 7, but for now we'll look at the *Growing Up in Ireland* indicators that are of particular relevance to childcare practitioners.

Growing Up in Ireland initially contained 42 child wellbeing indicators, including seven socio-demographic indicators. Four additional indicators were later added, which included quality of early childhood care and education, and nutritional outcomes. These last two indicators are of particular interest to childcare practitioners.

Nutritional Outcomes

This outcome ties in with existing childcare policies regarding the importance of good nutrition. Chapter 7 will examine the Health Promotion Unit's guidelines on nutrition.

Quality of Early Childhood Care and Education

This indicator was highlighted as a central measurement of positive outcomes for children: however, as Nóirin Hayes explains, this indicator has proved difficult to measure due to inconsistencies and confusion about how we distinguish between childcare and education:

> Policy and planning persists in drawing a distinction between childcare and education despite comprehensive and nuanced arguments encouraging government towards the development of a co-ordinated and integrated policy approach. (Hayes 2008, p. 17)

A critical difficulty in Irish policymaking, according to Hayes (2008) is the fact that in the main 'childcare' refers to two different service types:

1. For younger children, childcare has come to mean early childhood care and education and refers to the wide variety of settings, public and private, in which child-raising is shared with the family, including childminding and various forms of centre-based provision
2. For older children, generally up to about the age of 12 years, childcare refers to the variety of afterschool arrangements that exist to meet differing needs at different times.

We will examine information on childcare reported in the first and latest *State of the Nation's Children* reports (but bear in mind that two other reports have been published, in 2008 and 2010).

In Focus: *State of the Nation's Children* Reports 2006 and 2012

2006 Report

Measure
The number of children under 13 in various early childhood care and education arrangements, expressed as a proportion of all children in the same group. This can be subdivided into: (a) pre-school; (b) compulsory school; (c) centre-based care outside school hours; (d) crèche or day care; (e) professional childminder; and (f) family relative.

Key Findings
- Other than a parent/guardian, the main childcare arrangement for families with pre-school children was paid carer (12.1 per cent) and unpaid relative (9.7 per cent) for primary school children.

- Primary school children (78.5 per cent) were more likely to be cared for by a parent/guardian than pre-school children (59.7 per cent).
- 10.1 per cent of families with pre-school children used a crèche/Montessori as their main type of childcare in 2005. This compares with only 1.3 per cent of families with primary school children using this as their main type of childcare.

	Pre-school Children	
Main type of childcare (%)	2002	2005
Parent/guardian	62.1	59.7
Unpaid relative	10.5	11.5
Paid relative	4.6	4.5
Paid carer	12.0	12.1
Crèche/Montessori	9.3	10.1
Other	1.6	2.2

Percentage of families and main type of childcare arrangements 2002 and 2005 (CSO, Quarterly National Household Survey), quoted on p. 77 of http://www.dcya.gov.ie/documents/Publications/SONC_final.pdf

2012 Report

In the 2012 Report the 2006 measure was discontinued and replaced with the following indicator.

> **Measure**
> The percentage of Early Childhood Care and Education (ECCE) services under contract to deliver the free pre-school year scheme that meet basic and higher capitation criteria.

The 2012 measure is clearly focused on ECCE care provision in the form of the Free Pre-School Year Scheme; this represents a shift away from measuring how pre-primary and primary school children are cared for and to a focus on ECCE settings.

Key Findings

In 2011, a total of 4,162 ECCE services were under contract to deliver the Free Pre-School Year Scheme to 65,592 children. Of these ECCE services, 85.4 per cent met the basic capitation criteria and 14.6 per cent met the higher capitation criteria.

The number of ECCE services contracted to deliver the Free Pre-School Year Scheme increased by almost 10 per cent between 2010 and 2011.

It can be argued that the greater focus on ECCE witnessed in the 2012 measure is in part due to the establishment of the National Childcare Investment Programme (NCIP), which focused attention and demanded greater clarity within policy as to how we define and measure early childhood care and education. In addition to the NCIP, 2006 saw the introduction of the ten-year social partnership framework *Towards 2016*, which we will briefly overview before moving on to the NCIP.

> ### In Practice
>
> Reflect on how you feel the criteria for capitation impacts on skill mix and staff management.

TOWARDS 2016: A TEN-YEAR SOCIAL PARTNERSHIP FRAMEWORK 2006–2015

Launched in 2006, *Towards 2016* is a social partnership agreement that offered a blueprint to meet economic and social challenges facing the country. It is divided into two parts: economic issues and pay; and more social considerations about how best to meet challenges citizens face through the life cycle. Recognising the life cycle approach, Part 1 is divided into four sections dealing with: children; working-age people; older people; and people with disabilities.

It is the section on children that we will consider. *Towards 2016* was influenced by Ireland's ratification of the UNCRC and reflects the vision of the National Children's Strategy. *Towards 2016* pledged to create 50,000 new childcare places, including 10,000 pre-school places and 5,000 after-school places, as part of the €2.65 billion National Childcare Strategy 2006–2010.

The following are some of the 'priority actions' that were to be addressed in the first 27 months of the framework in the area of 'Early Childhood Development and Care':

- Create 50,000 new childcare places (including 10,000 pre-school places and 5,000 after-school places), as part of the National Childcare Strategy
- Develop a National Childcare Training Strategy to provide 17,000 childcare training places during 2006–2010
- Target the early childhood education needs of children from areas of acute disadvantage through DEIS (180 urban/town primary school communities)
- Deliver integrated care and education to children in disadvantaged communities through education-related professional support and training; and a curriculum and quality framework for early childhood education
- Publish the strengthened revised Pre-School Regulations, provide training for inspectors across the HSE, facilitate a national standardised inspection service and ensure that standardised inspection reports are publicly available
- Support and encourage school facilities being made available for after-school childcare provision as a key addition to the utilisation, development and support of local community facilities.

- Review the NCIP prior to its conclusion
- Extend the early childhood education component of the DEIS programme (to encompass the remaining 140 urban/town primary school under the School Support Programme).

In Practice

In planning for the future, what are the potential implications for ECCE settings and practice?

The Children's Rights Alliance, one of the social partners that submitted recommendations for *Towards 2016*, outlines the framework goals for children at: www.childrensrights.ie/ sites/default/files/submissions_reports/files/ChildCommitmentsSocialPartner2016_0. pdf.

The influence of the National Children's Strategy is acknowledged in *Towards 2016*, but of course these goals have to be funded, and this ties in with the launch of NCIP, also in 2006.

NATIONAL CHILDCARE INVESTMENT PROGRAMME 2006–2013

In terms of funding, the NCIP builds on the Equal Opportunities Childcare Programme (EOCP) 2000–2006 (DJELR 2000). As we saw in Chapter 1, the aim of EOCP was to create 40,000 childcare places as part of its investment programme. The NCIP, announced in Budget 2006, represented an investment of €575 million.

According to NCIP, it aimed to provide a proactive response to the development of quality childcare supports and services, which would be planned for and developed locally and centred on the needs of the child and the family. In keeping with *Towards 2016*, the goal of NCIP was to create 50,000 childcare places in addition to those already created under EOCP.

Key Objectives of NCIP

- Increase the supply and improve the quality of early childhood care and education services, part-time and full day care, school age childcare and childminding.
- Improve the supply of early childhood care and education services for 3- to 4-year-olds.
- Target the unmet need for school-age childcare services.
- Support families and break the cycle of disadvantage.
- Further develop the structures for co-ordination between statutory and non-statutory actors in the sector.

The programme aimed to achieve this goal through the following specific targets:
- 50,000 new childcare places, of which:

- ◆ 22,000 places in the private sector
- ◆ 28,000 places in the community and voluntary sector
- ◆ 20 per cent of new places were envisaged for children aged between 3 and 4 years to provide early childhood care and an education focus
- ◆ 10 per cent for children of schoolgoing age outside usual school times.
- Targets for childcare personnel, including:
  - ◆ 9,200 additional childcare workers
  - ◆ increasing the number of trained childcare personnel by 17,000.

As we saw in Chapter 1, one of the successes of EOCP was the creation of 33 City and County Childcare Committees (CCCs); it was envisaged that the CCCs would play an integral part in implementing NCIP.

We are now going to focus on policies that deal specifically with childcare: Síolta and Aistear.

CHILDCARE POLICY: SÍOLTA AND AISTEAR

Síolta – the National Quality Framework for Early Childhood Education (2006)

History

In Chapter 1 we discussed the White Paper on Early Childhood Education, *Ready to Learn*. Arguably, Síolta represents the coming to fruition of its aim to develop a high-quality system of early childhood education through a process of curriculum, training and qualifications. We will see in the next section that Aistear represents the curriculum aspect, but for now let's consider Síolta and its role in ECCE.

The Centre for Early Childhood Development and Education (CECDE) was responsible for initiatives to bridge the divide between education and care but also between early years settings and the formal education system. In pursuit of this aim it produced Síolta in 2006 after several years of consultation with stakeholders. CECDE was closed in 2008 and Síolta is now managed by the Early Years Education Policy Unit (EYEPU) in the Department of Children and Youth Affairs (DCYA). Síolta has a dedicated website of resources that can be accessed at www.siolta.ie.

What is Síolta?

Síolta aims to offer guidance on the provision of quality early education for young children as they journey through early childhood, a time which is crucially important for their development and learning. Síolta contains three strands:

- 12 Principles
- 16 Standards
- 75 Components of Quality.

In addition to providing the elements to guide practitioners, Síolta aims to assist them on many levels in practice situations:

- A support for individual professional practice and development
- A focus for team work and team development
- A tool for management, strategic planning and policy development
- A common base for the interactions of a varied team of professionals. (EYEPU 2013, p. 3)

Síolta's Principles

1. Early childhood is a significant and distinct time in life that must be nurtured, respected, valued and supported in its own right.
2. The child's individuality, strengths, rights and needs are central in the provision of quality early childhood experiences.
3. Parents are the primary educators of the child and have a pre-eminent role in promoting her/his well-being, learning and development.
4. Responsive, sensitive and reciprocal relationships, which are consistent over time, are essential to the wellbeing, learning and development of the young child.
5. Equality is an essential characteristic of quality early childhood care and education.
6. Quality early childhood settings acknowledge and respect diversity and ensure that all children and families have their individual, personal, cultural and linguistic identity validated.
7. The physical environment of the young child has a direct impact on her/his well-being, learning and development.
8. The safety, welfare and well-being of all children must be protected and promoted in all early childhood environments.
9. The role of the adult in providing quality early childhood experiences is fundamental.
10. The provision of quality early childhood experiences requires cooperation, communication and mutual respect.
11. Pedagogy in early childhood is expressed by curricula or programmes of activities which take a holistic approach to the development and learning of the child and reflect the inseparable nature of care and education.
12. Play is central to the well-being, development and learning of the young child. (www. siolta.ie/principles.php)

Síolta's Standards

Standard 1: Rights of the Child

Ensuring that each child's rights are met requires that she/he is enabled to exercise choice and to use initiative as an active participant and partner in her/his own development and learning.

Standard 2: Environments

Enriching environments, both indoor and outdoor (including materials and equipment) are well maintained, safe, available, accessible, adaptable, developmentally appropriate, and offer a variety of challenging and stimulating experiences.

Standard 3: Parents and Families

Valuing and involving parents and families requires a proactive partnership approach evidenced by a range of clearly stated, accessible and implemented processes, policies and procedures.

Standard 4: Consultation

Ensuring inclusive decision-making requires consultation that promotes participation and seeks out, listens to and acts upon the views and opinions of children, parents and staff, and other stakeholders, as appropriate.

Standard 5: Interactions

Fostering constructive interactions (child/child, child/adult and adult/adult) requires explicit policies, procedures and practice that emphasise the value of process and are based on mutual respect, equal partnership and sensitivity.

Standard 6: Play

Promoting play requires that each child has ample time to engage in freely available and accessible, developmentally appropriate and well-resourced opportunities for exploration, creativity and 'meaning making' in the company of other children, with participating and supportive adults and alone, where appropriate.

Standard 7: Curriculum

Encouraging each child's holistic development and learning requires the implementation of a verifiable, broad-based, documented and flexible curriculum or programme.

Standard 8: Planning and Evaluation

Enriching and informing all aspects of practice within the setting requires cycles of observation, planning, action and evaluation, undertaken on a regular basis.

Standard 9: Health and Welfare

Promoting the health and welfare of the child requires protection from harm, provision of nutritious food, appropriate opportunities for rest, and secure relationships characterised by trust and respect.

Standard 10: Organisation

Organising and managing resources effectively requires an agreed written philosophy, supported by clearly communicated policies and procedures to guide and determine practice.

Standard 11: Professional Practice

Practising in a professional manner requires that individuals have skills, knowledge, values and attitudes appropriate to their role and responsibility within the setting. In addition, it requires regular reflection upon practice and engagement in supported, ongoing professional development.

Standard 12: Communication

Communicating effectively in the best interests of the child requires policies, procedures and actions that promote the proactive sharing of knowledge and information among appropriate stakeholders, with respect and confidentiality.

Standard 13: Transitions

Ensuring continuity of experiences for children requires policies, procedures and practice that promote sensitive management of transitions, consistency in key relationships, liaison within and between settings, the keeping and transfer of relevant information (with parental consent), and the close involvement of parents and, where appropriate, relevant professionals.

Standard 14: Identity and Belonging

Promoting positive identities and a strong sense of belonging requires clearly defined policies, procedures and practice that empower every child and adult to develop a confident self- and group identity, and to have a positive understanding and regard for the identity and rights of others.

Standard 15: Legislation and Regulation

Being compliant requires that all relevant regulations and legislative requirements are met or exceeded.

Standard 16: Community Involvement

Promoting community involvement requires the establishment of networks and connections evidenced by policies, procedures and actions which extend and support all adult's and children's engagement with the wider community. (www.siolta.ie/standards. php)

In Practice

Consider how well your setting is implementing Síolta at present. How well do staff understand the complete process? Can you suggest ways in which their knowledge, understanding and application of Síolta can be enhanced?

Síolta is central to childcare regulation and practice; and Aistear is another critical piece of policy which has had an enormous impact on childcare and also on improving child learning and wellbeing.

Aistear: the Early Childhood Curriculum Framework (2009)

Aistear is Ireland's early childhood curriculum framework for all children from birth to 6 years. It was launched in 2009, following a process of consultation and partnership with stakeholders, by the National Council for Curriculum and Assessment (NCCA). This process included:

• Establishment of the Technical Working Group and Early Childhood Committee
• Consultation findings (2005)

- Portraiture study (2007)
- Four background papers.

We will return to the four background papers shortly, but first let's consider the origins of Aistear and how it relates to Síolta.

Aistear was developed by the NCCA and is designed to connect with Síolta: while Síolta is concerned with promoting quality in ECCE though its Standards, Aistear outlines a curriculum to guide ECCE practitioners on this path.

The principles that underpin Aistear are closely aligned with the principles underlying both Síolta and the primary school curriculum (1999). It could be argued that connecting these principles demonstrates an attempt to solidify and co-ordinate policy and to promote continuity across education.

In the development of Aistear, research was conducted into four main areas, the results of which was published in the following background papers. Examining these papers and their themes offers an insight into the key elements behind Aistear.

Background Research Papers

The research papers and their summaries can be accessed via NCCA's website: www.ncca.ie/en/Curriculum_and_Assessment/Early_Childhood_and_Primary_Education/Early_Childhood_Education/How_Aistear_was_developed/Research_Papers/. Here is a brief summary of each paper.

1. 'Perspectives on the Relationship between Education and Care in Early Childhood' (Hayes 2007)

According to Aistear, this paper highlights 'the key role the adult plays in a nurturing pedagogy'.

> **What is Pedagogy?**
> Pedagogy is usually defined as the science of teaching at its most simplistic. However, the following explanation of it from an early learning perspective explains it more thoroughly: 'Pedagogy is about learning, teaching and development, influenced by the cultural, social and political values and principles we have for children ... underpinned by a strong theoretical and practical base' (Learning and Teaching Scotland 2013).

This paper outlines how the adult can nurture pedagogy through interactions and collaborative learning, observing and interpreting the young child's words and actions and planning for future learning opportunities. The paper highlights how well-planned environments led by trained staff lead to positive outcomes for children.

2. 'Children's Early Learning and Development' (French 2007)

This paper's message relates to how children make connections as new learning builds on existing learning in a continuous process through language and play with others. These meaningful experiences allow children to make connections between learning, which supports their development.

3. 'Play as a Context for Early Learning and Development' (Kernan 2007)

The focus of this paper is evident from its title – play! Play is seen as a fundamental right for all children from birth onwards. The importance of time and space for play experiences is recognised. The paper outlines different types of play and their fundamental role in young children's development and learning. Elements identified as affecting how children play and the benefits they derive from it include the physical environment and the people and objects within that environment.

4. 'Supporting Early Learning and Development through Formative Assessment' (Dunphy 2008).

An emphasis is placed on the importance of assessment in supporting children's development and learning. Assessment forms the cornerstone of most educational endeavours, and this paper discusses formative assessment as collecting, documenting, reflecting on and using information to develop portraits of children as learners, allowing adults to 'see' and understand them. It guides the reader through a narrative approach to assessment to describe early learning using stories, photographs and samples of work to capture early learning and development.

In Practice

How do you see these key papers linking in to Síolta Standards?

Now let's see how the research papers translated into Aistear's framework.

Aistear contains 12 underpinning principles, and four themes with guidelines for their implementation. Let's look at the principles first.

Principles

Twelve principles of early learning and development are grouped into three sections:

Children and their lives in early childhood	Children's connections with others	How children learn and develop
• The child's uniqueness • Equality and diversity • Children as citizens	• Relationships • Parents, family and community • The adult's role	• Holistic learning and development • Active learning • Play and hands-on experiences • Relevant and meaningful experiences • Communication and language • The learning environment

Themes

Aistear presents children's learning and development using four interconnected, colour-coded themes:

- Well-being
- Identity and Belonging
- Communicating
- Exploring and Thinking.

The themes describe what children learn – their dispositions, attitudes and values, skills, knowledge, and understanding. Each theme begins with a short overview of its importance for children as young learners. The theme is then presented using four aims. Each aim is divided into six learning goals as shown in the diagram. Some of these goals may be more suited to children as they get older.

FIGURE 3.1 AISTEAR'S THEMES, AIMS AND LEARNING GOALS

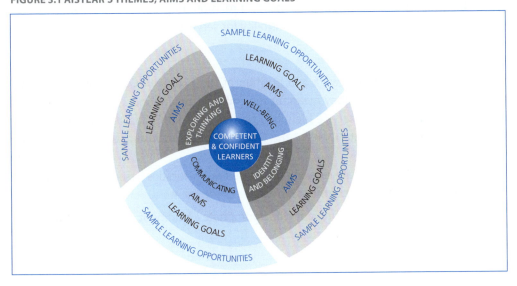

Principles and Themes	Guidelines on Good Practice
Principles Themes: • Well-being • Identity and Belonging • Communicating • Exploring and Thinking	• Partnership with Parents • Interactions • Play • Assessment

Source: NCCA (2009b)

In Focus: What is Quality in ECCE?

When discussing 'quality' it is useful to think of it as having two parts or aspects (La Paro *et al.* 2012):

1. **Structural quality:** includes classroom materials, curriculum, practitioner training and adult–child ratio.
2. **Process quality:** human interactions including practitioner to child and peer to peer.

The *Report on the National Forum for Early Childhood Education* identified a range of quality indicators that can be grouped under five key areas. These are:

1. **Child Indicators:** developmentally appropriate programmes, child progress assessments, programme assessment and the size of the group.
2. **Staff Indicators:** appropriately trained staff, appropriate pay and conditions, continuity of care and child–staff ratios.
3. **Physical Environmental Indicators:** health and safety standards, quality of space and physical resources.
4. **Social Indicators:** affordability, accessibility and parental and community involvement.
5. **National Indicators:** a national policy provision for regulation, provision and supervision, co-ordination of responsibility for services. (National Forum Secretariat 1998, pp. 55–6)

These indicators reflect the work and position of the European Commission Network on Childcare. But what do they mean for the childcare practitioner? Below are the key components in a quality service identified by the National Childcare Strategy (DJELR 1999). See if you can relate them to the UNCRC, Síolta and Aistear and to your daily practice.

• Offers both appropriate care and play-based opportunities based on the age and stage of development of the child.

• Provides a quality environment with appropriate equipment, materials, activities and interactions.

• Has a high adult to child ratio.

- Has suitably trained staff that are registered with the relevant lead agency.
- Offers continuity of relationships with adults and other children.
- Works in partnership with parents.
- Listens to and gives due consideration to the views and wishes of the children.
- Provides equal opportunities for all children attending as well as for staff.
- Recognises and promotes the cultural needs of children.
- Provides adequate remuneration for staff.
- Provides opportunities and support for in-service training of staff.
- Through a partnership approach with parents, links in with other community activities and services.
- Positively asserts the value of diversity.
- Is accessible for all. (DJELR 1999, p. 49)

In Practice

Take each component outlined above and evaluate how you and the service you work in meet it. Identify areas that could be improved upon. Consider other factors and measures you use to assess quality in your practice and in your setting.

The measurement of quality and the regulation of services are closely related. In Ireland, quality is currently measured or regulated through the Pre-School Regulations, which we discussed in Chapter 2. As you read the remaining chapters, see how these components of a quality service are reflected in policies, regulations and practices.

In relation to the development of ECCE policies, Dr Geraldine French (2008) identifies the following as promoting quality in ECCE:

1. Aistear
2. Síolta
3. The universal right to a Free Pre-School Year for children aged 3 and 4 years
4. Literacy and Numeracy Strategy
5. Regulation 5 and revised inspection systems

The final section of this chapter focuses on more recent policy developments.

NATIONAL EARLY YEARS STRATEGY

The National Early Years Strategy (NEYS) was officially launched in 2013 by the DCYA. An Expert Advisory Group, comprising parties representing early years and child protection, developed a consultation document that would form the basis of NEYS. A report, *Right from the Start*, which we look at below, was produced. NEYS is one of the three strands in the overarching national policy framework, *Better Outcomes Brighter Futures 2014–2020* (examined below).

NEYS is Ireland's first ever national strategy for early years and includes a range of topics such as child health and wellbeing, learning and development, play, parenting and family supports, and ECCE. It was informed not just by the findings of the Expert Advisory Group but also by findings of the *Growing Up in Ireland* studies and prevention and early intervention projects (PEIPs) such as Sure Start and the Rutland Project.

Key issues identified in NEYS are:
- the further development of early childhood care and education programmes
- the need to enhance quality provision, curricular support and workforce capacity in early years services
- support and regulation of the childminding sector
- the future development of early intervention, therapeutic and family support services to support young children and their parents.

At the Strategy's core is the recognition of the inherent benefits to be derived from early years supports and interventions.

Right from the Start

Right from the Start, which forms the basis of NEYS, is comprehensive in depth and coverage; its findings and recommendations are based on research and international best practice with an eye to developing future frameworks to support an early years strategy in Ireland. Only the briefest of summaries is possible here, but the full report can be accessed at www.dcya.gov.ie/documents/policy/RightFromTheStart.pdf.

The main body of the report consists of ten themes with accompanying recommendations pinpointed as essential to the success of NEYS. These are the themes, and we have listed just one recommendation for each theme to give an idea of the tone of the report.

1. **Economic rationale for increased investment**
   Raise significantly the amount of public investment in young children and their families.
2. **Supporting families**
   Develop a National Parenting Action Plan.
3. **Health and Well-being**
   Ensure that the timing and content of the core screening and vaccination programmes are consistent.

4. **Access to services and inclusion**
    Roll out the Diversity and Equality Guidelines for Childcare Providers nationally.
5. **Quality in services and supports**
    Develop a national plan for the phased, supported and simultaneous implementation of the Síolta and Aistear frameworks.
6. **Training and professional development**
    Ensure that all those working with young children and their families are required and supported to undertake regular continuing professional development.
7. **Regulation and support**
    Review the Pre-School Regulations and the new National Standards.
8. **Governance**
    Bring together in a single Government department all policy responsibility for early care and education services.
9. **Information, research and data**
    Ensure that the data collected by public health nurses related to early child development is used effectively to monitor the development of infants and toddlers.
10. **Implementation**
    Support staff and professionals working in early years services.

In total the report makes 54 recommendations across the ten themes. In addition, 'five peaks in five years' are identified, the 'peaks' referring to the challenges faced in making the kind of transformation in children's lives that is envisaged in the report. The 'peaks' that must be scaled within the next five years for this 'transformation' to happen are:

- Increasing investment
- Extending paid parental leave
- Strengthening child and family support
- Insisting on good governance, accountability and quality in all services
- Enhancing and extending quality early childhood care and education services.

The Appendices to the report contain five papers that give an overview of the following topics:

- Paper 1: Overview of government policy and comparable early years strategies internationally
- Paper 2: Early childhood care and education – key messages from research
- Paper 3: Child health, development and wellbeing in the early years in Ireland – key messages from research
- Paper 4: Supporting parents in the early years in Ireland – key messages from research
- Paper 5: Learning from the Prevention and Early Intervention Initiative.

A key message that resonates through this report is that there is so much to gain from early intervention and strong supports. We cannot encourage too strongly practitioners or anyone interested in early years to read this valuable report.

As mentioned above, this report forms the basis of NEYS, which itself is one strand of the national policy framework for children and young people, *Better Outcomes Brighter Futures*, to which we now turn our attention.

BETTER OUTCOMES BRIGHTER FUTURES, NATIONAL POLICY FRAMEWORK 2014–2020

While NEYS deals solely with the early years (0–6 years), *Better Outcomes Brighter Futures* is concerned with a national policy framework for all children and young people from birth to 24 years of age. *Better Outcomes Brighter Futures* builds on Ireland's earlier framework, the *National Children's Strategy*, which covered the period 2000 to 2010. Taking up from where it left off, *Better Outcomes Brighter Futures* outlines an ambitious strategy for improving children's lives. It was launched in 2014 by the DCYA and is the successor to the National Children's Strategy, carrying on the mantle of formulating a national vision to support children's lives. Below is the framework overview of *Better Outcomes Brighter Futures, 2014–2020*.

FIGURE 3.2 THE POLICY FRAMEWORK OF *BETTER OUTCOMES BRIGHTER FUTURES*

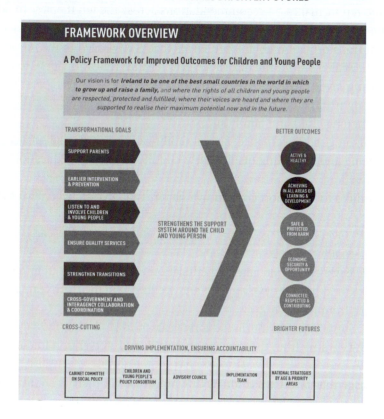

This strategy has been hailed as one of the most ambitious programmes for government. It spans health, education, child protection and poverty, committing government departments to work together to achieve five national outcomes for children.

FIGURE 3.3 *BETTER OUTCOMES BRIGHTER FUTURES* NATIONAL OUTCOMES

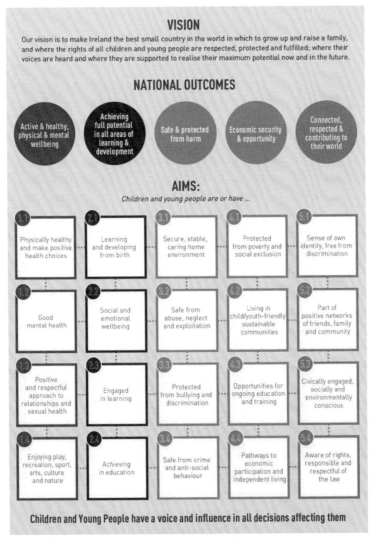

Five national outcomes for children and young people

This Policy Framework has adopted an outcomes approach based on five national outcomes for children and young people. These outcomes are interconnected and reinforcing. Four aims have been identified for each outcome [*see diagram below*]

VISION

Our vision is to make Ireland the best small country in the world in which to grow up and raise a family, and where the rights of all children and young people are respected, protected and fulfilled; where their voices are heard and where they are supported to realise their maximum potential now and in the future.

NATIONAL OUTCOMES

Active & healthy, physical & mental wellbeing

Achieving full potential in all areas of learning & development

Safe & protected from harm

Economic security & opportunity

Connected, respected & contributing to their world

AIMS:

Children and young people are or have ...

1.1	2.1	3.1	4.1	5.1
Physically healthy and make positive health choices	Learning and developing from birth	Secure, stable, caring home environment	Protected from poverty and social exclusion	Sense of own identity, free from discrimination
1.2	**2.2**	**3.2**	**4.2**	**5.2**
Good mental health	Social and emotional wellbeing	Safe from abuse, neglect and exploitation	Living in child/youth-friendly sustainable communities	Part of positive networks of friends, family and community
1.3	**2.3**	**3.3**	**4.3**	**5.3**
Positive and respectful approach to relationships and sexual health	Engaged in learning	Protected from bullying and discrimination	Opportunities for ongoing education and training	Civically engaged, socially and environmentally conscious
1.4	**2.4**	**3.4**	**4.4**	**5.4**
Enjoying play, recreation, sport, arts, culture and nature	Achieving in education	Safe from crime and anti-social behaviour	Pathways to economic participation and independent living	Aware of rights, responsible and respectful of the law

Children and Young People have a voice and influence in all decisions affecting them

Within these outcomes are five aims to be achieved through 'transformational goals' as outlined in the 'Overview' diagram (Figure 3.2).

Over the next seven years the priorities are to:
- Better support parents and families
- Focus more on children's early years
- Work together to protect young people at risk
- Enhance job opportunities for young people
- Tackle child poverty
- Promote positive influences for childhood
- Improve child health and wellbeing.

How does the government believe it will meet the priority of focusing more on children's early years? According to the strategy:

> Research in Ireland and internationally is increasingly pointing to the returns that can accrue from investing in the early years – from supporting children's early cognitive, social and emotional development, to enhancing school readiness and to generating longer term returns to the State and society. This Framework seeks to promote a shift in policy toward earlier intervention and to ensure the provision of quality Early Years services and interventions, aimed at promoting best outcomes for children and disrupting the emergence of poor outcomes. This will be achieved through commitments made to continue to raise the quality of early years care and education, to introduce a second free preschool year subject to resources becoming available and the provision of free GP care for those aged 5 years and under. The publication of Ireland's first-ever National Early Years Strategy will provide a detailed roadmap for the enhancement and coordinated provision of Early Years services and supports. (DCYA 2014, p. xi)

As we can see here, NEYS is heralded as the engine to drive energy and resource to supporting children's early years. We also see the linking of policies with each other, leading to greater coherence and co-ordination.

Finally, can you see the UNCRC running throughout this strategy? We started our discussion on policy with the UNCRC, and here its influence is quite clear. The box opposite illustrates UNCRC articles specifically relevant to the national outcomes identified earlier.

As with the section on NEYS, this has been only a brief summary of an extensive and detailed strategy. We would urge readers to read the strategy in full at: www.dcya.gov.ie/documents/cypp_framework/BetterOutcomesBetterFutureReport.pdf.

In terms of policy, *Better Outcomes Brighter Futures* marks a significant shift from a fragmented approach across several government departments towards early intervention through a co-ordinated approach.

FIGURE 3.4 THE UNCRC'S NATIONAL OUTCOMES

UNCRC Articles relevant for specific national outcomes

Active and healthy	Achieving full potential in learning and education	Safe and protected from harm	Economic security and opportunities	Connected, respected and contributing to their world
• Children have an inherent right to life and the State has an obligation to ensure to the maximum extent possible the survival and development of the child (Article 6). • Right to the enjoyment of the highest attainable standard of health possible and to have access to health services and the State is obliged to take steps to combat disease and develop preventative healthcare (Article 24). • Right to rest, engage in leisure, play and recreational activities, and participate in cultural and artistic activities (Article 31). • Right to protection from illicit drug use and involvement in drug production and trafficking (Article 33). • Children with a physical disability or learning difficulties have the right to special care, education and training designed to help them to achieve the greatest possible self-reliance and to lead a full and active life (Article 23).	• Right to education as a progressive and equal right; the State is obliged to make primary education compulsory and free to all; to develop different forms of secondary education and make it available and accessible to all; make higher education accessible to all on the basis of capacity; take measures to encourage regular school attendance and reduce drop-out rates, and to ensure school discipline is administered consistent with the child's dignity (Article 28). • Education should be directed at developing the child's personality and talents; fostering respect for human rights; own cultural, national values; and the environment (Article 29). • Right to freedom of thought, conscience and religion, subject to appropriate parental guidance and national law (Article 14). • Children with a physical disability or learning difficulties have the right to special care, education and training designed to help them to achieve the greatest possible self-reliance and to lead a full and active life (Article 23).	• Right to live and/or maintain contact with parents unless it is not in their best interests (Article 9). The State is obliged to foster and enable family re-unification (Article 10). • Right to protection from all forms of abuse (Article 19), exploitation (Article 36), including sexual exploitation, sexual abuse (Article 34) and armed conflict (Article 38). • The State has a duty to promote the recovery of child victims of abuse (Article 39) and to act to prevent child kidnapping (Article 11), abduction and the sale and/or trafficking of children (Article 35). • The State is obliged to assist a child without a family (Article 20); children have a right to a periodic review of their care placement (Article 25); and adoptions should only be carried out in the best interests of the child (Article 21). • The State is obliged to provide refugee children with appropriate protections (Article 22).	• Children have a right to a standard of living 'adequate for the child's physical, mental, spiritual, moral and social development'. Parents have the primary responsibility to provide this and the State has a duty to assist parents, where necessary, in fulfilling this right (Article 27). • The State has an obligation to recognise and promote the principle that both parents or legal guardians have common responsibilities for the upbringing and development of the child; the State shall support parents or legal guardians in this task through the provision of appropriate assistance (Article 18). • Right to benefit from social security (Article 26). • Right to be protected from harmful labour exploitation (Article 32).	• All the rights guaranteed by the UNCRC must be available to all children without discrimination of any kind and the State is obliged to protect children from discrimination (Article 2). • The child's view must be considered and taken into account in all matters affecting him or her, in accordance with their age and maturity (Article 12). • Right to his or her identity, which the State is obliged to protect and, if necessary, re-establish (Articles 7 and 8). • Right to protection from interference with privacy, family, home and correspondence, and from libel or slander (Article 16). • Children of minority communities and indigenous peoples have the right to enjoy their own culture, to practise their own religion and to use their own language (Article 30). • Right to obtain information and to express their own views, unless this would violate the rights of others (Article 13). • Right to meet with others and to join or set up associations, unless this would violate the rights of others (Article 15). • The State is obliged to make the rights contained in the UNCRC widely known to adults and children (Article 42).

It is noteworthy that not long before the publication of this strategy we had seen the establishment of Tusla (the Family and Child Agency), an increase in funding for early years, including the free pre-school year, and the launch an increase in funding in early years, including the free pre-school year, and the launch of *Right from the Start*. In terms of child protection, the government would point to the successful referendum it initiated on children's rights and the Children First Bill, in addition to including child protection in the *Better Outcomes* Strategy as evidence of action to strengthen child protection in this country.

Finally, in the arena of health and wellbeing, evidence offered of the government's ongoing commitment includes not only emphasis on health and wellbeing in NEYS and *Better Outcomes* but also the *Healthy Ireland* strategy, a blueprint for improving the health outcomes of the nation, and the introduction of free GP care for the under 5s. Early intervention and prevention is witnessed again in the government's promise of campaigns to tackle obesity and youth mental health. Certainly what has been promised is ambitious and has the potential to mark a real turning point in Ireland's history of child policy. Only time will tell if it has been successful.

References

CECDE (Centre for Early Childhood Development and Education) (2006) *Síolta: the National Quality Framework for Early Childhood Education*. Dublin: CECDE, http://www.siolta.ie

DCYA (Department of Children and Youth Affairs) (2006, 2012) *State of the Nation's Children*. Dublin: DCYA

DCYA (2013) *Right from the Start: Report of the Expert Advisory Group on the Early Years Strategy*. Dublin: Government Publications, http://www.dcya.gov.ie/documents/policy/RightFromTheStart.pdf

DCYA (2014) *Better Outcomes Brighter Futures: The National Policy Framework for Children and Young People 2014–2020*, http://dcya.gov.ie/documents/cypp_framework/Better OutcomesBetterFutureReport.pdf

DoHC (Department of Health and Children) (2000) *Our Children – Their Lives: National Children's Strategy*. Dublin: Stationery Office, http://www.dcya.gov.ie/documents/Aboutus/stratfullenglishversion.pdf

DJELR (Department of Justice, Equality and Law Reform) (1999) *National Childcare Strategy: Report of the Partnership 2000 Expert Working Group on Childcare*. Dublin: Stationery Office, http://www.justice.ie/en/JELR/Childcare1.pdf/Files/Childcare1.pdf

DJELR (2000) *Equal Opportunities Childcare Programme 2000–2006: General Guidelines for Funding*. Dublin: DJLER, http://www.justice.ie/en/JELR/Pages/Childcare_programme_funding_guidelines

Dunphy, E. (2008) 'Supporting Early Learning and Development through Formative Assessment', Aistear research paper. Dublin: NCCA

ESRI (Economic and Social Research Institute) and TCD (Trinity College Dublin) (various dates). *Growing Up in Ireland: National Longitudinal Study of Children*. Dublin: Department of Children and Youth Affairs, http://www.growingup.ie

EYEPU (Early Years Education Policy Unit) (2013) *Final Report on the Development and Implementation of the Síolta Quality Assurance Programme*. Dublin: DES, http://www. education.ie/en/Publications/Policy-Reports/S%C3%ADolta-Final-Report.pdf

French, G. (2007) 'Children's Early Learning and Development', Aistear research paper. Dublin: NCCA

French, G. (2008) *Supporting Quality Book 2: Guidelines for Professional Practice in Early Childhood Services – Enhancing Children's Learning and Development* (3rd edn). Dublin: Barnardos

Hayes, N. (2007) 'Perspectives on the Relationship between Education and Care in Early Childhood', Aistear research paper. Dublin: NCCA

Hayes, N. (2008) *The Role of Early Childhood Care and Education – An Anti-poverty Perspective*. Dublin: Combat Poverty Agency, http://www.combatpoverty.ie/ publications/TheRoleOfEarlyChildhoodCareAndEducation_2008.pdf

Kernan, M. (2007) 'Play as a Context for Early Learning and Development', Aistear research paper. Dublin: NCCA

La Paro, K.M., Thomason, A., Lower, J.K., Kintner-Duffy, V.L. and Cassidy, D.J. (2012) 'Examining the definition and measurement of quality in early childhood education: a review of studies using the ECERS-R from 2003 to 2010', *Early Childhood Research and Practice*, Volume 14(1), http://ecrp.uiuc.edu/v14n1/laparo.html

Learning and Teaching Scotland (2013). *Let's Talk about Pedagogy: Towards a Shared Understanding for Early Years Education in Scotland*, http://www.educationscotland. gov.uk/images/talkpedagogy_tcm4-193218.pdf

National Children's Office (2004) *Ready, Steady, Play! A National Play Policy*. Dublin: Department of Health and Children, http://www.dcya.gov.ie/documents/publications /NCOPlayPolicy_eng.pdf

National Forum Secretariat (1998) *Report on the National Forum for Early Childhood Education*. Dublin: Stationery Office

NCCA (National Council for Curriculum and Assessment) (2009a) *Aistear: the Early Childhood Curriculum Framework*. Dublin: NCCA.

NCCA (2009b) *Aistear: the Early Childhood Curriculum Framework and Síolta, The National Quality Framework for Early Childhood Education: Audit: Similarities and Differences*. http://www.ncca.ie/en/Curriculum_and_Assessment/Early_Childhood_ and_Primary_Education/Early_Childhood_Education/Aistear_Toolkit/Aistear_ Siolta_Similarities_Differences.pdf

OMC (Office of the Minister for Children) (2007) *The Agenda for Children's Services: A Policy Handbook*. Dublin: OMC, DoHC, http://www.childandfamilyresearch.ie/sites/ www.childandfamilyresearch.ie/files/cs_agenda_handbook_family_support_0.pdf

Child Protection: A Theoretical Introduction

In Chapter 2 we discussed legislation and regulations relating to the childcare setting. In this chapter we will consider the historical perspective of child abuse and child protection in Ireland. We will review the legislation guiding our practice in the area of child protection: bear in mind that it is essential that the practitioner is absolutely clear about their role and responsibilities. There are a number of key documents that provide us with guidance in our day-to-day work with children, and we shall examine these and relate them to day-to-day practice.

HISTORICAL PERSPECTIVE ON CHILD PROTECTION/ABUSE IN IRELAND

Over the last two decades we have learned many lessons from the child abuse cases which have come to light, and the inquiries that followed these revelations. Considerable changes in practice have come about to increase the protection of children. Here we will reflect on a number of these cases and explore what could have been done to prevent or limit the abuse of the children involved.

Kilkenny Abuse Case

The victim, who was referred to as 'Mary' in the court case, was physically and sexually abused by her father from 1976 to 1991. In late 1982/early 1983 she disclosed the abuse to a social worker. As she was over 16 years of age she was no longer legally considered a child, and no legal action was taken. At the age of 17 she had a baby boy.

Her father was the child's father. 'Mary' then left the family home with her son and went to live in a hostel. Her father discovered her whereabouts and with the assistance of the Gardaí she was persuaded to return home.

At the age of 27 she took legal action against her father. He was charged with rape, incest and assault, convicted and sentenced to seven years' imprisonment. It came to light that the Department of Health and Social Services had had over one hundred contacts with 'Mary' before the abuse stopped.

In hindsight it seems that in addition to appalling abuse by her father she was let down by the authorities in a most alarming manner. There are many questions to ask, for example:

- Mary was no longer a minor in the eyes of the law, but why did the authorities not investigate the alleged abuse of her when she was a minor?
- Why did the Gardaí help her father locate her? Were they not aware of the allegations she had made to the social worker?
- Did the Gardaí involve social services? Probably not, as she was not a minor at that stage. But if they had, they would not have assisted in returning her to an abusive home.

Kelly Fitzgerald Report

Kelly Fitzgerald died in a London hospital in 1993 at the age of 15 years, days after she arrived in Britain from her family home in Ireland. She was emaciated and in a critical state as a result of severe neglect. Her parents were found guilty of wilful neglect and were each sentenced to 18 months' imprisonment.

Prior to December 1990, the family had lived in England and when they moved back to Ireland Kelly remained with relations in England for some time. When she did move to Ireland in September 1992, UK social services alerted the Western Health Board to their concerns about Kelly and one of her siblings. When Kelly returned to the UK her relations took her to hospital from the airport because she was so unwell. She died within a matter of days.

Questions to be asked:

- Why was the Western Health Board so slow to engage with the family to assess Kelly's situation?
- Why, despite being alerted to Kelly's plight, did the authorities fail to take adequate steps to ensure her safety?

West of Ireland Farmer Inquiry

This inquiry was established in 1995 after a father received a very lengthy term of imprisonment following his conviction on charges of physical and sexual assaults of his children. Four of the six children in this family were subjected to horrific abuse, which began in 1976 when the three oldest children were aged 7 and 6 years old. In April

1982, a criminal case was taken against the father in relation to an assault on one of his children. The case was adjourned for six months and then struck out. In 1983, the eldest child was placed in voluntary care after he presented at the local Garda station with a teacher and stated his unwillingness to return home. While in care, the child disclosed that he and his sister had been sexually abused. Despite this, the child was returned to his home for weekend visits and after a number of months left the care home. There was no engagement between the family and social services between 1984 and 1993, when the full extent of the physical abuse was revealed by the children, three of whom were then adults.

Questions to be asked:
- How did the authorities not ensure the safety of these children?
- Why did none of the professionals involved have a clear picture of what was going on?
- Why did no one act as an advocate for the children?

Roscommon Report

Contact between child protection services and the family at the centre of the Roscommon Child Care Case began in 1989, shortly after the birth of the first child, and continued until May 2005, when care orders under Section 18 of the Child Care Act 1991 were granted in respect of all six children involved. In November 1996, more than eight years prior to the granting of the care orders, an application for supervision orders was discussed at the first case conference held in respect of this family, but no application was made to the court at this time. In October 2000, following discussions regarding a co-parenting arrangement with relations, the mother obtained an *ex parte* High Court order which restrained the Western Health Board from removing the children from her custody without a further order of the High Court. In July 2001, the Western Health Board applied for supervision orders in respect of the six children, but in March 2002, following a number of adjournments, the application was struck out at the request of the Western Health Board. In the summer of 2004, one of the children asked to be taken into care and in October 2004 the remaining five children were placed in care on foot of an emergency care order. A total of 12 case conferences were convened in respect of this family between November 1996 and November 2004. The mother was sentenced to a term of imprisonment of seven years in 2008, following her conviction on charges of incest, ill-treatment and neglect. The father was sentenced to a term of 14 years in 2010, following his conviction on charges of rape and sexual assault.

The following is an excerpt from the report on the **Roscommon Abuse Case** inquiry. It highlights the repeated failure of the professionals involved to ensure the safety of the children. It is vitally important that all professionals working with children fully understand what went wrong in previous cases to learn from them to ensure that every effort is taken to protect children.

The Inquiry Team concludes that the six children of the A family were neglected and emotionally abused by their parents until their removal from the home in 2003 and 2004. Some of the children have spoken of severe physical abuse by their parents. Some of the children were also sexually abused. There is no evidence that either parent understood or sought to consistently meet their children's needs. Both parents, but particularly Mr A, successfully resisted the efforts of professionals to work in a meaningful way with the children, while appearing to be cooperative on the surface. We have identified that while the WHB [Western Health Board] did recognise the neglect and indeed on occasions the emotional abuse of the children, it failed to follow up the decisions taken by the Core Group/Child Protection Management Team, in a way that offered the children better protection from the effects of that neglect, in a way that was lasting.

Staff utilised services to support the parents. The parents tended to agree readily to accept the support offered but the Inquiry Team did not find any evidence that any area of their parenting showed a positive consistent change over the eight year period from 1996 to 2004. The parents were both heavily dependent on alcohol and in the later years one parent had an additional dependence on prescription medication. This addiction and the use of the family income to support those addictions, rather than for the support and benefit of the children, were not fully taken on board in the planning in respect of this case.

There was a belief that these parents could, with support, meet the needs of their children. There was a focus on working with the parents. Progress was made at times in the general condition of the home but that progress was initiated by WHB staff, the actual clean-up was undertaken by the staff and then over time conditions again deteriorated. Until the children were taken into care there are few accounts of them as individuals on file although on one occasion in 2001 there was a proposal that their needs should be assessed and a plan put in place based on that assessment. That assessment was not undertaken. In families where ongoing and chronic neglect is occurring the services going into the family home must look at what day to day life is like for the children. We know from accounts given by the children since they came into care that this was not a home where 'good enough parenting' was available. We believe that the threshold as to what was considered 'good enough parenting' was set too low for these children.

We have concluded that, had there been a better insight and understanding of the condition and the needs of the children over a protracted period of time, the hope that this family could function in a positive way would have given way to serious concerns years earlier than it did and the children offered protection.

The views and opinions expressed, conclusions reached and recommendations made in this report are those of the Roscommon Inquiry. (Gibbons 2010)

In Practice

Key points to be taken from the above cases:

- The professionals involved were naive; at times they took what they saw at face value rather than exploring more deeply.
- Perhaps they were afraid or intimidated, which suggests that professionals need to be highly trained and experienced in order to recognise the more subtle indicators and also to be confident enough to question and challenge.
- In some cases the children were not spoken to and when they were they were not always believed. Instead they were suspected of making it up or exaggerating the facts. Sjöberg 2002 (cited in Barnardos 2010) found that children are often reluctant to disclose abuse and when they do they tend to minimise the experience rather than embellish it.
- Professionals involved need to have a very clear picture of what is 'good enough parenting' and at what point it is time to intervene to prevent or limit 'significant harm' to the child or children.

DEFINING ABUSE

In order to be in a position to determine whether or not a child is in an abusive situation, we must be very clear on what factors define the circumstances as abusive. In this chapter and in Chapter 5 we will examine the key indicators of abuse in detail to ensure that you have enough depth of knowledge and understanding to guide you in decision-making in the early years setting.

The World Health Organization (WHO) defines abuse as follows:

> Child maltreatment, sometimes referred to as child abuse and neglect, includes all forms of physical and emotional ill-treatment, sexual abuse, neglect, and exploitation that results in actual or potential harm to the child's health, development or dignity. Within this broad definition, five subtypes can be distinguished – physical abuse; sexual abuse; neglect and negligent treatment; emotional abuse and exploitation. (www.who.int/topics/child_abuse/en/)

Here are some relevant definitions from *Children First* (DCYA 2011):

- **Neglect:**
  - *'Wilful neglect'* occurs when there is direct and deliberate deprivation by a parent/carer of the child's basic needs, e.g. not providing food, shelter, warmth, clothing, contact with others.

- ◆ *'Circumstantial neglect'* usually occurs due to an inability of parent/carer to cope, e.g. stress/ill health/intellectual disability/addiction.
- **Physical abuse:** is that which results in actual or potential harm from an interaction, or lack of interaction, which is reasonably within the control of a parent or person in a position of responsibility, power or trust. There may be single or repeated incidents.
- **Emotional abuse:** is normally to be found in the relationship between the caregiver and the child rather than in a specific event or pattern of events.
- **Sexual abuse:** Occurs when a child is used by another person for his or her gratification or sexual arousal, or for that of others. (DCYA 2011, p. 9)

STATISTICAL EVIDENCE OF ABUSE
SAVI Report (2002)

The *Sexual Abuse and Violence in Ireland* report (McGee *et al.* 2002) was the first and remains the only significant research in Ireland into the incidence of sexual abuse in adults when they were children. Three thousand people were included in the data collection. The report is a landmark national study of Irish experiences, beliefs and attitudes concerning sexual violence. The report provides the results of the first national survey to assess sexual abuse and violence in Ireland, commissioned by the Dublin Rape Crisis Centre.

It details specific information about the prevalence of sexual violence in relation to age and gender for over 3,000 adults, and identifies the barriers to accessing law enforcement, medical and therapeutic services for those abused and their families. The sample group were chosen at random and were interviewed by telephone. The study focuses not only on the responses of those abused, but also includes attitudes and perceptions of the general public to sexual violence, and the myths and negative attitudes that make disclosure difficult. We strongly recommend that you take the time to read the summary of the report to gain a greater understanding of the findings. Here we present a number of the key findings for discussion.

SAVI Report Findings: Child Sexual Abuse

Child sexual abuse was defined in the report as sexual abuse of children and adolescents under the age of 17 years.

- **Girls:** One in five women (20.4 per cent) reported experiencing contact sexual abuse in childhood; a further one in ten (10 per cent) reported non-contact sexual abuse. In over a quarter of cases of contact abuse (i.e. 5.6 per cent of all girls), the abuse involved penetrative sex – vaginal, anal or oral sex.
- **Boys:** One in six men (16.2 per cent) reported experiencing contact sexual abuse in childhood with a further one in 14 (7.4 per cent) reporting non-contact sexual

abuse. In one of every six cases of contact abuse (i.e. 2.7 per cent of all boys), the abuse involved penetrative sex – either anal or oral sex.

- Almost one-third of women and a quarter of men reported some level of sexual abuse in childhood. Attempted or actual penetrative sex was experienced by 7.6 per cent of girls and 4.2 per cent of boys.

- Almost one-third of women and a quarter of men reported some level of sexual abuse in childhood. Attempted or actual penetrative sex was experienced by 7.6 per cent of girls and 4.2 per cent of boys. Equivalent rape or attempted rape figures in adulthood were 7.4 per cent for women and 1.5 per cent for men. Hence, girls and women were more likely to be subjected to serious sexual crimes than boys and men. Levels of serious sexual crimes committed against women remained similar from childhood through adulthood. Risks for men were lower as children than they were for women and decreased three-fold from childhood to adult life.

- Of those disclosing abuse, over one-quarter (27.7 per cent) of women and one-fifth (19.5 per cent) of men were abused by different perpetrators as both children and adults (i.e. 'revictimised'). For women, experiencing penetrative sexual abuse in childhood was associated with a sixteen-fold increase in risk of adult penetrative sexual abuse, and with a five-fold increase in risk of adult contact sexual violence. For men, experiencing penetrative sexual abuse in childhood was associated with a sixteen-fold increase in the risk of adult penetrative sexual violence, and an approximately twelve-fold increase in the risk of adult contact sexual violence. It is not possible to say that childhood abuse 'causes' adult revictimisation. Childhood sexual abuse is, however, an important marker of increased risk of adult sexual violence.

- Most sexual abuse in childhood and adolescence occurred in the pre-pubescent period, with two-thirds (67 per cent) of abused girls and 62 per cent of abused boys having experienced abuse by 12 years of age.

- In four of ten cases (40 per cent), the experience of child sexual abuse was an ongoing, rather than a single, abuse event. For many of those who experienced ongoing abuse (58 per cent of girls and 42 per cent of boys), the duration of abuse was longer than one year.

- A third (36 per cent) of those who had experienced sexual abuse as a child now believe that their abuser was also abusing other children at the time.

Abuse in All Categories

This section examines statistics from 2007–2011 for all four areas of abuse.

In 2011, there were 3,230 disclosures of emotional/physical or sexual abuse of children by callers to Women's Aid National Helpline, an increase of 55 per cent on 2011. (Women's Aid 2012)

The number of child welfare and protection reports to the HSE increased by almost 36 per cent between 2007 and 2011 (DCYA: *State of the Nation's Children* 2012).

In 2011, there were 31,626 child welfare and protection reports to the HSE (see the table below).

In Practice

Does this mean that the number of children being abused is increasing? We do not actually know, but what is most likely is that people are now more likely to come forward to report incidences of abuse than they were in the past. The increasing number of abuse cases being reported by the media has heightened the public's awareness of abuse and has also given victims of abuse the courage and confidence to seek help.

CHILD WELFARE AND PROTECTION REPORTS TO THE HSE, 2007–2011

	2007	2008	2009	2010	2011
Total	23,268	24,668	26,888	29,277	31,626
Type of report:					
Welfare	12,715	12,932	14,875	16,452	15,808
Physical	2,152	2,399	2,617	2,608	3,033
Sexual	2,306	2,379	2,594	2,962	3,326
Emotional	1,981	2,192	2,125	2,500	4,001
Neglect	4,114	4,766	4,677	4,755	5,458

Sources: CSO (2011); HSE *Reviews of Adequacy Reports*

From these figures we can see that neglect is consistently the most common category of abuse reported. Why? Is it really the most common form of abuse, or is it more 'visible' than other categories of abuse? We shall examine the indicators of abuse in detail in Chapter 5.

In Practice

Always be mindful that there may be a child in your setting who is being abused. As mentioned earlier, naivety has often been highlighted as a significant factor in failure to identify indicators of abuse. Because it is important for the early years practitioner to form a positive, open and friendly working relationship with parents/carers, we are at risk of thinking that abuse could not be happening in such a family. You must always be open to the possibility and ever vigilant for the signs of possible abuse.

HISTORICAL CHANGES

The last twenty years has seen many changes in child protection in Ireland. Some of the key milestones are:

1993 Kilkenny incest case. As a result of the investigation significant improvements were introduced in child protection services.

1994 Kelly Fitzgerald case brought to light the shortcomings in communications between social work departments.

1993–1996 Madonna House, Goldenbridge Orphanage and Trudder House were the first children's homes to be exposed for the abuse of the children in their care.

1994–present Disclosures of abuse by Roman Catholic clergy and religious orders.

1998 Protection of Persons Reporting Abuse Act.

1999 First publication of *Children First: National Guidance for the Protection and Welfare of Children*.

2002 Residential Institutions Redress Board established.

Garda Central Vetting Unit established.

Office of the Ombudsman for Children established. Its principal role is to promote the rights and welfare of children.

SAVI Report

2005 Ferns Report examined what took place and the handling of sexual abuse reports in the diocese of Ferns.

2007 Roscommon Abuse Case.

Recruiting and Training Staff

Every early years setting is now required to undertake the Garda Vetting screening of all staff employed in the setting. It is important to highlight that this only identifies people who have been found guilty of offences against children: remember, if someone has not been found guilty it does not mean that they are incapable of abusing children. You must always be vigilant for the possibility that one of your colleagues could abuse children. Women are as likely as men to abuse children.

PREDISPOSING FACTORS IN CHILD ABUSE

There are many views about the factors which can contribute to a child abuse situation arising. Increasing practical and academic knowledge has made us much more aware that traditional concepts of childhood as a series of predictable stages made up of set tasks is misleading, and it is now believed that there is no definitive set of needs. Research leads us now to consider that even if a child grows up in adverse circumstances they can go on to lead normal lives. Here we will consider the main factors which are still considered important identifying children who may be at risk. O'Brien (2011) has provided a useful overview of risk factors and protective factors involved in child abuse.

Examples of **risk factors**:

- Disabilities or mental retardation in children that may increase caregiver burden
- Social isolation of families
- Parents' lack of understanding of children's needs and child development
- Parents' history of domestic abuse
- Poverty and other socioeconomic disadvantages, such as unemployment
- Family disorganisation, dissolution and violence, including intimate partner violence
- Lack of family cohesion
- Substance abuse in the family
- Young, single, non-biological parents
- Poor parent–child relationships and negative interactions
- Parental thoughts and emotions supporting maltreatment behaviours
- Parental stress and distress, including depression or other mental health conditions
- Community violence.

Protective factors are the opposite of risk factors; they may reduce the risk of child maltreatment and they exist at individual, relational, community and societal levels.

Examples of **protective factors**:

- Supportive family environment
- Nurturing parenting skills
- Stable family relationships
- Household rules and monitoring of the child
- Parental employment
- Adequate housing
- Access to healthcare and social services
- Caring adults outside the family who can serve as role models or mentors
- Communities that support parents and take responsibility for preventing abuse. (Thomas *et al.* 2003, cited in O'Brien 2011)

It is important to recognise that both protective factors and risk factors, are cumulative – they gather or grow by gradual increases, potentially over the whole lifespan. Some factors can be related to, or more likely to occur in conjunction with, others; for example, where there is poverty some other factors are more likely to be present. This is illustrated in research by Sabates and Dex, who reflect, 'In the UK, the consequences of exposure to multiple risks have been investigated for children born in 1958 and in 1970 using the British birth cohort studies. For instance, early exposure to multiple risks in childhood has cumulative effects throughout the life course, influencing both behavioural adjustment during childhood and psychosocial functioning during adulthood' (2012, p. 4).

The above lists provide a helpful overview of factors to consider in the life of the child. The whole area of abuse is highly complex, and multiple factors play a part in determining the ability of the child to cope and the long-term effects of the abuse on their ability to function as a normal member of society. Buckley *et al.* (1997) have collated research relating to factors which contribute to the possibility of abuse. A greater knowledge and understanding of these factors will enable the early years practitioner to be more informed and thus better aware of what to look for in identifying children who may be at risk. Here is a summary of those factors. The key areas identified are:

- Age and gender
- Psychological health and wellbeing in childhood
- Changing family structures
- Parental mental illness
- Parental substance abuse and involvement in crime
- Marital discord
- Economic factors
- Educational success or failure (Buckley *et al.* 1997)

Age and Gender

Research found that children are better able to cope with stress as they get older and can understand the experience more. But of course how much they are exposed to this abuse can override their ability to deal with it. It was found that boys are more vulnerable to behavioural problems and more likely to offend as they grew older. Overall, males are more vulnerable to family disharmony. It is thought that because girls are more likely to discuss their feelings they cope better.

Psychological Health and Wellbeing in Childhood

Early behavioural disturbance has been cited as one of the strongest predictors of later problems, including psychological difficulties, involvement in crime and antisocial behaviour. Researchers found that a child who displays psychopathology in the early years is more likely to continue to experience difficulties into adulthood, although these difficulties may manifest themselves in various ways. Disruptive behaviour makes it more likely that they will have poor school attendance and leave school early.

Changing Family Structures

For most children the family provides the foundation on which they form relationships. We know from child development theory that the relationships formed in the first year of life determine our ability to form relationships throughout our life. The make-up of families in Ireland has changed quite considerably over the past twenty years. We now see a range of family types. Children are increasingly reared in lone-parent family units or in reconstituted families, although the majority of children still grow up in two-parent households. The research suggests that the most significant factor is the quality of the relationships and the economic resources available to the family. Studies have shown that children who live in single-parent households have a higher incidence of emotional problems and also problems at school compared to those living with both parents. It is thought that this is due to economic circumstances rather than parental marital status; in other words, there are more likely to be problems when poverty is an issue.

Many more mothers work outside the home than was the case even twenty years ago; their traditional role has changed. There is no evidence to suggest that this has had a negative effect on children; in fact research suggests that for many children it is a positive experience. A Danish longitudinal study by Christoffersen (2000, cited by Buckley *et al.* 1997) found that a long-term lack of employment of the mother could be a risk factor in the neglect and abuse of children.

Parental Mental Illness

There is considerable documentation to support the view that there is a strong link between parental mental illness and negative outcomes for children. It is thought that maternal depression undermines parenting ability and makes it more likely that the child will become disturbed. However, this relationship is not simple or straightforward and the impact of parental illness can be lessened when other resources are available to the child. There is widespread evidence of successful coping among children with parents who are mentally ill. The main risk factor when a parent suffers from psychological disorder appears to stem from the associated family discord, especially when the hostility directly involves the child. However, if there are healthy counterbalances, there is much less likely to be a negative effect on the children. This is also true when a child loses a parent due to death or separation. These potentially damaging situations, if successfully negotiated, can even benefit the child in the long term.

Marital Discord

Research has found that an increase in marital discord in the home is associated with an increased likelihood of referral to child psychiatric services and this is apparent in very young children. Yet, as with other adverse circumstances, marital disharmony does not in itself necessarily result in psychological difficulties in the child. If the child can gain support from other relationships outside the home it will off-set the effects overall. Very often it is not just one factor but the chain of negative events that are set in motion by the change in family structure.

Economic Factors

Economic factors play a key role in determining the overall health and social status of individuals throughout their lifespan and there is a well-established correlation between adverse socio-economic circumstances and the likelihood of problems with behaviour and school attendance. Relatively high rates of psychological distress have been found in a number of Irish studies based on lower socio-economic groups. A number of key factors have be identified as adversely affecting the child:

- Low-status parental occupation
- Lone parenthood
- Large family size
- Low level of maternal education.

Educational Success or Failure

We are all aware of the vital role of education in empowering people generally, and especially the opportunity it offers those who may be trapped in a cycle of unemployment and poverty. Research shows the importance of the impact of early learning experiences on the child's future. In Ireland all children have benefited from increased access to education, but some groups have gained more than others. Increasing retention levels are evident at second level (from 60 per cent in 1980 to 81 per cent in 1998), but socio-economic and gender differentials have emerged. Females are now outperforming males at most educational levels, while males are much more likely to drop out of the school system.

Extreme disadvantage will impact on the child's health overall and will affect their ability to attend and perform well at school. Yet children do overcome economic obstacles and become successful in the education system.

In Practice

Current experts recommend taking a flexible approach to every individual child rather than taking the same approach for every child who is disadvantaged. This is sound advice: each child is unique and therefore each will respond in a different way.

Reflect on how you can use the above to assist you and your colleagues in your practice with children to ensure the most positive outcomes for each child. (Modules 5 (Work Experience) and 6 (Supervision in Early Childhood Care) are relevant here.)

BREAKING THE CYCLE OF ABUSE

There is a clear cycle in maltreatment. Each life stage has moments where effective interventions can take place, but also where things can be made worse. Risk-taking behaviour as a result of early abuse, such as drug taking, can then impact on parenting behaviour and the social environment, which can then lead to further abuse. The cycle is not inevitable. There are many opportunities to break it by reducing risk factors and increasing protective factors, giving children the chance of a much brighter future.

Features of programmes that have shown to be effective in minimising the danger to children living in high-risk families include the following.

Bolstering Protective Factors

Strong family relationships and a positive social environment can make a real difference to the long-term outcomes for a child who has been physically abused. Work to strengthen families, to encourage clear boundaries with positive, non-physical discipline techniques, promoting mutual support between peers experiencing similar issues, and avoidance of peers involved in antisocial behaviour, criminal or substance-abusing behaviour, can be powerfully protective – even in the face of other adversities.

Strengthening Families

Relationships between children and their non-abusive parents can often suffer because of the violence within the family. Encouraging a warm and supportive relationship with the non-abusive parent or carer can make a world of difference in promoting strong attachments, repairing bruised relationships and restoring a child's self-esteem and emotional wellbeing.

Addressing Mental Health Issues

Focusing on the mental health of every family member has been shown to prevent recurrence of abuse and ensure better outcomes for the child.

Thinking 'Family'

When addressing problems such as mental illness, substance misuse and domestic abuse, adult services need to support their clients as parents and provide children with the help they need. Men can have a profound impact on families and need to be central in strategies for intervention. Professionals must consider and engage the key men in a child's life, to assess the risks they pose and the strengths they bring to family life.

Early Intervention

What is clear is the need to offer, at the earliest opportunity, preventive home visiting services to families at risk. It is essential for these services to be embedded across public services and policy.

In Practice

Research approaches aimed at reducing the risk of physical abuse in families, and discuss how you might implement these approaches in your practice. Consider Barnardos, ISPCC and NSPCC publications as part of your research; and also consult *Children First*.

ROLE OF SÍOLTA IN CHILD PROTECTION

Síolta was examined in some detail in Chapter 3. Here we will focus on the standards particularly relevant to child protection. Síolta is the national quality framework, and if it is clearly understood and effectively implemented by staff it is a most valuable tool in improving the provision for all children in the setting. It guides us to the areas on which we should particularly focus our attention in ensuring that every child's rights are met and upheld both in the setting and in the broader community.

Standard 1: Rights of the Child

The child is enabled to exercise choice and use their own initiative in relation to choices regarding their own development and learning.

If a child is being abused they lose their rights automatically as a result of the impact of the abuse on their development. By nature children are enthusiastic, curious and energetic. Abuse robs them of these characteristics, which are so vital in encouraging them to explore their world.

Standard 3: Parents and Families

Valuing and involving parents and families is vital to enrich the experience for the child and all adults involved in their development. The early years practitioner is in an excellent position to provide guidance and education to parents on all areas of child development. The development of an effective 'partnership with parents' is vital here. Communication should flow freely between the parents/carers and practitioners; each should value what the other has to offer and share the ultimate goal of meeting the child's needs. Working closely with parents and families will also help the practitioner to gain a fuller picture of the child's life. This will enable the practitioner to detect any changes in the child's behaviour that might need to be investigated: a good knowledge of what is happening in the child's life at home can help determine the possible cause of the changes. Remember, abuse takes place in every social class in our society – so never make assumptions.

Standard 11: Professional Practice

Practising in a professional manner requires the individual to have skills, knowledge and attitudes needed to achieve their role and responsibilities in the early years setting. Continuing professional development (CPD) and reflective practice are essential components. Regular ongoing training in child protection is necessary to maintain a clear awareness of what to observe from day to day.

Standard 12: Communication

Effective communication is vital in detecting possible child abuse. Very often it is like gathering pieces of a jigsaw, which gives us insight into the possibility of abuse. Sharing information with all stakeholders and keeping accurate, objective records is vital. Maintaining confidentiality is also vital to respect and protect all involved. Any child protection concerns should only be shared on a 'need to know basis'.

References

Barnardos (2010) *A Child Protection Guide for Early Years and School Age Childcare Services.* Dublin: Barnardos

Buckley, H., Skehill, C. and O'Sullivan, E. (1997) *Child Protection Practices in Ireland: A Case Study.* Dublin: Oak Tree Press, http://www.lenus.ie/hse/bitstream/10147/250811/1/ChildProtectionPracticesinIrelandaCaseStudy.pdf

CECDE (Centre for Early Childhood Development and Education) (2006) *Síolta: the National Quality Framework for Early Childhood Education.* Dublin: CECDE, http://www.siolta.ie

CSO (Central Statistics Office) (2011) *Census 2011.* Cork: CSO

DCYA (Department of Children and Youth Affairs) (various dates) *State of the Nation's Children.* Dublin: DCYA

DCYA (2011) *Children First: National Guidance for the Protection and Welfare of Children.* Dublin: DCYA, http://www.dcya.gov.ie/documents/Publications/ChildrenFirst.pdf

Gibbons, N. (2010) *Roscommon Child Care Case: Report of the Inquiry Team to the Health Service Executive.* Dublin: Stationery Office

HSE (Health Service Executive) *Reviews of Adequacy Reports.* Dublin: HSE

McGee, H., Garavan, R., de Barra, M., Byrne, J. and Conroy, R. (2002) *The SAVI Report: Sexual Abuse and Violence in Ireland.* Dublin: Liffey Press and Dublin Rape Crisis Centre

O'Brien, E. (2011) *Psychology for Social Care: An Irish Perspective.* Dublin: Gill & Macmillan

Sabates, R. and Dex, S. (2012) *Multiple Risk Factors in Young Children's Development.* London: Institute of Education

WHO (World Health Organisation) (2010) 'Understanding and Addressing Violence Against Women', www.who.int/iris/bitstream/10665/77434/1/WHO_RHR_12.37_eng.pdf

Women's Aid (2012) *Annual Report*, http://www.womensaid.ie/policy/publications/annual-report-2012/

CHAPTER 5

Child Protection: An Applied Approach

UNDERTAKING A RISK ASSESSMENT

This chapter will take you through the procedures for dealing with specific child protection issues when child protection concerns arise. It is not a definitive guide to all eventualities, but our aim is to prepare you by providing you with enough knowledge of theory and practice to make an informed decision when presented with a suspected or actual abuse case. The key aim of this section is to give you a clearly presented background to child protection in Ireland today and a step-by-step guide to dealing with child protection issues arising in the ECCE setting in order to safeguard every child and meet the legal requirements relating to child protection in practice.

It is vital that you, as an ECCE practitioner, are fully aware of your responsibility to uphold the legal requirements in the ECCE setting. In order to do this you must first know the relevant legislation and understand how to apply it to practice. The legal requirements are not optional: they place a statutory obligation on you to uphold the law at all times. Dealing with a suspected or an actual child abuse case is one of the greatest challenges for the early years practitioner. Adequate preparation will give you the knowledge and confidence to decide whether action must be taken to protect the child, and the procedures to be taken.

You will be guided through the completion of accurate documentation of concerns and all actions taken by ECCE staff following national guidelines set out in *Children First* (DCYA 2011) and *Our Duty to Care* (DoHC 2004). Case studies and critical incident analysis will be used to reinforce the reader's knowledge, understanding and analysis of situations. Correct completion of the official report form will be dealt with in detail and case studies will take the reader through each step, from initial concerns to completion of the report form and finally to follow-up.

It is important to remember that child protection is not just about dealing with actual abuse situations; it is also about ensuring that policies and procedures provide the early years practitioner with adequate support to guide their daily practices to ensure the safety of every child and staff member in their service. This section will deal with self-evaluation of relevant policies and procedures which safeguard children in ECCE settings. Undertaking a child protection audit is considered good practice in the ECCE setting. However, undertaking such an audit does require some specialist skills and knowledge, which we present in this book. **Síolta** includes a self-assessment approach enabling services to assess the quality of their service and practice against a quality framework. Throughout this book, practical application will be presented and reinforced. The expert childcare practitioner must have the knowledge and skills to deal with day-to-day practice and to ensure that all policies and procedures are followed in the case of actual or suspected abuse.

KEY LEGISLATION

Childcare legislation was discussed in considerable detail in Chapters 2 and 3, so here we shall provide a brief review. The relevant pieces of legislation are:
* Child Care Act 1991 (and Child Care Regulations 1996 and 2006)
* Domestic Violence Act 1996
* Freedom of Information Act 1997 and 2003
* Protection of Persons Reporting Child Abuse Act 1998
* Criminal Justice Act 2006
* Children First Bill 2014.

Child Care Act 1991

The purpose of this Act was to update the law in relation to the care of children who have been assaulted, ill-treated, neglected or sexually abused, or who are at risk. The main provisions of the Act are:
* Placing a statutory duty on the HSE to promote the welfare of children up to the age of 18 who are not receiving adequate care and protection
* Strengthening the powers of the HSE to provide childcare and family support services

- Improved procedures to facilitate immediate intervention by the HSE and An Garda Síochána where children are in danger
- Revised provisions to enable the courts to place children who have been assaulted, ill-treated, neglected or sexually abused, or who are at risk, in the care of or under the supervision of the HSE
- Introduction of arrangements for the supervision and inspection of pre-school services
- Revised provisions in relation to the registration and inspection of residential centres for children.

The Child Care Regulations 1996 and 2006 present the requirements of the legislation in a format which practitioners can use in their daily work.

Domestic Violence Act 1996

This Act introduced major changes in the legal remedies for domestic violence. Two main remedies are available:

1. **Safety Order:** Prohibits a person from further violence or threats of violence. It does not oblige that person to leave the home. If the parties live apart, the order prohibits the violent person from watching or being in the vicinity of the home.
2. **Barring Order:** Requires the violent person to leave the family home.

The legislation gives the HSE the power to intervene to protect individuals and their children from violence. Section 6 of the Act empowers the HSE to apply for Orders on behalf of a person who is deterred from doing so through fear or trauma. The consent of the victim is not a prerequisite for such an application, although he or she must be consulted. Under Section 7 of the Act the Court may, where it considers it appropriate, adjourn proceedings and direct the HSE to undertake an investigation of the dependent person's circumstances with a view to:

1. Applying for a Care Order or Supervision Order under the Child Care Act 1991
2. Providing services or assistance for the dependent person's family or
3. Taking other action in respect of the dependent person.

Freedom of Information Act 1997 and 2003

The Freedom of Information Act 1997 and the Freedom of Information (Amendment) Act 2003 allow members of the public to obtain access to the greater extent possible, consistent with the public interest and the right to privacy, to information in the possession of public bodies.

Protection of Persons Reporting Child Abuse Act 1998

The main provisions of the Act are:

1. The provision of immunity from civil liability to any person who reports child abuse 'reasonably and in good faith' to the designated officers of the HSE or to any member of An Garda Síochána
2. The provision of significant protections for employees who report child abuse. These protections cover all employees and all forms of discrimination up to, and including, dismissal
3. The creation of a new offence of false reporting of child abuse, where a person makes a report of child abuse to the appropriate authorities 'knowing that statement to be false'. This is a new criminal offence, designed to protect innocent persons from malicious reports.

Criminal Justice Act 2006

Section 176 introduced the criminal charge of 'Reckless endangerment of children', which states:

A person, having authority or control over a child or abuser, who intentionally or recklessly endangers a child by–

a. Causing or permitting any child to be placed or left in a situation which creates a substantial risk to the child of being a victim of serious harm or sexual abuse, or

b. Failing to take reasonable steps to protect a child from such a risk while knowing that the child is in such a situation, is guilty of an offence.

Children First Bill 2014

The proposed legislation includes mandatory reporting, which means that any adult who is employed and tasked with responsibility for children is legally required to report any suspected or actual abuse. Failure to do so will result in legal action being taken against the practitioner (once the Bill has been enacted).

KEY PRINCIPLES GUIDING PRACTICE

Children First (DCYA 2011) identifies key principles of best practice in child protection and welfare.

(i) The welfare of the child is of paramount importance.
(ii) Early intervention and support should be available to promote the welfare of children and families, particularly where they are vulnerable or at risk of not

receiving adequate care or protection. Family support should form the basis of early intervention and preventive interventions.

(iii) A proper balance must be struck between protecting children and respecting the rights and needs of parents/carers and families. Where there is conflict, the child's welfare must come first.

(iv) Children have a right to be heard, listened to and taken seriously. Taking account of their age and understanding, they should be consulted and involved in all matters and decisions that may affect their lives. Where there are concerns about a child's welfare, there should be opportunities provided for their views to be heard independently of their parents/carers.

(v) Parents/carers have a right to respect and should be consulted and involved in matters that concern their family.

(vi) Factors such as the child's family circumstances, gender, age, stage of development, religion, culture and race should be considered when taking protective action. Intervention should not deal with the child in isolation; the child's circumstances must be understood within a family context.

(vii) The criminal dimension of any action cannot be ignored.

(viii) Children should only be separated from parents/carers when alternative means of protecting them have been exhausted. Re-union should be considered in planning for the child's future.

(ix) The prevention, detection and treatment of abuse or neglect requires a coordinated multidisciplinary approach, effective management, clarity of responsibility and training of personnel in organisations working with children.

(x) Professionals and agencies working with adults who for a range of reasons may have serious difficulties meeting their children's basic needs for safety and security should always consider the impact of their adult client/patient's behaviour on a child and act in the child's best interest. (DCYA 2011, p. 4)

Here we will explore some of these key principles and discuss how the practitioner should implement them in practice. We will also consider actual cases and hypothetical cases to further emphasise application of these principles to practice.

Principle of Paramountcy

The welfare of the child is of paramount importance.

When dealing with a child protection situation the protection/needs of the child experiencing the abuse must come first. At times the practitioner may be concerned about how reporting the abuse will impact on the rest of the family. However, the experts tell us that the child in question must come first. (DCYA 2011)

> ### *In Practice*
>
> At times the practitioner may be faced with the difficult scenario of the impact of raising a child abuse suspicion/concern on the other members of the family, possibly resulting in the break-up of the family unit. In addition, other parents may perceive it as a possible threat to their family if they are themselves experiencing difficulties at home. Adhering to this principle ensures that the child's needs are met regardless of the circumstances. Making new families aware of your child protection policy and day-to-day procedures through one-to-one discussion and information packs for new families will certainly help to alleviate any concerns they may have. Most parents/carers will be very supportive once they realise that practitioners are acting in the best interests of every child and that they want parents to be fully informed and involved.

Early Intervention

Early intervention and support should be available to promote the welfare of children and families, particularly where they are vulnerable or at risk of not receiving adequate care or protection. Family support should form the basis of early intervention and preventive interventions.

> ### *In Practice*
>
> Early recognition is key to early intervention. The practitioner must have the knowledge, skills and confidence to be constantly observing every child in their service. Child abuse is not confined to certain social classes; it can occur in any family type. Working in partnership with parents is a vital factor in providing the best possible early years experience for the child, but this must not cloud the practitioner's view of the family and possible indicators of abuse within that family. There is no room for naivety; there have been abuse cases where naivety led to insufficient action, with catastrophic results for the child. For example, in the Roscommon abuse case (Chapter 4), despite considerable involvement by Social Services over a number of years none of the children was ever actually spoken to by the social workers. Perhaps if they had spoken to the children they would have gained greater insight into their plight and taken more effective action.
>
> Children who are abused are unlikely to disclose (Barnardos 2010). Sjöberg (2002, cited in Barnardos 2010) found that abused children are unlikely to disclose the abuse and even when they do, they minimise their experiences. This may be because they are afraid or perhaps do not fully realise that what they experiencing is not normal. However, it does not negate the responsibility of all professionals involved to gather all information available to assist them in making an informed decision about a given situation.

Parents'/Carers' Rights

Parents/carers have a right to respect and should be consulted and involved in matters that concern their family.

In Practice

It must be remembered that neglect and abuse take place for many reasons. If all involved keep in mind that the ultimate aim of any intervention is to work towards the most positive outcome for the child, any prejudicial views about perceived 'parental inadequacies' must be put aside in order to work towards what is best for the child.

Family Context

Factors such as the child's family circumstances, gender, age, stage of development, religion, culture and race should be considered when taking protective action. Intervention should not deal with the child in isolation; the child's circumstances must be understood within a family context.

In Practice

Ireland today is a multicultural country. It is important that the practitioner has a knowledge and understanding of the cultural backgrounds of the children in their service in order to meet the unique needs of each child. At times there may be practices around childcare and behaviour management which are deemed unacceptable, e.g. excessively punitive disciplinary measures for behaviour management. For example, some years ago a situation arose where a 4-year-old child told the early years manager that his mum locked himself and the baby in the house when she went out shopping. This proved to be true. The mother said that in the country they came from everyone did it as it was far safer than taking your children with you. The manager had no choice but to contact Social Services. She informed the mother that she had no choice but to do so, but assured the mother that Social Services would merely visit to ensure that she understood that this could not happen again. Never assume – always check it out.

Criminal Dimension

The criminal dimension of any action cannot be ignored.

> ## *In Practice*
>
> As we shall see later in this chapter, an understanding of legislation is essential in order to comply with it. When the Children First Bill is passed it will place a mandatory requirement on all persons working with children to report any actual or suspected abuse. Failure to do so will result in legal action being taken against those who fail to act. This will place considerable responsibility on all those working with children. However, if childcare practitioners understand the policies and procedures to be followed they will realise that support is available to help them take the correct action.

Separation as a Last Resort

Children should only be separated from parents/carers when alternative means of protecting them have been exhausted. Re-union should be considered in planning for the child's future.

> ## *In Practice*
>
> This relates to such situations as a parent with a mental health illness or addiction problem that renders them incapable of caring for their child. Removing the child/children from the home may not be necessary if arrangements are made for a responsible adult (either a relation or someone paid by the HSE) to help the parent care for the child/children safely in the home.

TYPES OF ABUSE

The World Health Organisation (WHO) defines abuse as follows:

> Child maltreatment, sometimes referred to as child abuse and neglect, includes all forms of physical and emotional ill-treatment, sexual abuse, neglect, and exploitation that results in actual or potential harm to the child's health, development or dignity. Within this broad definition, five subtypes can be distinguished – physical abuse; sexual abuse; neglect and negligent treatment; emotional abuse and exploitation. (www.who.int/topics/child_abuse/en/)

Children First defines abuse as occurring when the child is exposed to one incident or repeated incidence of abuse which effects their normal development (DCYA 2011).

Significant Harm

It can be difficult to decide when a behaviour or action towards a child becomes abuse. The question to ask is whether the action or inaction potentially or actually causes **significant harm** to the child. *Protecting Children* (2010) defines significant harm as follows:

> The threshold of significant harm is reached when the child's needs are neglected to the extent that his or her well-being and/or development are severely affected. (Conroy & Kingston 2010, p. 21)

Neglect

It is thought that neglect is the most common category of abuse, both in Ireland and internationally; it is certainly the most commonly reported form of abuse. It is also recognised as the most damaging: it will result in lifelong harm, for example serious neglect in infancy will have a serious negative impact on brain development. It is closely correlated with low socio-economic factors and parental inabilities.

- **Wilful neglect** occurs when there is direct and deliberate deprivation by a parent/carer of the child's basic needs, e.g. not providing food, shelter, warmth, clothing, contact with others.
- **Circumstantial neglect** usually occurs due to an inability of the parent/carer to cope, e.g. stress/ill health/intellectual disability/addiction. (DCYA 2011)

Neglect is 'usually a passive form of abuse involving omission rather than acts of commission' (Skuse & Bentovim 1994). Neglect of the child's physical needs and a lack of supervision generally results in failure to meet the child's developmental needs.

Neglect should be suspected in cases of:
- Abandonment or desertion
- Child persistently being left alone without adequate care and supervision
- Malnourishment, lack of food, inappropriate food or erratic feeding
- Lack of warmth
- Lack of adequate clothing
- Inattention to basic hygiene
- Lack of protection and exposure to danger, including moral danger or lack of supervision appropriate to the child's age; persistent failure to attend school
- Non-organic failure to thrive
- Failure to provide adequate care for the child's medical and developmental problems
- Exploitation, overwork. (DCYA 2011)

Dubowitz (1999) categorised neglect into three types:
1. **Disorganised or chaotic neglect** inconsistent parenting, disorganised and crisis-prone families, resulting in lack of certainty and routine. This results in attachment disorders. The child may suffer from anxiety manifesting in disruptive and attention-seeking behaviour. There may also be a high incidence of accidents in the home due to inadequate safety measures.

2. **Depressed or passive neglect** is the stereotypical scenario characterised by bleak and bare accommodation, poor hygiene, minimal comfort and little or no social or psychological stimulation. This type of neglect is characterised by lack of food, no clean clothes, young children spending long periods in a cot/pushchair, broken, age-inappropriate toys and a strong sense of hopelessness and lack of drive to improve the situation. Children in this situation frequently miss school, are poor at completing homework and are at risk of major developmental delay.

3. **Chronic deprivation** is most likely in situations where there is an absence of key attachment figures, such as in large institutions/orphanages. Theories proposed by Bowlby, Ainsworth, etc. support this view (Meggitt 2011).

Neglect generally becomes apparent in different ways over a period of time rather than at one specific point. A pattern involving the indicators below will build up over a period of time.

Indicators of Emotional Abuse and Neglect

- Abandonment or desertion
- Children persistently being left alone without adequate care and education
- Lack of warmth
- Lack of adequate clothing
- Lack of protection and exposure to danger, including moral danger, or lack of supervision appropriate to the child's age
- Persistent failure to attend school
- Non-organic failure to thrive – when the child is not gaining weight because of malnutrition and also emotional deprivation
- Failure to provide adequate care for child's medical needs/problems
- Exploitation, overwork. (Conroy & Kingston 2010)

In Practice

The practitioner should be looking out for the following on a day-to-day basis; building up pieces of evidence into a full picture is vital. The following indicators are taken from Barnardos' *Protecting Children* (2010).

- A child whose health needs are unmet, for example when they are ill, or failing to attend routine health assessments, vaccinations, etc. It is important that practitioners keep a record of these appointments so that they are aware of any failure on the part of the parent/carer. Do remember that at times it can be difficult for small children to receive the full programme of vaccinations (due to illness, for example), and some parents may need prompting/health promotion activities to remind and encourage them.

- A child who is inadequately dressed for the weather. Do not confuse this with the child who insists on wearing her princess dress in the snow; what this means is the child who is consistently dressed unsuitably, e.g. clothes too small, shoes too small, no socks or underwear.

- A child who is unwashed and wearing dirty clothes. Do remember that as a society we are at times over zealous about small children being in spotless clothes. A happy child is often a grubby child after a day of playing and exploring their environment. Here we are talking about a child who smells because they, or their clothes, have not been washed for some days or longer.

- Babies/toddlers whose nappies have not been changed frequently enough, resulting in a very sore bottom. Remember, a teething baby can be very prone to a sore bottom, so be sure to check out other possible causes first. Also remember that you are looking for a number of indicators, not just one, before you draw any conclusions.

- A child who is persistently hungry and looks thin and malnourished. Small children go through phases of having a healthy appetite alternating with bouts of poor eating; this should not be mistaken for the above scenario. Check for other indicators.

- A child who is constantly so tired that they are falling asleep during the day. Be mindful of the child who may not be getting adequate sleep at night due to illness, or a child who is going through a phase of interrupted sleep at night. You would expect that the child's parents will inform you of this, as they too will be concerned.

- Failure of the parent/carer to seek medical assistance for the child even when you have advised them of a need (e.g. persistent cough, conjunctivitis, failure to thrive). Practitioners sometimes report that parents/carers are reluctant to take their child to a doctor because of the cost and hope the child will recover without medical attention. The expertise of the early years practitioner, coupled with a positive working relationship with parents, is of great importance here in guiding the parents/carers to make the right decision about their child's health.

- A parent who is under the influence of drugs or alcohol, rendering them incapable of caring for their child adequately. The early years practitioner may find themselves in a situation where a parent comes to collect their child under the influence of drugs or alcohol. Without exception the practitioner cannot allow the parent to take their child and must insist that another responsible adult is called. If necessary they may need to call the Gardaí rather than allow an unfit person to take responsibility for the child.

Record keeping is key to putting together the pieces of the jigsaw that may lead you to the conclusion that a child is being neglected, resulting in significant harm to them. Each early years setting will have their own policies and procedures for recording and storing such important observations, which can be easily accessed as a picture is building up.

Accurate observation of a child's developmental progress provides an objective view of the child.

EMOTIONAL ABUSE

Emotional abuse is normally found in the relationship between the caregiver and the child rather than in a specific event or pattern of events. Typically the home is lacking in emotional warmth. The parent's relationship with the child may be without empathy and devoid of emotional responsiveness (DCYA 2011). The parent/carer may be unable to or unaware of how to meet their child's emotional and developmental needs.

Emotional abuse is not easy to recognise because it builds up over time and there is no one indicator to suggest conclusively that there is abuse taking place. Every child is unique, and where one child may be deeply affected by a parent/carer's failure to meet their emotional needs, another child may not be nearly so badly affected.

Examples of emotional abuse include:

- Persistent criticism, sarcasm, hostility or blaming. Child development theory highlights the importance of providing a positive environment for children. They need to be encouraged and praised as much as possible. Persistent criticism erodes the child's self-esteem very quickly.
- Conditional parenting: the level of attention is determined by the child's behaviour/performance. Examples of this may be unrealistic expectations of how a small child can manage their behaviour. A child may be pressured to perform well at school and affection and praise are withheld if they do not.
- Premature imposition of responsibility on the child, e.g. being expected to behave in a certain way when they are incapable of doing so, or being expected to care for younger siblings when they are unable to do so.
- Under- or over-protection of the child. Commonly we consider lack of care as abuse, but being excessively over-protective can also have a negative effect on a child's development.
- Use of unreasonable or overly harsh disciplinary measures with a child. Some parents instinctively know how to manage their child's behaviour in a positive manner. Unfortunately some parents do not, and here the role of the early years practitioner is vital in acting as a positive role model and educator for the parents.
- Emotional unavailability by the parent/carer. This may be due to the poor parenting they experienced themselves, mental health problems, physical health problems or addiction problems.

- Exposure to domestic violence. The child may be the subject of the violence or may witness it being directed at others.
- Failure to show interest in or provide age-appropriate opportunities for the child's cognitive and emotional development. This does not mean providing an extensive range of activities and experiences for the child, just normal opportunities for play and exploration of the world around them.

The threshold of *significant harm* is reached when abusive interactions become typical of the relationship between the child and the parent/carer. (Conroy & Kingston 2010)

In Practice

The practitioner should look out for the following signs and symptoms, which may indicate that a child is suffering from emotional abuse. Remember, building up the pieces of the jigsaw is vital: it is unlikely that any one indicator will cause emotional abuse but more likely that a cluster of indices over a period of time will result in significant harm to the child.

- Rejection by the parent(s)/carer
- Lack of comfort and love to the child
- Lack of attachment (as proposed by Bowlby and Ainsworth)
- Lack of proper stimulation, e.g. fun and play
- Lack of continuity of care, e.g. frequent house moves, school moves, especially if they are unplanned
- Ongoing lack of praise and encouragement
- Serious over-protectiveness
- Inappropriate non-physical punishment, e.g. locking the child in their room, excluding the child from the family
- Family conflict and/or violence
- Every child who is abused physically, sexually or who is neglected is automatically emotionally abused
- Inappropriate expectations of a child in relation to their behaviour relative to their age and stage of development

---

PHYSICAL ABUSE

Physical abuse of a child is that which results in actual or potential physical harm from an interaction, or lack of interaction, which is reasonably within the control of a parent or person in a position of responsibility, power or trust. There may be single or repeated incidents. (DCYA 2011, p. 9)

Physical abuse may present as:

- Severe physical punishment
- Beating, slapping, hitting or kicking
- Pushing, shaking or throwing (e.g. shaken baby syndrome, in which a very young baby can suffer brain damage from being shaken)
- Pinching, biting or hair pulling
- Terrorising with threats, such as threats of physical harm to the child or someone important to them
- Observing violence taking place between other persons
- Use of excessive force in handling the baby/child
- Deliberate poisoning
- Suffocation
- Fabricated/induced illness or injury (FII) – this is a recognised psychological condition where a person complains of illness for which there is no evidence, suggesting that the individual is seeking attention. FII by proxy occurs when the parent/carer (usually mother) inflicts injury or brings about the child's symptoms to gain attention for themselves
- Allowing or creating a substantial risk of injury to a child.

In Practice

The early years practitioner should look out for the following signs and symptoms/indicators. Where there is an unsatisfactory explanation or inconsistencies in explanation, or clustering of a group of these events, the practitioner should be alerted to the possibility of physical abuse of the child.

- **Bruising:** It is not uncommon for small children to have a range of bruises in many areas of their body. However, determining which bruises occur through daily rough and tumble and which should be viewed with suspicion is very important.
- **Fractures** in any part of the body. Experts advise that any fracture of the long bones (upper and lower arm and leg) in a child who does not yet walk must be treated with great concern as it would take very considerable impact to fracture such a bone.
- **Swollen joints:** Be mindful of the possibility of some underlying medical condition which should be ruled out during the investigation.
- **Burns/scalds:** Unfortunately young children all too often have accidents leading to burns and scalds. Usually the parents/carers are very distressed and self-blaming. Listen closely for inconsistencies in the account of how the injury occurred. Is the history/story of what happened in keeping with the actual injury?
- **Abrasions/lacerations:** These may be caused by the child being dragged along the floor/carpet, causing friction burn marks.
- **Haemorrhage:** Retinal or subdural. Retinal haemorrhage, which shows up in the whites of the eyes (sclera), can be consistent with injury. Subdural haemorrhage is

bleeding inside the brain. This can lead to increased pressure in the brain, possibly resulting in loss of consciousness/coma and long-term brain injury/damage.

- **Bite marks:** Are the marks from adult teeth or from other small children?
- **Damage to body organs** as a result of beating, which can injure the kidneys and/or liver, resulting in an acute medical condition or long-term damage which may not be immediately evident.
- **Poisoning:** Administering prescribed drugs inappropriately to babies/children; giving alcohol or illegal drugs; giving babies/small children totally unsuitable food. There have been instances of parents weaning babies on liquidised takeaway Chinese food, fish and chips, etc., which could contain high levels of chemicals that would be highly toxic for babies and would quickly result in serious illness and possible death. If a child has taken a poisonous substance, check how they were able to access this substance. Has this happened on more than one occasion?
- **Failure to thrive:** The baby/child is visibly malnourished and when weighed and measured falls well below normal percentile ranges for their age. Do remember that there are medical conditions that can cause this and that must be eliminated as a possible cause.
- **Coma/unconsciousness/death:** May result from a number of these forms of abuse.

A child who is being physically abused and who needs medical attention as a result of this abuse may be taken to different doctors or emergency departments to avoid the abuse being detected. (Unfortunately we do not have a national database which would alert healthcare professionals to children presenting in different hospitals/GP practices.) All healthcare professionals must be aware of this possibility and should observe closely both children and parents if they detect any inconsistency in the history being given versus how the injury/illness presents. Following any child presenting at either a private or public emergency or minor injury clinic/unit the normal procedure is that the unit will write to the family GP advising them of the child's condition/treatment. The parent/carer who is trying to conceal the injury may give false information about their GP; and, unless the GP already has concerns about the child, they might quickly read the letter and file it away, not realising that there is a possible reason for concern.

SEXUAL ABUSE

Children First gives the following definition and examples of sexual abuse:

Sexual abuse occurs when a child is used by another person for his or her gratification or sexual arousal, or for that of others.

(i)   Exposure of the sexual organs or any sexual act performed in the presence of a child.

(ii)   Intentional touching or molesting of the body of a child whether by a person or object for the purpose of sexual arousal or gratification.

(iii) Masturbation in the presence of the child or the involvement of the child in an act of masturbation.

(iv)   Sexual intercourse with the child, whether oral, vaginal or anal.

(v)   Sexual exploitation of a child, which includes inciting, encouraging, propositioning, requiring or permitting a child to solicit for, or to engage in, prostitution or other sexual acts. Sexual exploitation also occurs when a child is involved in the exhibition, modelling or posing for the purpose of sexual arousal, gratification or sexual act, including its recording (on film, video tape or other media) ... It may also include showing sexually explicit material to children, which is often a feature of the 'grooming' process by perpetrators of abuse. (DCYA 2011, p. 9)

Signs and Symptoms of Sexual Abuse

Child sexual abuse often covers a wide spectrum of abusive activities. It rarely involves just a single incident and usually occurs over a number of years. Child sexual abuse most commonly happens within the family. Cases of sexual abuse principally come to light through:

- Disclosure by the child or his or her siblings/friends
- The suspicions of an adult
- Physical symptoms.

Colburn Faller (1989, cited in DCYA 2011) provides a description of the wide spectrum of activities by adults which can constitute child sexual abuse. These include:

- Non-contact sexual abuse
- 'Offensive sexual remarks', including statements the offender makes to the child regarding the child's sexual attributes, what he or she would like to do to the child and other sexual comments
- Obscene phone calls
- Independent 'exposure' involving the offender showing the victim his/her private parts and/or masturbating in front of the victim
- 'Voyeurism' involving instances when the offender observes the victim in a state of undress or in activities that provide the offender with sexual gratification. These may include activities that others do not regard as even remotely sexually stimulating
- Sexual contact involving any touching of the intimate body parts. The offender may fondle or masturbate the victim, and/or get the victim to fondle and/or masturbate them. Fondling can be either outside or inside clothes. Also includes 'frottage', i.e. where offender gains sexual gratification from rubbing his/her genitals against the victim's body or clothing.

- Oral-genital sexual abuse involving the offender licking, kissing, sucking or biting the child's genitals or inducing the child to do the same to them.
- Interfemoral sexual abuse, sometimes referred to as 'dry sex' or 'vulvar intercourse', involving the offender placing his penis between the child's thighs.
- Penetrative sexual abuse, of which there are four types:
  - Digital penetration – putting fingers in the vagina or anus, or both. Usually the victim is penetrated by the offender, but sometimes the offender gets the child to penetrate them
  - Penetration with objects – penetration of the vagina, anus or occasionally mouth with an object
  - Genital penetration – involving the penis entering the vagina, sometimes partially.
  - Anal penetration – involving the penis penetrating the anus
- Sexual exploitation involves situations of sexual victimisation where the person who is responsible for the exploitation may not have direct sexual contact with the child. Two types of this abuse are child pornography and child prostitution.
  - Child pornography includes still photography, videos and movies, and, more recently, computer-generated pornography.
  - Child prostitution for the most part involves children of latency age or in adolescence. However, children as young as 4 and 5 are known to be abused in this way.

The sexual abuses described above may be found in combination with other abuses, such as physical abuse and urination and defecation on the victim. In some cases, physical abuse is an integral part of the sexual abuse; in others, drugs and alcohol may be given to the victim.

In Practice

Just thinking about the above fills us with horror and disbelief. However, it is essential to be aware of what can happen to a child who is being sexually abused to ensure that such possibilities are considered. Naivety or innocence on the part of the practitioner is of no help to the abused child. We must be aware of such horrendous occurrences in order to recognise the possible signs. Past cases have shown us that having a positive working relationship with parents/family may actually cloud the ability of the professionals, leading them to discounting the possibility of sexual abuse because they could not believe it of the adults they know.

Behavioural and emotional changes the practitioner may observe include:
- Mood changes – the child becomes withdrawn, fearful of adults and starts 'acting out'

- Lack of concentration, which may be evident in changes in their performance at school
- Bed wetting and soiling by a child who is toilet trained
- Psychosomatic complaints such as pains or headaches
- Skin disorders
- Nightmares, changes in sleep patterns
- Refusing to go to school or other activities
- Separation anxiety
- Loss of appetite
- Isolation (lack of involvement with other children)
- Disclosure by the child
- Sexual knowledge inappropriate for their age
- Sexual role-play with dolls or other children
- Drawing pictures which show sexual knowledge
- Using sexually explicit language
- Being overly affectionate in a sexual way. (DCYA 2011)

What to Do if You Suspect Abuse

If there are reasonable grounds for suspicion of abuse, the practitioner **must** take action.

A Word of Warning

It is very likely that once you become involved in a child abuse case you will not feel good about the action you take. Taking action is likely to cause great distress to all involved, but this must not stop you taking appropriate action. As we have emphasised, **care of the abused child is paramount**.

Also remember that the person reporting the concern is not responsible for deciding if abuse is actually taking place.

Designated Liaison Person

This person is vital in dealing with any child protection concern. They act as both a resource and a support to all involved. The role should be undertaken by a senior member of the team in the early years setting who has suitable experience and training. The designated liaison person should be readily available to staff should a child protection concern arise. It is usual, but not essential, for this person to have undertaken the HSE two-day Child Protection Training course.

Key Roles

- In collaboration with the staff member who reports the suspicion of abuse, decides whether the HSE should be notified.
- Establishes contact with the senior member of Children and Family Social Services.
- Provides information and advice on child protection issues in their service.
- Ensures that child protection policies and procedures are followed.
- Ensures that all documentation is completed correctly when a referral is made.
- Liaises with the HSE, Gardaí and other agencies.
- Keeps relevant people in the service informed.
- Provides support for staff who are dealing with a child protection case.
- Provides support for staff against whom an allegation of abuse has been made.

Grounds for Concern

Reasonable grounds for concern include:

- A disclosure or specific indication from the child that suggests they have been or are being abused
- A disclosure from a parent that they were abused as a child
- A staff member actually witnessing the abuse of a child. This could take place in the early years setting, outside the setting or in the child's home where the practitioner may be visiting as part of their role
- The report of a third party who has actually witnessed the child being abused. This could be a parent, another child, a member of the public or another professional
- An injury or behaviour which is consistent with a child being abused and is unlikely to have been caused by other means
- The accumulation of indicators over a period of time which suggest that a child is suffering from emotional abuse or physical neglect
- A dysfunctional behaviour which, coupled with knowledge of the child's history, causes concern
- An injury which causes concern irrespective of the parent/carer's explanation
- An injury or behaviour that is consistent with both abuse and an innocent explanation, but where there are corroborative indicators supporting the concern that it may be a case of abuse
- Consistent indication over a period of time that a child is suffering from emotional or physical neglect
- Admission or indication by someone of an alleged abuse
- A specific indication from a person who saw the child being abused
- An account from a person who saw the child being abused
- Evidence (e.g. injury or behaviour) that is consistent with abuse and unlikely to have been caused in any other way. (HSE 2011)

A referral to Children and Family Services should always be made in the following circumstances:

- A concern about a child at risk of sexual abuse
- Physical injury caused by assault or neglect which may or may not require medical attention
- Children who suffer from persistent neglect
- Children who live in an environment which is likely to have an adverse effect on their emotional development
- Where parents' own emotional impoverishment affects their ability to meet their child's emotional and/or physical needs, regardless of material/financial circumstances and assistance
- Where parents' circumstances adversely affect their capacity to meet the child's needs because of domestic violence, drug and/or alcohol misuse, mental health problems, intellectual disability
- A child living in a household with, or having significant contact with, a person at risk of sexual offending or with previous convictions for offences against children
- An abandoned child
- Children left home alone
- Bruising/injury to a pre-mobile baby
- Pregnancy where children have been previously removed
- Suspicion of fabricated or induced illness
- Where a child under one year old is present in a home where domestic violence is a concern. (HSE 2011)

The above list is a very useful guide, but do remember that there may be a range of other circumstances when it is deemed necessary to make a referral.

In addition to the above, Barnardos (2010) offer the following questions as a useful guide:

- Is the child behaving normally for his or her age and stage of development?
- Does the child present a change in behaviour?
- For how long has this behaviour been observed?
- How often does it occur? Where does it occur?
- Has something happened that could explain the child's behaviour?
- Is the child showing signs of distress?
- Does the behaviour happen everywhere or just in the school or childcare setting?
- Is the child suffering?
- Does the behaviour restrict the child socially?
- Does the behaviour interfere with the child's development?
- What effect, if any, does it have on others?
- What are the child's parents' view, if known?

A suspicion which is not supported by any objective signs of abuse would not constitute a reasonable suspicion or reasonable grounds for concern. However, these suspicions should be recorded internally and future suspicions may lead to the decision to make a report. (French 2008)

Action to be Taken

Children First offers the following advice:
- If a disclosure, listen carefully to the child. Give them time to tell you. Do not ask any leading questions. Do not comment on the alleged abuser.
- Stay calm. You may be very distressed yourself by what the child has told you.
- If the child tells you they want to keep it a secret you must explain that you cannot as you may need to get someone to help with the situation. You can reassure the child that confidentiality will be maintained and only those who really need to know will be told.
- Reassure the child that they have done the right thing in telling you.
- Do not ask probing questions beyond what you need to know to make a decision on the seriousness of the situation.
- Consult the policy relating to child protection.
- Report to Designated Liaison Person.
- Make a decision together as to whether a report to social services is indicated. It is possible to contact social services and get their advice on whether a formal report should be made. Remember it is better to take advice and recommended action than to place a child at risk. At times even the experts can find it difficult to decide if a child is being abused. If in doubt seek advice.
- Record what you have been told/observed. Remember, it is vital that anything written must be objective and not contain subjective comments.
- Reassure the child.
- Maintain confidentiality. A suspected child abuse situation must only involve people on a need to know basis. (DCYA 2011)

Your role is now to help support this child by communicating with them, offering them comfort and if possible allowing them to continue with their usual routine in your setting.

The following form should be completed in as much detail as possible and sent by fax to the relevant social services office. National contacts for HSE Children and Family Services are listed in Appendix 2 of *Children First* (DCYA 2011).

FIGURE 5.1 HSE STANDARD REPORT FORM

FORM NUMBER: CC01:01:01

STANDARD REPORT FORM
(For reporting CP&W Concerns to the HSE)

HSE

HSE Feidhmeannacht na Seirbhíse Sláinte
Health Service Executive

A. To Principal Social Worker/Designate: _____

1. Date of Report _____

2. Details of Child

Name:		Male ☐ Female ☐	
Address:		DOB	Age
		School	
Alias		Correspondence address (if different)	
Telephone		Telephone	

3. Details of Persons Reporting Concern(s)

Name:		Telephone No.	
Address:		Occupation	
		Relationship to client	
Reporter wishes to remain anonymous ☐		Reporter discussed with parents/guardians ☐	

4. Parents Aware of Report

		Yes	No
Are the child's parents/carers aware that this concern is being reported to the HSE?	- Mother	☐	☐
	- Father	☐	☐
Comment			

5. Details of Report

(Details of concern(s), allegation(s) or incident(s) dates, times, who was present, description of any observed injuries, parent's view(s), child's view(s) if known.)

6. Relationships

Details of Mother		Details of Father	
Name:		Name:	
Address: (if different to child)		Address: (if different to child)	
Telephone No's:		Telephone No's:	

7. Household composition

Name	Relationship	DOB	Additional Information e.g. School/Occupation/Other:

8. Name and Address of other personnel or agencies involved with this child

	Name	Address
Social Worker		
PHN		
GP		
Hospital		
School		
Gardaí		
Pre-School/Crèche/YG		
Other (specify):		

9. Details of person(s) allegedly causing concern in relation to the child

Relationship to child:		Age		Male ☐	Female ☐
Name:			Occupation		
Address:					

10. Details of person completing form

Name:		Occupation:	
Address:		Telephone No's:	
Signed		Date:	

Role of the Social Worker

- Investigate the report of child abuse.
- Check records to determine if there is a history in relation to the family or alleged abuser.
- Assess the risk to the child and decide what action should be taken, or if no action is to be taken.
- Liaise with all relevant authorities: Gardaí, medical personnel, referring personnel.
- Form a relationship with the child and provide him/her with ongoing support.
- Keep relevant authorities informed of progress in the case.
- Maintain support and ongoing contact with parents.
- Provide reports for case conferences and court hearings.

Role of the Gardaí

- Check records to see if the alleged abuser has a record of child abuse/violence.
- Investigate whether a crime has been committed.
- Institute criminal proceedings against alleged abusers.
- Provide back-up support for professionals involved, e.g. social worker, public health nurse, GP if needed.
- Remove child/children from immediate harm, if necessary.
- Participate in strategy meetings, case conferences and reviews.

Possible Outcomes of Referral

This will usually be determined by the category of abuse. Emotional abuse does not usually involve immediate action. It is more likely to require the early years practitioner to work closely with the child's parents to support them in recognising how their child's needs are not being met. Similarly, neglect is more likely to involve ongoing support and possibly resources to bring about improvement in the situation for the child. This may be additional financial support, housing or the provision of a competent adult going into the home to ensure the child/children's care needs are met and the parent(s) provided with support and guidance. However, as discussed before, a realistic view of the situation is vital.

If it appears that a child is in immediate risk of harm, emergency action can be taken by the HSE or the Gardaí. This may involve having the child medically examined and/or removing the child to a safe environment such as a foster home or to the home of relatives. This may take place with the parents' consent or may require an Emergency Care Order under the Child Care Act 1991.

- **Emergency Care Order:** Authorises the placement of a child in the care of the HSE where there is reasonable cause to believe they will suffer significant harm if not removed immediately. The Gardaí can remove a child to safety without a warrant if they consider the child's health or welfare to be at risk.

- **Interim Order:** Maintains a child in the care of the HSE until an application for a Care Order has been processed.
- **Supervision Order:** Authorises the local HSE to have a child's health and welfare checked out and supervised where there is reasonable grounds for believing that a child is at risk.
- **Care Order:** Places a child under the care of the HSE, which takes over the rights and responsibilities of the parents and has legal responsibility to look after the health and welfare of the child.

Child Protection Meetings

Three types of meeting may be organised by the HSE during the management of a case:

1. **Strategy meeting:** The main aim is to plan a strategy for early intervention and assessment.
2. **Child Protection Conference:** To facilitate the sharing and evaluation of all available information from the different professionals involved in the case, as well as parents/carers, and to formulate a **child protection plan**. Practitioners working in an early years or school setting may be asked to attend as they will have relevant information about the child. A child protection plan is an inter-agency plan that outlines the action to be taken by professionals and agencies directly involved with the family necessary to ensure the child's continuing protection and wellbeing.
3. **Child Protection Review:** Considers the current situation. These meetings are held every six months and are attended by the core professionals involved in the case. Each professional is required to submit a written report in advance.

Actions to be Taken

When dealing with an actual or suspected child abuse situation we must identify short-, medium- and long-term actions to be taken.

Short-term actions include:

- Reassure the child.
- Consult policies and procedures for guidance on steps to take.
- Report to designated liaison person.
- Make a referral to a social worker.
- Contact the child's parent(s) if they are not aware of the situation, but not if there is risk of the parent(s) absconding with the child.
- Ensure the child's immediate safety, which may involve removing the child immediately from the abuser.
- Seek medical assistance.
- Identify whether any other children are at risk.

Medium-term actions:
- Support the child and parents/carers.
- Provide a safe and normal environment for the child in the ECCE setting.
- Undertake observation of child.
- Work with parents/carers.
- Liaise with social workers.

Long-term actions:
- Continuously monitor child's progress/development.
- Work with parents/carers.
- Liaise with social workers.

CASE STUDIES

Case studies are an excellent way to examine a scenario and consider the actions to be taken in light of the evidence. At times it can be difficult to be sure of the validity of your concerns, so it is vital to be as objective as possible. Refer to the indicators of abuse and also decide whether the situation could be leading to significant harm for the child. Even experts can at times find it hard to be absolutely sure that a child is being abused. It is better to err on the side of caution rather than not take action.

Case Study 1

Recently a 3½-year-old girl started in your crèche. Her parents told you that she is going through a tantrum phase at present but did not make anything of it. The mum collects the little girl and the dad drops her off in the morning. She has settled in with you very well and is happy and contented. She has now been coming to you every day for three weeks. For the last three mornings she has had a tantrum as soon as the dad says he is going. The first morning he was patient and caring towards her. Yesterday and today he was shouting at her to stop and today he told her if she did not stop they would not come back for her; he then slapped her on the bottom. He was in a rage. You told him to go and that you would look after her, then he just stormed out.

Questions to consider:
1. What should you do immediately?
2. Is this an abuse case?
3. Should you report it to your designated child protection officer/designed person?
4. What should you say to the parents?

Answers:
1. Calm the little girl and reassure her that everything is fine.

2. No: based on the evidence given in the case study there are no reasonable grounds to suspect that this is an abuse case. However, if the father's behaviour is repeated you would need to assess the impact on the little girl's development to determine whether it is affecting her overall development, i.e. is it causing significant harm?

3. Report it to your line manager as the behaviour of the father is totally inappropriate and must be addressed to ensure that it does not happen again.

4. The parents must be invited to a meeting as soon as possible to discuss what took place, the effect the father's behaviour will have on the child and how the staff could support the father/family in dealing with the little girl's tantrums. Do not be judgemental about the father – you never know what is going on in people's lives, and the support of caring staff could make a great difference to the lives of all members of this family.

Case Study 2 (Home Setting)

You are on work placement in the community. You and your supervisor visit a one-year-old child in his home to undertake a developmental assessment. The mother is required to undress the child and you notice bruising on his back, legs and inside his upper arms. When you weigh the little boy you find that he is underweight, and he does not meet his physical development milestones. He appears pale, tired and not interested in you or your supervisor.

Do you suspect possible abuse?
1. Consult the indicators given earlier in the chapter. How many possible indicators can you tick?
2. Does this help you to decide that there is suspected abuse?
3. What should you do now?

Answers:
2. Yes, there are grounds to suspect possible abuse. But there may be some medical reason for the child's failure to thrive, which must also be considered.
3. An immediate referral to social services is necessary as his overall condition is so poor, in addition to the bruising. Your designated liaison person should be informed immediately to move the process forward without delay. It would not be appropriate to discuss this with the mother as there may be a possibility that she could abscond with her son.

Case Study 3

Practitioners observed over a period of time that Paul (aged 2½) was not reaching his developmental milestones. They spoke to his mum and dad about making a referral for an assessment. His parents were unwilling to accept any suggestion that their child needed an assessment, despite practitioners gently discussing it with them on several occasions. It was in Paul's best interests to have an assessment as early as possible, but both parents were reluctant and unable at that time to come to terms with the possibility that their child may need extra support or might have a developmental delay.

Questions to ask:
1. Are you concerned about this little boy?
2. Do you think he is at risk?
3. Is he being abused?
4. What happens now?

Answers:
1. There is reason to be concerned because he is not meeting his developmental milestones.
2. If his needs are not met in the near future he will be at risk of neglect.
3. No, he is not being abused.
4. It is very important for the early years practitioners to work closely with Paul's parents to help them come to terms with the possibility that he has a significant problem. It may be necessary in the future to advise the parents that you may have to involve social services of your concerns if they are unable to accept your concerns and as a result not meet his needs.

ALLEGATIONS AGAINST STAFF

We all like to think that the people we work with are as professional, kind and caring to the children as we are. Unfortunately, at times this is not the case. Two cases in particular ring alarm bells: the female manager of an early years setting in the UK was found to have been sexually abusing babies in the setting, with her male partner; and in June 2013 RTÉ televised a programme entitled *Breach of Trust* in which a reporter with a hidden camera gained a position as a childcare practitioner in a number of crèches and recorded the most appalling treatment of children. These examples show that it is essential to keep an open mind at all times about our colleagues and to be alert to behaviour or actions which are inappropriate to the child or situation.

Key components to safeguard children from abuse and staff against allegations of abuse include:

- A clear child protection policy and procedures that are known to both practitioners and parents/carers
- Staff training in child protection awareness
- Adequately qualified staff
- Safe practices followed by all, for example:
  ◆ Nappy changing area visible to other members of staff
  ◆ Never closing the toilet door when assisting a small child
  ◆ Avoiding, where possible, being in a one-to-one situation with a child where you cannot be seen by other members of staff. Use of glass panels in doors and walls is very important here. Some crèches have CCTV.
- Recruitment of staff:
  ◆ Garda vetting
  ◆ Checking references
  ◆ Ensuring staff are suitably qualified for the position.

In the event of an allegation of child abuse by a staff member, the employer has dual responsibilities – to the child and the employee. Two different members of senior management should carry out independent investigations. Every early years service has its own policies and procedures for dealing with both the allegation of abuse of the child and the allegation of abuse by the practitioner.

Our Duty to Care recommends the following guidelines:

- The principle of paramountcy must always apply. The protection of the child must come first.
- Different persons have responsibility for dealing with the reporting issues and the worker issues.
- Workers may be subject to malicious or unfounded allegations, therefore any allegations should be dealt with sensitively and support provided for the staff member, including counselling if necessary.
- Management should report the allegation to the HSE and the Gardaí and liaise with both regarding the investigation. (DoHC 2004)

Our Duty to Care identifies several other factors which management will need to consider:

- Possible reactions of other members of staff in the service, including anger, disbelief, doubt, fear, guilt, shock, anxiety and confusion.
- The effects on the alleged abuser of the service's own internal disciplinary proceedings, the child protection investigation and the criminal investigation.
- The reaction of other staff and other children towards a child who has been abused or whose allegation is being investigated.

- The reaction of parents/carers and other family members of the child.
- During child protection training it is extremely valuable to discuss what might happen in such a situation. It will give everyone the confidence to take action if necessary. (DoHC 2004)

References

Barnardos (2010) *Protecting Children: A Child Protection Guide for Early Years and School Age Childcare Services*. Dublin: Barnardos

Conroy, A. and Kingston, C. (2010) *Protecting Children: A Child Protection Guide for Early Years and School Age Childcare Services*. Dublin: Barnardos

DCYA (Department of Children and Youth Affairs) (2011) *Children First: National Guidance for the Protection and Welfare of Children*. Dublin: DCYA, http://www.dcya.gov.ie/documents/Publications/ChildrenFirst.pdf

DoHC (Department of Health and Children) (2004) *Our Duty to Care: The Principles of Good Practice for the Protection of Children and Young People*. Dublin: DoHC

Dubowitz, H. (1999) *Neglected Children: Research, Practice, and Policy*. Sage

French, G. (2008) *Supporting Quality: Guidelines for the Professional Practice*. Dublin: Barnardos Training and Resource Service

HSE (Health Service Executive) (2011) *Child Protection and Welfare Practice Handbook*. Dublin: HSE.

Meggitt, C. (2011) *Child Development: An Illustrated Guide* (3rd edn). Pearson

Skuse, D. and Bentovim, A. (1994) 'Physical and Emotional Maltreatment' in M. Rutter, E. Taylor and L. Hersor (eds), *Child and Adolescent Psychiatry* (3rd edn). Oxford: Blackwell Scientific

CHAPTER 6
Equality and Diversity

INTRODUCTION

Our vision is to make Ireland the best small country in the world in which to grow up and raise a family, and where the rights of all children and young people are respected, protected and fulfilled; where their voices are heard and where they are supported to realise their maximum potential now and in the future. (DCYA 2014)

In this chapter we examine the concepts of equality and diversity with the aim of helping you to gain a greater understanding of these concepts and their application to the childcare setting. The chapter will explore the theory underpinning our day-to-day practice with children from an equality and diversity perspective. The relationship between legislation, regulation and policy and its application, through best practice and national guidelines, to the ECCE setting will be outlined. In overviewing issues of diversity and equality in childcare, you will be encouraged to reflect on your professional development and consider implications of equality and diversity in your daily practice.

This chapter is written against the backdrop of the *Diversity and Equality Guidelines for Childcare Providers* developed in 2006 under the aegis of the National Childcare Co-ordinating Committee (OMC 2006).

Why do we need to address diversity and equality issues in early childhood care? We are all aware that we should treat others fairly and reasonably. In the last twenty years

Ireland has undergone considerable demographic change with the arrival of people from a wide range of other countries who have chosen to make their homes here. In this chapter we will look at how the early years practitioner can increase their knowledge and understanding of different attitudes in our society and how they can affect both individuals and society. Greater knowledge and understanding will enable the early years practitioner to have a deeper understanding of our multicultural society and how to meet children's needs within it.

> To be able to develop understanding of others you have to know who you are, overcome biases you have learned about other groups and have a highly developed sense of empathy and justice. (Derman-Sparks & Olsen Edwards 2010)

Before we examine our own attitudes and beliefs later in the chapter, we'll explore some definitions and concepts associated with equality and diversity issues.

DEFINITIONS AND CONCEPTS

Diversity refers to the diverse nature of Irish society, for example in terms of social class, gender, returned Irish emigrants, family status, minority groups and the majority group (Tilmouth *et al.* 2011). It also refers to the differences in our experiences, beliefs and values which must be recognised in order to ensure that each person's unique needs are identified and met.

Equality refers to the importance of recognising different individual needs and of ensuring equity in terms of access, participation and benefits for all children and their families. It is therefore not about treating people the 'same' (Tilmouth *et al.* 2011).

Prejudice: Barron and Byrne (1991) define prejudice as an attitude (usually negative) towards the members of a group that is based solely on their membership of that group. Bandura (1977) suggested that we learn prejudice in the same way as we learn other attitudes and values – by observing the behaviours of others through association, reinforcement and modelling. The early years practitioner has a great responsibility to provide an environment in which equality is clearly evident to staff, children, parents and any others who enter the setting.

Discrimination means acting on prejudiced beliefs, treating an individual or group negatively and differently from how we would treat others (Tilmouth *et al.* 2011).

Ethnicity is a term used to denote groups of people who share a culture of values and beliefs, national origins, customs and traditions (Tilmouth *et al.* 2011).

Race 'usually refers to a category of people sharing biologically transmitted traits' (Macionis & Plummer 2002, p. 259). However, the following definition of **racism** identifies the complexities involved:

> Racism is a multidimensional and complex system of power and powerlessness; it is a process through which powerful groups are able to dominate. It operates at micro and macro levels, is developed through specific cognitions and actions, and perpetuated and sustained through policies and procedures of social systems and institutions. This can be seen in the differential outcomes for less than powerful groups in accessing services in the health and welfare, education and housing and legal systems. (Thompson 2006)

Reading this definition we immediately sense the negativity. We as human beings and as childcare professionals must be constantly vigilant to ensure that such behaviour is not allowed to take place in our early years settings as it has such a negative impact on all involved.

Stereotyping is a set of beliefs we hold about groups of people based on the characteristics they have. These beliefs are often inaccurate, but they do help us to make sense of our world (Tilmouth *et al.* 2011).

Bias is any attitude, belief or feeling that results in and helps to justify unfair treatment of an individual because of his/her identity (Murray & O'Doherty 2001).

Anti-bias is an active approach to challenging prejudice, stereotyping and bias. It actively intervenes to challenge and counter the personal and institutional behaviours that keep oppression alive (Murray & O'Doherty 2001). The anti-bias approach covers more than cultural diversity: it includes gender, differences in abilities, class and language. It is based on children's developmental tasks as they construct identities and attitudes. Teaching about diversity is integrated into everyday activities and children from all backgrounds can come to value and celebrate comparisons between their own lives and those of children from other cultures and backgrounds (Murray & O'Doherty 2001).

> The concept of equality between individuals and between groups, involves respect for identity, both personal and cultural identity. 'Diversity' involves issues relating to culture, ethnicity, race, colour, nationality, language, gender, ability (disability), marital status, family status, sexual orientation, religion, membership of the Travelling community and socio-economic circumstance. (Barnardos 2002, p. 2)

In the 2006 *Guidelines* the term 'minority group' includes but is not limited to:
• People with a disability
• Members of the Traveller community
• Black Irish
• Irish language speakers
• Refugees

- Asylum seekers
- Children with gay or lesbian parents
- Families of minority religious faith. (OMC 2006)

HISTORICAL AND INTERNATIONAL INFLUENCES

Article 40.1 of the Irish Constitution states, 'All citizens shall, as human persons, be held equal before the law.' This statement is very clear and leaves us in no doubt as to its intention. Equally clear is the Universal Declaration of Human Rights (1948), which says that 'all human beings are born free and equal in dignity and rights' (Article 1). The Declaration of Human Rights was drawn up as a response to the genocide of the Jewish people in Germany and Poland during World War II. It was intended to prevent such a holocaust ever happening again. As we know from recent history and current events, we as human beings have not succeeded in upholding human rights. Every day the media remind us of the appalling injustices and lack of humanity in many places around the world.

UN Convention on the Rights of the Child

The UN Convention on the Rights of the Child (UNCRC) (see also Appendix A) classifies the rights of the child under four headings:

1. **Survival rights:** including the child's right to life and to their most basic needs of nutrition, shelter, warmth and hygiene.
2. **Development rights:** including the right to education, play, leisure, cultural activities, access to information, and freedom of thought, conscience and religion.
3. **Protection rights:** ensuring that children are safeguarded against all forms of abuse, neglect and exploitation.
4. **Participation rights:** encompassing children's freedom to express opinions, to have a say in matters affecting their own lives, to join associations and to assemble peacefully. As their capacities develop, children should have increasing opportunity to participate in the activities of society, in preparation for adulthood.

The UNCRC includes four articles, also known as 'general principles', that are given special emphasis. These articles are the bedrock for securing the rights in the Convention:
- All the rights guaranteed by the UNCRC must be available to all children without discrimination of any kind (Article 2).
- The best interests of the child must be a primary consideration in all actions concerning children (Article 3).
- Every child has the right to life, survival and development (Article 6).
- The child's view must be considered and taken into account in all matters affecting him or her (Article 12).

Implementing the UNCRC

When the Irish state signed the UN Convention on the Rights of the Child, the Government agreed to be assessed periodically by the UN on its progress in implementing the rights in the Convention. This means that every few years the State submits a progress report to the UN Committee on the Rights of the Child and agrees to an oral examination by the Committee members. The Children's Rights Alliance also submits an independent report on behalf of non-governmental organisations (NGOs). This is known as the 'shadow report' and we have done this twice before; in 1998 and in 2006. Ireland is due to report again within the next few years to the Committee on the Rights of the Child. (CRA website)

By ratifying the UNCRC in 1990, Ireland committed to:

respect and ensure the rights set forth in the present Convention to each child within their jurisdiction without discrimination of any kind, irrespective of the child's or his or her parent's or legal guardian's race, colour, sex, language, religion, political or other opinion, national, ethnic or social origin, property, disability, birth or other status. (Article 2)

And to:

take all appropriate measures to ensure that the child is protected against all forms of discrimination or punishment on the basis of the status, activities, expressed opinion, or beliefs of the child's parents, legal guardians, or family members. (Article 2)

Legislation and Policies

The most important pieces of Irish legislation, and national and international policies, for equality and diversity are:
• Irish Constitution (Bunreacht na hÉireann) (1937)
• UN Declaration on the Elimination of All Forms of Racial Discrimination (1963)
• International Convention on the Elimination of All Forms of Racial Discrimination (1965)
• UNCRC (1989)
• Child Care Act 1991
• *Children First: National Guidance for the Protection and Welfare of Children* (1999, 2011)
• Employment Equality Acts 1998 and 2004
• Equal Status Acts 2000 to 2004

- Education (Welfare) Act 2000
- National Children's Strategy 2000–2010
- Children Act 2001
- Official Languages Act 2003
- Disability Act 2005

For further information on legislation and policy guidelines, see the first three chapters of this book and Appendix B.

The following is a brief summary of some important developments in legislation and policy.

Commission on the Status of People with Disabilities

Established in 1993, the commission examined the status of people with disabilities. It produced a report in 1996 containing 402 recommendations. A progress report on its recommendations was published in 1999.

Refugee Act 1996

This Act placed a statutory obligation on the Irish State to consider applications from people fleeing persecution in their home countries and applying for refugee status in Ireland. Section 7 of the Act established the Office of the Refugee Applications Commissioner.

People with Disabilities Ireland

Formed in 1997, this group comprises people with disabilities, representatives of parents, carers and partners, advocates, local groups of people with disabilities and representatives of special needs organisations. It lobbies government and statutory authorities on the rights of people with special needs.

National Consultative Committee on Racism and Interculturalism

Established in 1998, this is a partnership of non-governmental organisations, state agencies, social partners and government departments. Its objectives are to develop an integrated approach against racism and towards interculturalism.

Equal Status Acts

Under the Equal Status Acts 2000 to 2004, discrimination in the supply of goods and provision of services is prohibited on nine grounds:

- Gender
- Marital status
- Family status
- Sexual orientation

- Religious belief
- Age
- Disability
- Race
- Membership of the Traveller community

Human Rights Commission (2000)

The Human Rights Commission was established following the Good Friday Agreement. Among the functions of these dependent bodies (set up North and South) is to challenge discrimination and to develop a strong anti-racism/intercultural dimension to their roles.

DIVERSITY AND EQUALITY GUIDELINES

The *Diversity and Equality Guidelines for Childcare Providers* (OMC 2006) support the practitioner to:

- Improve knowledge and understanding of diversity, equality and discrimination issues
- Challenge one's own thinking, assisting critical reflection and the development of new thinking
- Understand why diversity and equality policies and practice are important and relevant to childcare services
- Generate ideas for discussion at team and network meetings
- Develop ideas to tackle discriminatory or difficult issues that arise in practice
- Discover ways to assess and critically reflect on the childcare environment and daily practice
- Learn how to access information on racism, equality, and diversity approaches in childcare
- Find out how to source and/or develop resources and activities
- Gain new skills to support all levels of work on diversity and equality issues
- Create policies and procedures on equality and diversity.

Aims and Objectives of the Guidelines

The Guidelines aim to:

- Support childcare practitioners, early childhood teachers, managers and policymakers in their exploration, understanding and development of diversity and equality practice
- Foster awareness about diversity and equality issues
- Stimulate discussion about bias and discrimination
- Encourage the development of services that are inclusive of all children and their families. (OMC 2006)

The approach establishes four goals for adults and children. These are briefly outlined below, together with guidelines on how to achieve them. Each goal addresses a particular area of growth and builds upon and interacts with the others.

Children	Adults
To support children's identity and sense of belonging	To be conscious of one's own culture, attitudes and values and how they influence practice
To support children to become comfortable with difference	To be comfortable with difference and engage effectively with families
To foster each child's critical thinking about bias	To critically think about bias and discrimination
To empower children to stand up for themselves and others in the face of bias	To confidently engage in dialogue around issues of bias and discrimination

How do Early Years Practitioners Address Diversity and Equality?

Our National Equality and Diversity Strategy 2006 states that we should create an environment where each child feels a sense of belonging and where they are proud to be who they are. The early years practitioner should be vigilant in observing how children play and how adults interact with them, and identify any bias or discrimination. The practitioner should deal with this immediately in a positive manner. The perpetrator of the bias or discrimination may be a member of staff or a child. As you will have found, we often make assumptions about what a small child knows or understands and are then surprised to discover that we misjudged their level of understanding.

Louise Derman-Sparks and Julie Olsen Edwards, two American educationalists, undertook research in the area of equality and diversity; their findings emphasise the importance of actively providing an anti-bias curriculum (Derman-Sparks & Olsen Edwards 2010). Some early years settings may think that they do not have any problems with equality or discrimination and therefore do not actively address the issue. However, as well as addressing our own views, we also need to assist the children in our care to become more aware of the uniqueness of others.

The research by Denman-Sparks and Olsen Edwards, which was further developed by the Diversity in Early Childhood Education and Training (DECET) European Network and Glenda MacNaughton of Melbourne University, aims to help adults working with young children to critically reflect on and change, where necessary, their attitudes to 'difference'. Derman-Sparks sets out initial steps for understanding the daily lives of all children in the setting, followed by ideas for changing programme activities. The approach was developed to help people appreciate diversity more and consider changes they need to make to their practice as something positive rather than negative. This particular approach establishes four goals for adults and children. These are outlined briefly below, together with guidelines towards achieving the goals. We recommend that you spend time undertaking further reading on this approach to enhance your understanding further, thereby enabling you to actually implement this excellent programme in your day-to-day practice. Each goal addresses a particular area of growth and builds upon and interacts with the others.

Goal 1

Each child will demonstrate self-awareness, confidence, family pride, and positive social identities.

This is the starting place for all children in all settings. A basic goal of quality early childhood education work is to nurture each child's individual, personal identity. Anti-bias education adds to that goal the important idea of nurturing social (or group) identities. Goal 1 strengthens social, emotional, and cognitive development. As children develop a strong sense of both individual and group identity, they also develop more tools for success in school and in life.

Goal 2

Each child will express comfort and joy with human diversity; accurate language for human differences; and deep, caring human connections.

In an anti-bias approach, encouraging children to learn about how they are different from other children and how they are similar go hand in hand. These are never either/ or realities because people are simultaneously the same and different from one another. This is at the heart of learning how to treat all people caringly and fairly.

From infancy on, children notice and are curious about all kinds of differences among people. They also develop their own (often surprising) explanations for the differences that they observe and experience. By preschool, children have already developed ideas about many aspects of human diversity, including ideas that may seem quite strange to adults. Moreover, many children have already begun to develop discomfort about or even fear of specific kinds of difference.

Some teachers and parents are not sure whether they should encourage children to 'notice' and learn about differences among people. They think it is best to teach only about how people are the same, worrying that learning about differences causes prejudice. While well intentioned, this concern arises from a mistaken notion about the sources of bias.

Differences in and of themselves do not create the problem.

Children learn prejudice from prejudice – not from learning about human diversity.

Goal 3

Each child will increasingly recognise unfairness, have language to describe unfairness, and understand that unfairness hurts.

Help children to think critically about the world as this strengthens their resilience later in life, it increases their sense of self. Spend time finding out about their misconceptions about people and how they stereotype others. This may be done through drawing, art or play in younger children who do not have the language to explain their thoughts. Holding planned conversations asking questions or showing pictures and asking them to explain their understanding of what they see will help the child to examine their views.

Goal 4

Each child will demonstrate empowerment and the skills to act, with others or alone, against prejudice and/or discriminatory actions.

This fourth building block of anti-bias education is about helping every child learn and practise a variety of ways to act when:

- another child behaves in a biased manner toward her or him
- a child behaves in a biased manner toward another child
- unfair situations arise in the setting or in the children's immediate community.

Elimination of unfairness strengthens their growth on the other three goals. If a child is the target of prejudice or discrimination, she needs tools to resist and to know that she has worth (Goal 1). When a child speaks up for another child, it reinforces his understanding of other people's unique feelings (Goal 2). When children are helped to take action, it broadens their understanding of 'unfairness' and 'fairness' (Goal 3). Biased behaviours among children such as teasing, rejection, and exclusion based on some aspect of a child's identity are a form of aggressive behaviour and are just as serious as physical aggression. The old saying 'Sticks and stones may break my bones, but names will never hurt me' does not apply. Children's developing sense of self is hurt by name-calling, teasing, and exclusion based on identity. And children who engage in such hurtful behaviours are learning to be bullies. An anti-bias approach calls on teachers to gently but firmly intervene, support the child who has been hurt by the biased behaviour, and help children learn other ways of interacting. Anti-bias education is a necessary partner of conflict-resolution education.

In Practice

Group Activity: Discuss how you see the above goals being implemented day to day in your early years setting. What factors can impede effective implementation? How could you circumvent these factors?

Work Experience 6N1947: this would be an excellent subject for a work experience diary entry.

Supervision in Early Childhood Care 6N1973: Explore how these goals will impact on practice and how you can influence the practice of staff under your supervision.

ANTI-BIAS POLICIES

As you are aware, policies and procedures guide our daily practice to enable us to meet the requirements of legislation, regulations and best practice standards.

An anti-bias policy can:

- Promote equality of access, participation and outcome for all
- Address racism and discrimination at organisation/management level and individual level
- Look at development of identity and attitudes in young children
- Ensure that minority and majority groups are involved equally
- Provide guidelines on how to create an anti-bias environment
- Encourage the development of a caring and definite understanding of diversity.

Policy Statements

A policy statement provides a public statement of commitment and a framework for developing practice. The policies themselves should be drawn up in collaboration with staff and parents/guardians. The approach requires a willingness and commitment on the part of the management and staff to incorporate diversity into every aspect of the curriculum and, by doing so, to provide a truly inclusive setting. Adopting an anti-bias approach requires that stereotyped notions or behaviours are continuously challenged.

Points to consider in developing an anti-bias/anti-discrimination policy:

- Develop a plan to challenge negative attitudes and behaviours that have been learned.
- Develop a plan to support positive attitudes and behaviours towards those who are different in the service.
- Set up a means to review, examine and assess the plans which have been put in place.
- Develop policies that address areas of employment, involvement of volunteers, admissions, curriculum, etc.
- Draw up a programme for implementing policy, including timescale and responsibilities.
- Assess the need for staff training in the area.
- Ensure an appropriate procedure is in place for addressing any discrimination found.
- Arrange regular meetings of management, staff and families to review, address and consider policies.
- Try to be as comprehensive as possible in including relevant information on personal and family names, ethnicity, home language and important requirements for children on the initial registration forms.
- Ensure that new parents understand the policies that are in place.

The service should ensure that:

- All children are respected and valued equally in the group
- All children's positive identities are fostered
- All families are respected and valued
- All children are assisted to learn about difference and learn to interact with others comfortably
- All children's home languages and traditions are acknowledged and respected
- All children's abilities are positively affirmed
- Children see (through the anti-bias approach) that acting in a biased way towards others is unfair and hurtful
- Ongoing communication with families is encouraged and valued
- Materials are available to depict a variety of backgrounds or cultures
- Non-stereotypic intercultural materials and posters are on display in the early years setting and those which are stereotypical are removed.
- All staff are aware of the short- and long-term effects of discrimination on children
- Children are empowered to resist discrimination
- Anti-bias activities are planned and carried out. (Murray & O'Doherty 2001)

We are all prejudiced as human beings. We are constantly attempting to make sense of the world around us and in order to do so we draw on our past experiences, whether positive or negative.

Self-assessment

Use the following questionnaire devised by Willoughby (2004) to reflect on your own practice in relation to an anti-bias environment. Examine the extent to which you are happy with your result and consider the steps you may need to take to further enhance an anti-bias environment.

In my childcare service I use resources and provide activities that reflect and support:

All the children, families, students/trainees, staff members in my group.

Always ☐   Sometimes ☐   Never ☐

Children and adults at work and at play from the major ethnic groups living in my community, region and country.

Always ☐   Sometimes ☐   Never ☐

Diversity within each group, e.g. a range of languages, especially those spoken by families and children in the group.

Always ☐   Sometimes ☐   Never ☐

People from class, cultural or ethnic groups that are different from my own without encouraging or reinforcing stereotypical thinking.

Always ☐   Sometimes ☐   Never ☐

Women and men from various ethnic backgrounds doing a range of tasks in the home and having professional, manual, managerial, artistic or administrative jobs or who are unemployed.

Always ☐   Sometimes ☐   Never ☐

Older people of various backgrounds doing a variety of activities.

Always ☐   Sometimes ☐   Never ☐

I use materials and provide activities that reflect and support:
Differently abled people of various class, ethnic and cultural backgrounds working and being with their families and playing.

Always ☐   Sometimes ☐   Never ☐

Diversity in family lifestyles including single mothers or fathers; mothers in jobs outside the home and fathers at home; fathers in jobs outside the home and mothers at home; families with grandparents or other relatives and no parents; families with two mothers or two fathers; middle-income and low-income families; families with differently abled members; foster families; and families whose members come from different ethnic and cultural groups.

Always ☐   Sometimes ☐   Never ☐

* For every 'Always' answer give yourself 2 points
* For every 'Sometimes' answer give yourself 1 point
* For every 'Never' answer give yourself 0 points

Now total your points and examine the results:
* If you scored between 14 and 16 you are operating out of an anti-bias approach with regard to your environment.
* If you scored between 11 and 13 you are engaging an anti-bias approach in some areas of your environment.
* If you scored between 5 and 10, you may be operating out of what Louise Derman-Sparks calls a 'tourist approach' i.e. introducing cultural activities at special times, seeing other cultures as 'exotic' and not incorporating them into all aspects of the programme. The 'tourist approach' does not support children or give them the tools they need to comfortably, empathically and fairly interact with diversity.
* If your score is 4 or below, you are reflecting the dominant culture's point of view in the environment and ignoring the experiences and views of people from groups different from your own.

(Willoughby 2004, pp. 6–7)

GUIDELINES FOR EARLY YEARS PRACTITIONERS

We have already looked briefly at the aims of the *Diversity and Equality Guidelines for Childcare Providers* (OMC 2006).

> The guidelines detail steps for providers to develop and adhere to a diversity and equality policy, and include sections on accessibility, partnering opportunities, environmental considerations, gender, religion, discipline, traditions, and bullying. While these guidelines are clear, comprehensive and accessible, the key issue is their full implementation. (Barry & Sherlock 2008, p.9)

In Practice

In our early years settings our practices relating to equality and diversity are determined by policies and procedures, as we have seen in earlier chapters. These policies and procedures act as our guidelines; they are there to ensure that we meet both Irish and international legislation and national policy. Familiarise yourself with the policies in your setting which relate to equality and diversity. Once you have read this chapter, reflect on how well those policies address the broad areas explored here. Is it time to review your policies?

We have a great responsibility to ensure that we offer an environment which clearly values the uniqueness of every child and their family. In order to do this the early years practitioner must have sufficient knowledge and understanding of the child's cultural and religious background.

> Diversity and equality issues affect everyone, so we must support all children in their development as active citizens. Practitioners need the empathy, understanding and skills to help children achieve a positive sense of themselves and of others. Our role: to protect and value all children in the setting, foster empathy and provide accurate information about difference to enable children to think critically about and challenge bias. (OMC 2006)

Legislation and social policy clearly place a requirement on the early years practitioner to have some level of knowledge of the background of each child in their setting. We have already discussed the importance of recognising each child as a unique person with unique needs, and in order to do this the early years practitioner needs to have a degree of knowledge and understanding of the child's background. We can see from the table on the next page that a considerable number of people living in Ireland were born in other countries and also that people in Ireland hold a range of religious beliefs.

POPULATION OF IRELAND BY RELIGION AND NATIONALITY, 2011

Religion	Nationality										All
	Irish	Non-Irish	UK	EU27 excl. Irish & UK	Other Europe	African	Asian	American	Other nationality	Not stated, incl. no nationality	
Roman Catholic	3,525,573	282,799	49,761	184,066	2,222	9,770	19,420	13,706	3,854	22,815	3,831,187
Church of Ireland, England, Anglican, Episcopalian	93,056	30,464	21,477	4,228	174	2,571	783	628	603	925	124,445
Muslim (Islamic)	18,223	29,143	823	1,445	2,049	8,777	15,376	170	503	764	48,130
Orthodox (Greek, Coptic, Russian)	8,465	34,854	271	22,108	8,901	815	2,299	154	306	684	44,003
Other Christian	24,023	15,258	2,112	3,165	300	5,506	2,556	1,325	294	371	39,652
Presbyterian	14,348	8,311	3,619	1,494	67	1,758	349	743	281	176	22,835
Apostolic or Pentecostal	5,520	8,182	183	2,320	37	5,013	364	166	99	174	13,876
Other stated religions	34,867	40,227	6,598	11,845	621	4,967	12,620	2,891	685	561	75,655
No religion	173,180	82,194	25,620	37,463	1,478	1,154	10,179	4,188	2,112	1,456	256,830
Not stated	29,888	12,925	1,795	6,371	458	1,311	1,633	913	444	25,855	68,668
All religions	3,927,143	544,357	112,259	274,505	16,307	41,642	65,579	24,884	9,181	53,781	4,525,281

Source: CSO, http://cso.ie/en/statistics/population/populationclassifiedbyreligionandnationality2011/

> ### *In Practice*
>
> How relevant, do you think, are these statistics to your early years setting?
> Are you surprised by any of these statistics?
> What do you know about the countries immigrants to Ireland have come from?
> What do you know about the range of religious beliefs shown in the table? How might a variety of religious views in the early years setting impact on a child's life?

THE ÉIST PROJECT: AN IRISH PERSPECTIVE

The éist Project, funded under the Equal Opportunities Childcare Programme (EOCP) (DJELR 2000), sub-measure 3 (Quality Improvement Programme), was developed to examine how early years practitioners should be provided with appropriate training on equality and diversity.

The project was funded for a three-year period and set out to raise awareness of the need for a comprehensive equality and diversity training approach relevant to the early years sector and to develop such a programme. The éist Project worked closely with County Childcare Committees to develop awareness-raising packages and training. They also developed materials depicting Irish children from minority backgrounds, produced four jigsaws depicting the life of the Traveller and provided resource lists on diversity issues and equipment for early childhood practitioners.

PRE-SCHOOL EDUCATION INITIATIVE FOR CHILDREN FROM MINORITY GROUPS 2011–2012

This initiative was funded by the Department of Education and Skills; the Early Years Education Policy Unit (under Dormant Accounts), and since then has grown to offer a wide variety of activities and projects undertaken by various agencies and organisations.

The objectives of the initiative were:

- To **train**, in a co-ordinated manner, staff from 160 early childhood care and education (ECCE) services in 32 City/County Childcare Committee areas in the FETAC Level 5 award Diversity and Equality in Childcare
- To **mentor** the participants attending this training in order to support them to implement the learning from the training in their services
- To **work** towards each participating ECCE service **implementing** the anti-bias method of practice
- To **form** local equality and diversity networks developed from the core group of trained ECCE services
- To **link** to Síolta, the National Quality Framework for Early Childhood Education (CECDE 2006), the *Diversity and Equality Guidelines for Childcare Providers* (OMC 2006) and Aistear, the Early Years Curriculum Framework (NCCA 2009)

- To **evaluate** the effectiveness of the programme informing current and future policy and practice.

SÍOLTA

We have seen in earlier chapters that Síolta is the quality framework that must guide and be clearly evident in every aspect of our daily practice in the early years setting.

Standard 1: Rights of the Child

Ensuring that each child's rights are met requires that she/he is enabled to exercise choice and to use initiative as an active participant and partner in her/his own development and learning.

> **Component1.1:** Each child has opportunities to make choices, is enabled to make decisions, and has her/his choices and decisions respected.
>
> *Signpost for Reflection:* How does your setting match its care routines to the child's own routines and needs?

In Practice

Looking at this Standard, Component and Signpost for Reflection from an equality and diversity perspective, what factors will influence how you will support a child in meeting this standard? You might, for example, think about care routines that acknowledge the child's parents' wishes and respect the child's personal choice and decisions.

Consider what changes you may need to make in your setting to meet the child's choices and decisions if they do not fit in with your plans for a particular activity. You may have a child who does not like painting and you have to alter the activity to enable them to participate in a manner which meets their needs.

Practitioners should recognise bias or discrimination as it is happening, and know how to respond sensitively and appropriately, for example when a child makes a statement or asks a question that reveals bias or when a child teases or excludes another child. Practitioners also need to be able to work with and challenge discriminatory issues with adults.

Remember, we all form prejudices based on our life experience. The first step is to examine ourselves: becoming more aware of our own prejudices will make us conscious of ensuring that they do not lead us to discriminate against anyone in the early years setting.

Dealing with Discriminatory Incidents

Here are some ideas from the *Diversity and Equality Guidelines*:

- Make it a rule that exclusion or name-calling is not acceptable and discuss this with the children in a sensitive and unauthoritative manner.
- When a child says something hurtful to another child that refers to difference, intervene immediately and remind her or him of the rule. Do not ignore.
- Determine the real reasons for the conflict or exclusion.
- Children may call other children names that have racist connotations without fully understanding what they say. They still need to understand that hurt was caused. On the other hand, research shows that children can know exactly when to use a derogatory term to hurt another child.
- Comfort the child who was a target of discrimination and help him/her verbalise their feelings. Equally support the child who caused the hurt. Children need to be helped to recognise what is happening and learn that it is equally unacceptable for them to be a target or to target others.
- If fear or prejudice is the underlying reason, try to learn more about the child's bias and make a long-term plan to address the issue. This will involve discussion with the families and other staff.
- Intervention should be immediate and will need to be followed up with both children.
- Use puppets or dolls to demonstrate a situation of name-calling or exclusion, and ask the children about the feelings involved. (OMC 2006)

In Practice

If a new child only eats a particular type of food (e.g. follows a macrobiotic diet), how can you ensure that you meet their needs but also do not treat them differently in a manner which could have a negative impact on the child? How can you source the correct food? Would you ask the parents to provide all the child's food? You would not make a major issue out of the fact that their food is different from the other children's, so what do you say to the other children about the difference in food?

Component 1.2: Each child has opportunities and is enabled to take the lead, initiate activity, be appropriately independent and is supported to solve problems.

Signposts for Reflection: Responding quickly to a baby who is crying or needs attention. Routines are organised to ensure the child gets regular and frequent individual attention. Providing individualised care for every child.

Component 1.3: Each child is enabled to participate actively in the daily routine, in activities, in conversations and in all other appropriate situations, and is considered as a partner by the adult.

Signposts for Reflection: How do you enable each child to participate fully with their peers, including a child with special needs? How do you ensure each child joins in sharing activities in a way that suits her/his own disposition?

Standard 14: Identity and Belonging

Promoting positive identities and a strong sense of belonging requires clearly defined policies, procedures and practice that empower every child and adult to develop a confident self and group identity, and to have a positive understanding and regard for the identity and rights of others.

Component 14.1: The setting has written records of all policies, procedures and practice regarding the promotion of positive identities and a strong sense of belonging within the setting and makes them available to all stakeholders.

Signposts for Reflection: What policies and procedures within your setting relate to the promotion of positive identities and belonging in the best interests of the child?

In Practice

Do you have policies to guide practice in relation to Inclusion, Access to the setting, Behaviour Management, Anti-discrimination/anti-bias practice? Does everyone have access to these policies; do they understand them? Do they follow the good practice set out to guide their daily practices?

Component 14.2: The setting promotes a confident self and group identity through the provision of an appropriate environment, experiences and interactions within the setting.

Signposts for Reflection: How does the environment reflect and promote the culture and background of all children present in the setting, avoiding stereotypical role models and cultural images?

Some ideas might include:
- Having toys, games and resources that depict a range of cultures, family structures and socio-economic statuses.

- Strategies to support and maintain the child's first language, e.g. staff learning a few key words, labelling items using the child's language, and contact with the family to help with this.
- Inviting parents into the setting to give a short talk or demonstration to everyone, especially around the time of a special religious or cultural celebration.
- Ensuring assessment techniques used are free from cultural and gender bias.

> **Component 14.3:** The setting promotes positive understanding and regard for the identity and rights of others through the provision of an appropriate environment, experiences and interactions within the setting.
>
> *Signposts for Reflection:* How does the environment promote positive understanding and regard for the identity and rights of others?

Suggestions here include:
- Images of family/community life (e.g. photos, pictures, posters, children's drawings, etc.)
- A range of toys, computer software, books and materials which present people from various races and cultures, family structures, socio-economic groups, etc.
- Avoid depicting stereotypical role models and cultural images
- Encourage staff to become more aware of their own beliefs, values and attitudes to diversity in the setting. This may take place using 'critical incident analysis' following a problem, but formal training to prevent any such incidents arising would be most helpful to all involved.

AISTEAR

Aistear's theme Identity and Belonging has four aims:

Aim 1

Children will have strong self-identities and will feel respected and affirmed as unique individuals with their own life stories.

In partnership with the adult, children will
1. build respectful relationships with others
2. appreciate the features that make a person special and unique (name, size, hair, hand and footprint, gender, birthday)
3. understand that as individuals they are separate from others with their own needs, interests and abilities
4. have a sense of 'who they are' and be able to describe their backgrounds, strengths and abilities

5. feel valued and see themselves and their interests reflected in the environment
6. express their own ideas, preferences and needs, and have these responded to with respect and consistency.

Aim 2

Children will have a sense of group identity where links with their family and community are acknowledged and extended.

In partnership with the adult, children will

1. feel that they have a place and a right to belong to the group
2. know that members of their family and community are positively acknowledged and welcomed
3. be able to share personal experiences about their own families and cultures, and come to know that there is a diversity of family structures, cultures and backgrounds
4. understand and take part in routines, customs, festivals, and celebrations
5. see themselves as part of a wider community and know about their local area, including some of its places, features and people
6. understand the different roles of people in the community.

Aim 3

Children will be able to express their rights and show an understanding and regard for the identity, rights and views of others.

In partnership with the adult, children will

1. express their views and help make decisions in matters that affect them
2. understand the rules and the boundaries of acceptable behaviour
3. interact, work co-operatively, and help others
4. be aware of and respect others' needs, rights, feelings, culture, language, background, and religious beliefs
5. have a sense of social justice and recognise and deal with unfair behaviour
6. demonstrate the skills of co-operation, responsibility, negotiation, and conflict resolution.

Aim 4

Children will see themselves as capable learners.

In partnership with the adult, children will

1. develop a broad range of abilities and interests
2. show an awareness of their own unique strengths, abilities and learning styles, and be willing to share their skills and knowledge with others

3. show increasing confidence and self-assurance in directing their own learning
4. demonstrate dispositions like curiosity, persistence and responsibility
5. experience learning opportunities that are based on personal interests, and linked to their home, community and culture
6. be motivated, and begin to think about and recognise their own progress and achievements. (NCCA 2009)

In Practice

What activities would you plan in the child's curriculum to address these aims?

Obviously activities must be age and stage appropriate for the child; for example, with a very young child you might do something as simple as using mirrors and reflective toys to enable them to recognise themselves. Here are some more ideas:

- Show daily routines through photographs of the babies and children undertaking the activities.
- Observe each child's individual likes, needs and wishes. For example, you might notice that they dislike colouring but recognise that it is important for pencil control leading to writing skills. How can you offer a similar useful activity which will appeal to the child?
- Spend time one to one with each child to make them feel special and valued.
- Use materials and resources which reflect children's families, backgrounds, abilities and cultures, e.g. books and puzzles which represent different family types, homes, dolls with different skin tones and hair types.
- Work closely in partnership with parents/families to identify the unique needs of each child.
- Support toddlers to help them manage their behaviour appropriately and to know what behaviour is acceptable.
- Provide opportunities that enable children to become aware of their community. For older children, this might include walking around the area, visiting the local library, or drawing a map of the local area and marking on it areas of interest in a very simple, easily understood format.

References

Bandura, A. (1977) *Social Learning Theory*. Englewood Cliffs, NJ: Prentice Hall

Barnardos (2002) *Diversity: Information Pack*. Dublin: Barnardos' Training and Resource Service, http://barnardos.ie/assets/files/information-pack/Diversity_IP.pdf

Barron, R.A. and Byrne, D. (1991) *Social Psychology: Understanding Human Interaction* (6th edn) Boston, MA: Allyn & Bacon

Barry, U. and Sherlock, L. (2008) *Provision of Childcare Services in Ireland*. UCD School of Social Justice Working Papers 8(1): 1–31, http://researchrepository.ucd.ie/handle/10197/2037

CECDE (Centre for Early Childhood Development and Education) (2006) *Síolta:the National Quality Framework for Early Childhood Education*. Dublin: CECDE, http://www.siolta.ie

CRA (Children's Rights Alliance) (website) 'The United Nations Convention on the Rights of the Child', http://childrensrights.ie/childrens-rights-ireland/un-convention-rights-child

DCYA (Department of Children and Youth Affairs) (2011) *Children First: National Guidance for the Protection and Welfare of Children*. Dublin: DCYA, http://www.dcya.gov.ie/documents/Publications/ChildrenFirst.pdf

DCYA (2014) *Better Outcomes Brighter Futures: The National Policy Framework for Children and Young People 2014–2020*. Dublin: DCYA

Derman-Sparks, L. and Olsen Edwards, J. (2010) *Anti-Bias Education for Young Children and Ourselves*. Washington, DC: National Association for the Education of Young Children

DJLER (2000) *Equal Opportunities Childcare Programme 2000–2006: General Guidelines for Funding*. Dublin: DJLER, http://www.justice.ie/en/JELR/Pages/Childcare_programme_funding_guidelines

Macionis, J. and Plummer, K. (2002) *Sociology: A Global Introduction* (2nd edn). Prentice Hall

Murray, C. (n.d.) *Promoting Diversity and Equality in Early Childhood Care, Education and Training: The 'éist' Project*. Dublin: CECDE, www.cecde.ie/english/pdf/Questions%20of%20Quality/Murray.pdf

Murray, C. and O'Doherty, A. (2001) *'éist': Respecting Diversity in Early Childhood Care, Education and Training*. Dublin: Pavee Point

NCCA (National Council for Curriculum and Assessment) (2009) *Aistear: the Early Childhood Curriculum Framework*. Dublin: NCCA

OMC (Office of the Minister for Children) (2006) *Diversity and Equality Guidelines for Childcare Providers*. Dublin: OMC

Thompson, N. (2006) *Anti-discriminatory Practice* (3rd edn). Basingstoke: Palgrave

Tilmouth, T., Davies-Ward, E. and Quallington, J. (2011) *Foundation Degree in Health and Social Care*. London: Hodder Education

Willoughby, M. (2004) *Every Child Matters: Developing Anti-discriminatory Practice in Early Childhood Services*. Dublin: Barnardos' National Children's Resource Centre, http://www.barnardos.ie/assets/files/publications/free/Every%20Child%20Matters%281%29.pdf

CHAPTER 7

Introduction to Child Health and Wellbeing

INTRODUCTION

This chapter takes an applied approach to policy and legislation, highlighting their centrality to childcare practice. An overview of child health and wellbeing is given and linked to Síolta Standards. Different factors in health and wellbeing are linked with policy, legislation, research and Síolta Standards, and the chapter includes 'In Practice' suggestions on how each factor can be implemented in childcare practice. The chapter ends by taking a theoretical approach – Bronfenbrenner's ecological theory – to understanding the interplay of many factors in children's health and wellbeing. A case study further illustrates this relationship.

In Chapters 1 and 3 we explored the development of policies relevant to ECCE, including policies of national importance, such as the National Children's Strategy (DoHC 2000). If you have not already done so, it would be useful to read those chapters before continuing.

It is arguable that concepts of child wellbeing are relatively recent; legislation criminalising animal cruelty was enacted before the criminalisation of child cruelty. In

America in the 1870s, in order to prosecute a mother who was physically abusing her ten-year-old daughter, Mary Ellen McCormack, a case had to be brought by the American Society for the Prevention of Cruelty to Animals because there were no laws protecting children from parental physical abuse. In the UK in 1881, the Reverend George Staite summed up the inhumanity of the era: 'whilst we have a Society for the Prevention of Cruelty to Animals, can we not do something to prevent cruelty to children?' This was at a time when children were viewed differently from how we think of them now: they did not have rights, and indeed the prevailing attitude was 'spare the rod and spoil the child'.

Ireland has a shameful history in our treatment of children (discussed in Chapter 4). Thankfully things have changed and continue to do so: signs of this change are touched on in earlier chapters on policy and legislation, the United Nations Convention on the Rights of the Child (UNCRC) and the recent successful referendum on children's rights.

WHAT IS CHILD HEALTH AND WELLBEING?
Needs versus Rights

Another development that has radically changed the lives and wellbeing of children is the move from a **needs**-led approach to a **rights**-based one. Why is this important? A needs-led model is based on a notion of charity; a rights-based model acknowledges that the individual – whether a child, someone with a disability, etc. – has a **right** to protection, support and equality. This is a fundamental shift as in the past children were often seen as miniature adults and as the 'property' of their parents. The UNCRC challenged this notion and insisted on the recognition that children are entitled to individual rights. This shift to a focus on rights has had a profound effect on how we view children's health and wellbeing.

> ### Think about it!
> How would you define and explain child health and wellbeing? Which areas of health would you include? What would you leave out? How would you measure child health and wellbeing?

It's not so easy to settle on a definition when you start to consider how wide the scope is, especially for wellbeing. Did you include physical wellbeing in your definition? How about cognitive development and functioning? Social relationships probably featured when you thought about wellbeing, but how would you measure them? Would spiritual wellbeing be included in your definition? Did you restrict your conception of wellbeing to immediate influences on the child, or did you acknowledge 'external' factors such as poverty or access to education?

One definition of child wellbeing is:

[H]ealthy and successful individual functioning (involving physiological, psychological and behavioural levels of organisation), positive social relationships (with family members, peers, adult caregivers, and community and societal institutions, for instance, school and faith and civic organisations), and a social ecology that provides safety (e.g., freedom from interpersonal violence, war and crime), human and civil rights, social justice and participation in civil society. (Andrews 2002, cited in Hanafin & Brooks 2005, p.15)

As we can see, child wellbeing covers a wide range of factors from immediate influences on the child to more distant ones, such as community and civil rights. The UNCRC reinforced the importance of children's voices being heard, and this is enshrined in the National Children's Strategy, so maybe a worthwhile endeavour would be to ask children what wellbeing means to them. A significant piece of research did just that.

What does Wellbeing Mean to Irish Children?

Encouraging research into children's lives is one of the aims of the Department of Children and Youth Affairs (DCYA). In pursuit of this aim, the DCYA commissioned some innovative research by Nic Gabhainn and Sixsmith (2005) exploring Irish children's understandings of wellbeing. The children in the study were asked to take pictures of things that represented wellbeing to them. Several findings emerged from the study regarding children's understanding of wellbeing:

A number of specifically interesting factors emerged. ... The centrality of interpersonal relationships with family and friends (including school friends) emerges strongly, as does the value of activities or things to do. During all phases, children discussed how aspects of the various categories made them feel; how relationships (with people and pets/animals) and the activities within or context of those relationships gave them a sense of belonging, being safe, loved, valued and being cared for ... These categories illustrate the extent to which children interact with the natural world around them, as well as the interpersonal environment in which they are located. These factors certainly deserve further attention from researchers, policymakers and practitioners. (Nic Gabhainn & Sixsmith 2005, p. 64)

This piece of research is quite special: hearing children's voices gives us a better understanding of and insight into their world, bringing us back to the UNCRC, which demands that children's voices are recognised, and linking to **Síolta Standards 1 and 4**. It is clear that children appear more focused on the things and relationships that bring them happiness and joy within their immediate and more distant environment.

In Practice

1. As a childcare practitioner, how can you ensure that children's voices are listened to and their opinions integrated within ECCE settings? How can you use 'consultation' with children during your daily practice? In listening to children's expression of their needs, what skills can be utilised and supports offered to meet those needs?

2. From a policy perspective we can see several Síolta Standards reflected here, e.g.:

- **Standard 2: Environments**. Enriching environments, both indoor and outdoor (including materials and equipment) are well maintained, safe, available, accessible, adaptable, developmentally appropriate, and offer a variety of challenging and stimulating experiences.

- **Standard 6: Play**. Promoting play requires that each child has ample time to engage in freely available and accessible, developmentally appropriate and well-resourced opportunities for exploration, creativity and 'meaning making' in the company of other children, with participating and supportive adults and alone, where appropriate.

What other standards can you see?

3. Nic Gabhainn and Sixsmith talk about how children interact with the natural world around them. Do you feel that children in ECCE settings have enough interaction with the natural world? How would you rate the quality of access to 'outdoor' play? Can you do more to facilitate this interaction, either through children's access to the physical world around them or through their learning about the natural world?

The research also highlights the centrality of relationships in children's lives, which links to two of the 12 principles of learning and development that underpin **Aistear** regarding children's connections with others:

- Relationships
- Parents, Family and Community

Think about it!

As practitioners, what lessons can be learned from this research in terms of your own learning and the environment you create to support child wellbeing?

Now we have a better understanding of what child wellbeing is, but what are the factors that influence it?

FACTORS INFLUENCING CHILD WELLBEING

What is a factor? At its simplest, it is something that influences or produces a result or outcome.

A child's health, development and wellbeing are shaped by a range of factors such as child and family characteristics, and the broader social, economic and physical environments in which the child is raised. Earlier chapters outlined child protection, protective and risk factors, but this is just one area where we see factors at play; other outcomes can include education, health and happiness.

Factors can be either 'risk' or 'protective' and can affect all areas of an individual's life throughout the lifecycle. Added to this is our recognition that experiences early in life affect later development, that early years is a critical and sensitive period that can have massive ramifications throughout the remainder of a child's life.

Risk factors are factors that can have an adverse impact on an individual person or their immediate and distal (distant) environments and that have a potentially negative influence on their development or behaviour. Where one risk factor is present there are often likely to be others; for example, children born with low birth weight (biological risk) may also be born to mothers with low education levels and who live in poverty (psychosocial risks). This phenomenon is sometimes called a 'double jeopardy'. The more risk factors that accumulate, the longer these factors last and the more severe the factors, the greater the impact on the individual and their development (as an illustration, see the case study at the end of this chapter).

Offset against this are **protective factors**, which operate in a similar fashion to risk factors. To put it simply, the more protective factors you have the better 'protected' you are and the more likely you are to enjoy better outcomes. Intervention programmes, such as Young Ballymun, the Incredible Years Programme and Springboard, operate by targeting children and families who are vulnerable for a variety of reasons by putting support mechanisms in place. These programmes are protective in and of themselves and their ideology reflects the need to target at-risk populations by increasing protective factors to offset risk factors and thus improving outcomes.

The following table lists the protective and risk factors that were used in developing the child wellbeing indicators for Ireland (Hanafin & Brooks 2005, p. 18).

RISK FACTORS AND PROTECTIVE FACTORS

	Child	Family	School	Life Events	Community and Culture
Risk factors	• Prematurity • Low birth weight • Disability • Pre-natal brain damage • Birth injury • Low intelligence • Difficult temperament • Chronic illness • Insecure attachment • Poor problem-solving • Beliefs about aggression • Poor social skills • Low self-esteem • Lack of empathy • Alienation • Hyperactivity/ disruptive behaviour • Impulsivity	• Teenage mothers • Single parents • Psychiatric disorders • Substance abuse • Criminality • Anti-social models • Family violence/ disharmony • Marital discord • Disorganised environment • Negative interaction/ social isolation • Large family size • Father absence • Long-term parental unemployment • Poor supervision and monitoring of child • Discipline style • Rejection of child • Abuse • Lack of warmth/ affection • Low involvement in child's activities • Neglect	• School failure • Normative beliefs about aggression • Deviant peer group • Bullying • Peer rejection • Poor attachment to school • Inadequate behaviour management	• Divorce and family break-up • War or natural disasters • Death of a family member	• Socio-economic disadvantage • Population density and housing conditions • Urban area • Neighbourhood violence and crime • Cultural norms concerning violence as an acceptable response to frustration • Media portrayal of violence • Lack of support services • Social or cultural discrimination

	Child	Family	School	Life Events	Community and Culture
Protective factors	• Social competence • Social skills • Above average intelligence • Attachment to family • Empathy • Problem-solving • Optimism • School achievement • Easy temperament • Internal locus of control • Moral beliefs • Values • Self-related cognitions • Good coping style	• Supportive caring parents • Family harmony • More than two years between siblings • Responsibility for chores or required helpfulness • Secure and stable family • Supportive relationship with other adult • Small family size • Strong family norms and morality	• Positive school climate • Responsibility and required helpfulness • Sense of belonging/bonding • Opportunities for some success at school and recognition of achievement • School norms concerning violence	• Meeting significant person • Moving to new area • Opportunities at critical turning points or major life transitions	• Access to support services • Community networking • Attachment to the community • Participation in church or other community group • Community/cultural norms against violence • Strong cultural identity and ethnic pride

Source: Hanafin & Brooks (2005, p. 18) (adapted from Developmental Crime Prevention Consortium 1999, p. 150–3, cited in Commission for Children and Young People 2002, pp. 18–19).

> **Think about it!**
> Can you think of examples where 'family' as a factor could potentially have a negative impact on a child's development or wellbeing (parental addiction, perhaps) or a positive one? Does where you live or grow up impact on your development? If so, in what way (physically, socially)? All these factors interact with each other to influence our wellbeing in a variety of domains of development.

In the sections that follow we shall look at a number of factors:
• Family structure
• Community
• Culture
• Education and health
• Social services
• Social status.

At the beginning of each factor we'll focus, where applicable, on relevant policies along with links to Síolta Standards. As meeting children's needs is an essential role for the childcare practitioner, at the end of each factor we shall, where possible, suggest some ideas on how to support and meet those needs. Later we shall look at a case study, with Bronfenbrenner's ecological theory, to offer a framework for understanding this complex interaction of factors.

FAMILY STRUCTURE

UNCRC Article 5: Parental guidance
Governments should respect the rights and responsibilities of families to direct and guide their children so that, as they grow, they learn to use their rights properly…It does place on governments the responsibility to protect and assist families in fulfilling their essential role as nurturers of children.

- *Strengthening Families for Life* (Commission on the Family 1998)
- *Strategies for Strengthening Families* (CECDE 2004)
- Family Support Agency Act 2001
- Child and Family Agency Act 2013

Síolta Standard 3: Parents and Families. Valuing and involving parents and families requires a proactive partnership approach evidenced by a range of clearly stated, accessible and implemented processes, policies and procedures.

Policy and Families

Family is fundamental to children's development, health and wellbeing. The family is the primary agent of socialisation, teaching children social norms, rules and behaviour. The centrality of families and parents is captured by the Centre for Early Child Development and Education (CECDE) in their policy document *Strategies for Strengthening Families*:

The strengthening of families forms an inherent part of this brief, the family forming the primary unit within which the majority of children develop and learn. As part of the development of the NQF [National Quality Framework] (Síolta), parental involvement is cited within our Programme of Work (CECDE 2001) as one of the core areas for the development of guidelines and standards. (CECDE 2004, p.2)

Another policy document, *Strengthening Families for Life* (Commission on the Family 1998), placed the importance of families at the forefront. Its core themes related to:
- Building strengths in families
- Supporting families in carrying out their functions – the caring and nurturing of children

- Promoting continuity and stability in family life
- Protecting and enhancing the position of children and vulnerable dependent family members.

These core themes can be traced through policy and initiatives, culminating in the establishment of Tusla (the Child and Family Agency) in January 2014 under the Child and Family Agency Act 2013. Under Section 8 of the Act, Tusla is required to:

- Support and promote the development, welfare and protection of children, and
- Support and encourage the effective functioning of families.

Some Research Findings

Let's look at some findings which elaborate on how early experiences within the family can affect a child's development throughout their life. A recent study (Fahey *et al.* 2012), using data from *Growing Up in Ireland* (ESRI & TCD),explored the theme of 'Family Relationships and Family Wellbeing'. In this study the authors defined wellbeing in terms of children's physical, socio-emotional and cognitive outcomes at age 9. One focus was on family type or structure. Figure 7.1 shows the different types of family structure seen in the study.

FIGURE 7.1 FAMILY TYPES BY STRUCTURE

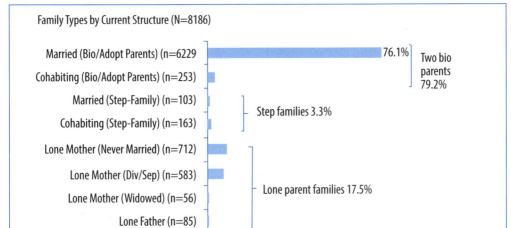

From this figure you can see that the majority of children in this study belong to married parents, with 17.5 per cent coming from lone-parent families. Figure 7.2 shows how family structure or type impacts on child wellbeing.

FIGURE 7.2 INDICATORS OF CHILD WELLBEING BY FAMILY TYPE

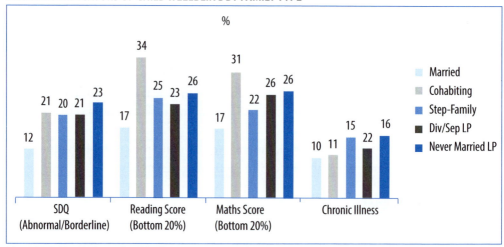

Note: SDQ (Strengths and Difficulties Questionnaire) is a commonly used measure of social and emotional development in children.

According to Fahey *et al.*:

> Here we can see that children in intact married families have an advantage on all outcomes – they are less likely to have poor social and emotional adjustment, low reading ability, low maths ability or chronic illness than children from other family types. The advantage among these children is smallest in regard to chronic illness and is more substantial for the social-emotional and cognitive outcomes. The key contrast here is not between one-parent and two-parent families, since children in married two-parent families have a consistent advantage over those in cohabiting and step-families, both of which also constitute two-parent families. Thus the main contrast is between the traditional family of father and mother who are married to each other versus the rest. (2012, pp. 67–8)

It would be easy to assume from such findings that the traditional married two-parent family type is the one which produces the best results for children. However, this is where we need to think *why* the results might be as they are. We know from research that children in lone-parent families are at higher risk of poorer outcomes, but this doesn't necessarily indicate that it is the type of parenting that is the difficulty: there may be other forces at play. For example, lone parents are more likely to face poverty than two-parent families, since there can be only one income stream. Lone parents are more likely to be unemployed, and as we have seen in earlier chapters the cost and relative lack of access to quality childcare is an identified issue. We must always think about the *why*! It is interesting to note that two-parent families other than the traditional, e.g. step and cohabiting, don't seem to have as positive outcomes, suggesting that having two parents is not a protective factor *per se*; it is the 'type' of two-parent family that appears to make a difference.

> ### *Think about it!*
> Next time you read research findings, question the processes and mechanisms behind the finding rather than taking the results at face value. Why might children of non-traditional two-parent families not do as well as children of married parents?

Other factors associated with 'family' can have an impact on children's health and wellbeing, and one powerful factor is the quality of the relationship between parent and child.

Key Features of the Parent–Child Relationship

> The nature and quality of family experiences influence not only how a child copes with life growing up, but also help to determine the quality of their relationships, parenting and mental health in adulthood. (Gilligan 1995)

Each child has a unique relationship with its parents and siblings. Guralnick (1997, cited in Brady *et al.* 2004, p.10) highlights three features of the parent–child relationship as important:

- The quality of parent–child interaction.
- The extent to which the family provides the child with diverse and appropriate experiences within the surrounding social and physical environment.
- The way in which the family ensures the child's health and safety.

According to the Irish College of Psychiatrists there is a clear and documented relationship between mental wellbeing and early experiences, especially in the realm of attachment relationships. Further, 'Interventions specifically targeting this age group [0–5 years] can have preventive/protective value and have been shown to be successful' (Irish College of Psychiatrists 2005, p.17)

As we have seen here and in the chapters on child protection, family is a crucial factor in influencing child wellbeing. As family is so instrumental, interventions have been developed to support at-risk children and their families. One such family support intervention is Springboard.

Springboard: Family Support Interventions

The Springboard Family Support Projects for children at risk is the first major family support initiative of its kind in Ireland. It was established by the Department of Health and Children in 1998, with approval from the Cabinet Committee on Social Inclusion. According to the Department of Health and Children, the intention of the initiative is to provide a valuable framework for tackling child and family difficulties at local community level and a baseline for quality service provision in supporting troubled families.

In their evaluation of a Springboard project, Holt *et al.* note:

> The type or structure of a family is just one influence on children's wellbeing; parenting style and the role of fathers are among other factors too numerous to cover here. It is clear, however, that family is the primary and arguably most powerful influence and it is unsurprising that we have seen so many policies and initiatives aimed at supporting families emerge. (Holt *et al.* 2002, p.78)

The Benefits of Partnership with Parents

As a childcare practitioner, you will know that Síolta and Aistear emphasise the importance to children of family and relationships; and they also highlight partnership between practitioners and parents/guardians. As childcare practitioners we can support parents through partnership. According to Aistear:

> Partnership involves parents, families and practitioners working together to benefit children. Each recognises, respects and values what the other does and says. Partnership involves responsibility on both sides. (NCCA 2009, p.7)

Think about it!

From your own experiences, can you identify how partnership with parents is supported and encouraged in ECCE settings? What steps could you take to build such partnerships and support relationships between child and parent/guardian? (At the end of this section we will explore just how to do that.)

Partnership with parents, colleagues and other stakeholders is central to Aistear and can be seen in Síolta Standards too. As we've been looking as family as a factor, let examine what benefits are possible when practitioners and parents work together. The Aistear booklet *Building Partnerships between Parents and Practitioners* lists the following benefits.

Parents:
- Feel valued and respected
- Are more involved in their children's learning and development
- Can share information about their children
- Feel their family's values, practices, traditions, and beliefs are understood and taken into account
- Feel comfortable visiting the setting, talking to, and planning with practitioners
- Know more about their children's experiences outside the home and use this information to support their learning and development more effectively
- Understand why early childhood care and education is important
- Have increased confidence in their own parenting skills.

Practitioners:
- Understand better the children and families in their settings and use this information to make learning more enjoyable and rewarding for all children
- Can help children develop a sense of identity and belonging in the setting by actively engaging with and finding out about family values, traditions and beliefs, and building on these where appropriate
- Benefit from parents' skills and expertise
- Can provide a more emotionally secure environment for children.

Children:
- Feel more secure and benefit more from the educational opportunities given to them
- Move from one setting to another with greater confidence
- See learning as more enjoyable when their home life is 'visible' in the setting
- Enjoy hearing and seeing their home language in the setting when their home language is neither English nor Irish
- Experience more connections between the different services that support them. (NCCA 2009d, p. 18, Table 1)

Reflect on your practice
1. How can I gather and use information from parents to improve children's experiences?
2. What steps can I take to help parents support their children's learning and development?
3. What resources do I have that I could share with parents? (NCCA 2009d, p. 10)

One of the principles underpinning Aistear is 'family, parents and community', recognising that families exist within their community and therefore community itself is an influence on wellbeing. Community as a factor and how it links to families is clear – the Springboard intervention, for example, was aimed at community level. 'Community' is pivotal in supporting – or failing to support – child health and wellbeing.

COMMUNITY

If we want our communities to be strong, if we want our families to be strong, we have to have strong kids, who turn into strong adults – problem solvers, not problems. (McAleese 2011)

- *Ready, Steady, Play!*
- Social capital

Solta Standard 16: Community Involvement. Promoting community involvement requires the establishment of networks and connections evidenced by policies, procedures and actions which extend and support all adult's and children's engagement with the wider community.

Aistear contains 12 principles in three groupings. Community can be seen in two of these principles:
- Children as citizens
- Parents, family and community.

What does 'Community' Mean?

'Community' is a broad term and can involve many different aspects, from the physical environment itself to the people who inhabit it; and more philosophical ideas such as social capital.

Social Capital

McPherson *et al.* outline the following approach to defining social capital:

> Putnam defines social capital as a key characteristic of communities. In Putnam's definition, social capital extends beyond being a resource to include people's sense of belonging to their community, community cohesion, reciprocity and trust, and positive attitudes to community institutions that include participation in community activities or civic engagement. (McPherson *et al.* 2013, p.2)

Social capital is considered a key factor in child health and wellbeing. Irwin *et al.*, in a World Health Organisation (WHO) report, *Early Child Development: A Powerful Equaliser*, highlight the importance of family and community relationships and resources in stimulating the physical, emotional and social development of children and young people at key life stages, and comment:

> The environments that are responsible for fostering nurturant conditions for children range from the intimate realm of the family to the broader socioeconomic context shaped by governments, international agencies, and civil society. ...

These environments and their characteristics are the determinants of ECD (early child development); in turn, ECD is a determinant of health, wellbeing, and learning skills across the balance of the lifecourse. (Irwin *et al.* 2007, p. 5)

According to McPherson *et al.* (2013), high quality and cohesion in community social capital such as schools and neighbourhoods are associated with better health and wellbeing outcomes.

> ### *Think about it!*
> Do you believe that pre-schools, crèches and childminders also form part of the fabric of the community and contribute to community social capital? How would you support your answer?

How do we actually measure or judge child wellbeing within a community? Costello (1999, p. 37) offers the following indicators:
- Availability of quality play space and a clean environment
- Level of contact with peers
- Access to preferred leisure/play areas
- Proximity of community resources to the family home
- Level of geographic mobility of child
- Level of social capital within community.

> ### *Think about it!*
> Using these indicators, how would you rate the community you live and work in: positively or negatively? Are there any other measures you would use to evaluate how a community influences child health and wellbeing?

Can we see community and social capital addressed in Irish policies on child wellbeing? *Ready, Steady, Play!* is one policy initiative which clearly links physical environment and community to child health and wellbeing. Let's see how.

Physical Environment and Access to Play

Space and the physical environment has been identified as an aspect of community involved in child health and wellbeing (Costello 1999). Costello argues that children need to have access to recreation spaces to play outside the home; and, further, such spaces create opportunities to develop relationships/friendships with their peers.

The idea of physical environment and access to recreational pursuits links in with

Ready, Steady, Play!, the national play policy, which recognises the centrality of play to children's development. As a result of this recognition, funding for the refurbishment and creation of playgrounds around the country was put in place to ensure greater access to play opportunities and its associated benefits for children within their communities.

In Practice

How can you, as a childcare practitioner, integrate 'community' into your practice? Aistear (NCCA 2009) suggests the following learning opportunities in developing young children's **awareness of the community in which they live**:

- Include the children in making decisions and in participating in community activities such as concerts, assemblies and displays
- Visit places in the community and facilitate visits from, and interactions with members of the community
- Discuss the roles of people in the community such as a garda, a nurse, a social welfare officer, a librarian, a teacher, a lollipop person
- Work on projects such as 'Our Community' – involving where to go and what to do, making maps or posters of the local area with pictures of significant features such as a sculpture, a castle or a mountain; make a community wall.

CULTURE

UNCRC Article 2: Non-discrimination
The right of all children to enjoy all the rights in the Convention without discrimination.

- Equality Act 2004
- Disability Act 2005
- *Diversity and Equality Guidelines for Childcare Providers* (OMC 2006)

Síolta Standard 14: Identity and Belonging. Promoting positive identities and a strong sense of belonging requires clearly defined policies, procedures and practice that empower every child and adult to develop a confident self- and group identity, and to have a positive understanding and regard for the identity and rights of others.

Aistear includes two relevant principles:
- the child's uniqueness
- equality and diversity.

The Royal College of Nursing notes that different cultural practices may manifest in different ways: 'A Christian family may wish to have the baby christened, a Hindu family might wish to write the mantra "Om" on the baby's tongue with honey, while a Muslim family may wish that a male relative whisper the Islamic call to prayer into the baby's ear and perhaps attach an amulet round the baby's neck or wrist' (RCN 2004). In Chapter 6, Equality and Diversity, we explored concepts of cultural diversity and the role of childcare settings and practitioners in supporting diversity.

> ### *Think about it!*
> Consider cultural diversity in your neighbourhood or among the children you work with. List the various ethnic and cultural backgrounds you are aware of. Have you seen or encountered different child-rearing and parenting practices? Reflect on how such differences might have implications for your childcare practice.

How does 'culture' impact on child health and wellbeing? One powerful example of the influence of culture can be found in recent research which examined the health outcomes of an indigenous ethnic group: *Our Geels: The All Ireland Traveller Health Study* (Pavee Point 2010). This study showed that members of the Traveller community have poorer health outcomes than settled people. According to Pavee Point, 'Travellers require special consideration in health care because they are a distinct cultural group with different perceptions of health, disease and care needs.' The study found that the Traveller community has significantly lower life expectancy figures (61.7 years for men; 70.1 years for women) and poorer health outcomes. Let's compare those figures with the figures for Ireland as a whole, collected by the WHO, which regularly monitors life expectancy figures throughout the world. Ireland has seen a steady increase in life expectancy rates:

	1990	2000	2012
Male	72	74	79
Female	78	79	83

What do you think accounts for such vast differences in life expectancy? As Pavee Point indicated, cultural differences in perceptions surrounding health is a factor. Other factors would include social exclusion of and discrimination against Travellers in accessing State services, including health, education and employment. Maycock *et al.* (2009), in a study of another marginalised group, lesbian, gay, bisexual and transgender (LGBT) people, proposed the concept of 'minority stress' as a factor in poorer health outcomes experienced by minority groups, whose experiences of prejudice and discrimination result in a deleterious effect on their health and wellbeing.

Census 2011: Religious and Ethnic Demographics
The link below is to a Census 2011 report focusing on religion, ethnic or cultural background and the Irish Traveller community in Ireland. The findings relating to education outcomes in the Traveller community make for grim reading and highlight the need for universal access to early childhood education.
http://www.cso.ie/en/media/csoie/census/documents/census2011profile7/
Profile,7,Education,Ethnicity,and,Irish,Traveller,entire,doc.pdf

We're now going to examine another group in Ireland who have been and, arguably, continue to be marginalised and discriminated against. By the end of this section it will be clear how changes in cultural and societal attitudes can and have led to improvements in wellbeing and in health for those with disabilities.

Prejudice is a negative attitude towards a group; and **discrimination** is the behaviour that comes from that attitude. People with disabilities have suffered the most appalling prejudice and discrimination for centuries – this will become clear from the 1943 survey of learning disabilities we shall look at below. But does prejudice and discrimination affect health and wellbeing?

Cohort Effect and Disability

Glen Elder developed a theory to capture how social change can influence individuals' lives. It is called the **cohort effect** and it is 'one of the ways in which lives can be influenced by social change. History is experienced as a cohort effect when social change and culture differentiate the life patterns of successive cohorts' (Elder 2001, p.37).

What does this mean? Let's take the example of a child born with Down Syndrome in Ireland. Compare and contrast the likely experience of that child if they had been born in the 1940s. What do you imagine their life would have been like then?

Dr Louis Clifford: Survey of Learning Disability (1943)

The following is an extract from Griffin and Shevlin's 2007 book *Responding to Special Educational Needs: An Irish Perspective*. It highlights the attitudes and experience of those born with a disability in the 1940s:

> Having a disabled child, according to Clifford, was widely seen by parents of the time as a disgrace and a reflection on the family. The more affluent and socially superior the family, the more the condition was resented and abhorred. Families from lower socio-economic backgrounds were usually more philosophical about their misfortune. In his account, Dr Clifford records that disabled children were sometimes hidden away in top rooms and seldom taken out except at night. (Griffin & Shevlin 2007, p.39)

From this perspective, it would have been hard to imagine at the time that children and adults would be participating in an event such as the Special Olympics (the global Special Olympics began in 1968), yet change does occur.

Does a child born today with Down Syndrome face a different experience from that of a child born in the 1940s? If your answer is Yes, this represents the 'cohort effect' – the life experience of one generation differs from that of another, due to social changes. It also demonstrates the power and influence that social change can produce. This is particularly important in areas where people experience prejudice and discrimination, such as those with disabilities or marginalised groups.

One could argue that children are another group whose life experiences have improved from generation to generation, reflecting societal and cultural changes. Research is clearly showing that people with disabilities such as Down Syndrome have longer life expectancies and better health outcomes than previous generations. Mainstreaming in early education settings or primary schools is becoming a reality for some, though arguably not enough. Participation in sporting and social events such as the Special Olympics offers individuals with disabilities increased quality of life and improved wellbeing. This illustrates that we have the power to support and improve children's health and wellbeing through inclusive and supportive practices that embrace diversity.

Think about it!

Are there children from diverse backgrounds in your setting? What steps can you take to ensure that every child feels included and supported?

In Practice

To meet the needs of 'Identity and Belonging' and learning opportunities for toddlers, Aistear suggests using resources and materials which reflect toddlers' families, genders, abilities, backgrounds, and cultures:

- Provide books and puzzles which represent a variety of family types, homes and occupations, including those of the toddlers' parent/s, taking account of abilities, disabilities and cultures, beginning with who is in the setting and then extending it to the community
- Play with toddlers using dolls, including those with anatomically correct features that have a range of skin tones and hair types, provide a range of colours in crayons and paints, and encourage toddlers to show different skin tones in their pictures
- Play and respond to culturally appropriate and relevant music
- Read books about people of different appearances and abilities (including those with special needs), for example people who wear glasses or hearing aids, people

who use wheelchairs, crutches or Zimmer   e who are on the autistic
spectrum, or people with illnesses such as A   s or Parkinson's disease
- Plan the pretend play area to reflect the lifestyle of all toddlers attending, for example dress-up clothes, utensils, food, and cooking items in the pretend play area that are familiar to the toddlers, especially if they are from culturally diverse homes.

EDUCATION

UNCRC Article 29: Aims of Education

Education shall aim at developing the child's personality, talents and mental and physical abilities to the fullest extent. Education shall prepare the child for an active adult life in a free society and foster respect for the child's parents, his or her own cultural identity, language and values, and for the cultural background and values of others.

- *Ready to Learn:* White Paper on Early Childhood Education (DES 1999)
- *Síolta: the National Quality Framework for Early Childhood Education* (CECDE 2006)
- *Thematic Review of Early Childhood Education and Care Policy in Ireland* (OECD 2004)
- *Delivering Equality of Opportunity in Schools* (DEIS 2006)
- *Aistear: the Early Childhood Curriculum Framework* (NCCA 2009)
- *Developing the Workforce in the Early Childhood Care and Education Sector: Background Discussion Paper* (DES 2009)

Education is so central to child wellbeing outcomes that, along with the care of the child, education and learning are central to policy and practice. In Aistear, the curriculum for early years learning, education is pivotal. Education is enshrined in the UNCRC as a child's right. As we shall see, quality early years education is associated with better outcomes for children.

Is High-quality ECCE a Factor in Children's Wellbeing?

There is strong evidence that positive or negative consequences of care and education can last well into adulthood ... A recent review of the international literature, undertaken on behalf of the National Audit Office in the UK (2003), showed that high-quality childcare for disadvantaged children in the first three years of life resulted in benefits in the areas of cognitive, language and social development. This review also concluded, however, that low-quality childcare produced either no benefits or had negative effects. (DCYA 2006, p. 76)

The Effective Provision of Pre-School Education (EPPE) project, the first major European study of child development between the ages of 3 and 7, found that high-quality ECCE does impact positively on children's development. The study found that:

- Pre-school experiences (age 3–4) improved all-round development in children.
- Better intellectual development was associated with an earlier start (under age 3).
- Disadvantaged children benefited significantly from good quality pre-school experiences, especially where there was a mix of children from different backgrounds.
- High-quality pre-schooling is related to better intellectual and social/behavioural development for children.
- Settings that have staff with higher qualifications have higher-quality scores and their children make more progress. (Sylva *et al.* 2004)

Other studies have found additional positive outcomes for children who attend quality early childhood programmes, such as:

- Being better prepared to make the transition to school
- Being less likely to drop out of school or repeat
- Having greater access to health care and improved physical health.

Another important dimension of ECCE services is that they can produce a multiplier effect on the families of the children and on their communities. For example, studies have shown that mothers whose children participated in quality early child development programmes display lower levels of criminal behaviour and less behavioural impairment due to alcohol and drugs (NESF 2005).

We've seen that education plays a pivotal role in child outcomes. Now let's take another approach and explore how the lack of education is a risk factor in outcomes. We can see in everyday life that there is a direct relationship between poorer education and attainment for the individual: it's harder to get employment, to make enough money to maintain a comfortable lifestyle, and so on. However, the following piece of research demonstrates that there is an **intergenerational** impact. This means that a risk factor for one generation has a negative effect on the next generation.

Growing Up in Ireland (2010) Infant Cohort Key Findings – Pregnancy and Birth

Here are some of the findings of the national longitudinal study relating to the impact of level of maternal education on pregnancy and birth weight.

Mothers with the lowest education have the lightest babies:

- The average weight for babies at birth was 3.5 kg; 5% of babies could be classified as of 'low birth weight' (below 2.5 kg).
- On average, mothers with the lowest level of education tended to have slightly lighter babies. (ESRI/TCD 2010)

It's hard to imagine that a mother's level of education could affect the weight of her baby. Here is another opportunity to think of the **why**. How does education as a factor impact on birth weight? We need to think of the inter-relatedness and 'double jeopardy' of factors. If you have a lower education level, it's harder to find work; or perhaps the person left school early. Are people more likely to become involved in risky behaviours if they left school as young teenagers? Might they get involved in drug use? Smoking and drugs can result in low birth weight. Can you begin to see the complexity behind this finding?

Síolta and Aistear are both fundamental to education as a factor. Síolta provides standards to encourage quality in early years education; as we've seen, quality in education is central to ensuring successful outcomes for children. Aistear, the curriculum for early years, acts as a framework for practitioners to plan children's learning. Revisit Chapter 3 for a more in-depth discussion on these two policies.

In Practice: Features of 'Quality' in ECCE

The evidence shows that early care and education only has strong developmental benefits where it is of sufficient quality. The following features promote quality and meet the needs of the whole child:

- Young children having opportunities to make choices about their own activities and immediate environment and to make discoveries for themselves. In our vision, young children would be active participants in their own care and education.
- A central role for play, with a combination of child-led and adult-led play, and with lots of opportunities for outdoor activity, including exploration of nature and the local environment.
- Settings that are attractive, comfortable, homely and fun – not just safe – and in which young children are able to take risks: running, jumping, climbing, splashing, exploring ...
- Continuity for children in the adults around them, which is essential for young children to develop positive and trusting relationships. Continuity is helped by practices such as key-workers, high adult–child ratios, and low staff turnover.
- Support for parents to engage with and participate in services regularly, breaking down some of the boundaries between home and services outside the home.
- A strong emphasis on respect for diversity, including diversity in children's social and ethnic backgrounds and in their physical abilities, and also diversity in the workforce, including a much larger proportion of men in the workforce. (Start Strong 2010, p. 41)

It is interesting to note that several factors we have already discussed – role of parents, equality and diversity, environment and play – are featured here in relation to meeting needs and promoting quality.

> **_Think about it!_**
>
> Does the childcare environment in which you work promote the features outlined above? List how these needs are met and link them to Síolta and Aistear where possible. Are there features that could be improved upon? Draw up a list and the steps needed to improve them.

HEALTH

UNCRC Article 24: Health and health services

Children have the right to good quality health care – the best health care possible – to safe drinking water, nutritious food, a clean and safe environment, and information to help them stay healthy. Rich countries should help poorer countries achieve this.

- Child Care (Pre-School Services) Regulations 1996 and Child Care (Pre-School Services) (No. 2) Regulations 1997
- *Our Children – Their Lives: National Children's Strategy* (DoHC 2000)
- *Food and Nutrition Guidelines for Pre-school Services* (HPU 2013)
- Child Care (Pre-School Services) Regulations 2006
- *Immunisation Guidelines for Ireland*, 2013 (HSE 2013a)
- *Better Outcomes Brighter Futures: The National Policy Framework for Children and Young People 2014–2020* (DCYA 2014)
- *Healthy Ireland:* blueprint for improving the health outcomes of the nation (HSE 2013b)
- Introduction of free GP care for the under 5s.

Like education, health is a powerful factor in child wellbeing and development. Healthcare is recognised as central to developing babies, and the infant healthcare entitlements aimed at improving health outcomes include the following:

Maternity and Infant Care Scheme provides free antenatal and postnatal care in Ireland, mother and baby are entitled to two visits to a general practitioner (GP) after a baby is born, the first when the baby is two weeks old and the second at six weeks. At six weeks, the baby's weight, length, head circumference and hips are examined, along with an enquiry into their feeding patterns and general health.

Public Health Nurse & the Child Health Record. A public health nurse (PHN) visits parents of new infants in their homes shortly after discharge from hospital. In 2012, 83.6% of infants were visited by a PHN within 48 hours of discharge from hospital.

Immunisations. Under the Childhood Immunisation Programme, vaccinations are provided free of charge to all children in Ireland. The schedule for babies born since 1st July 2008 is as follows:

- At birth: The BCG vaccination (a vaccine to protect against tuberculosis) is normally administered in the maternity hospital where the baby is born.
- 2, 4 and 6 months: The '6 in 1' vaccination against diphtheria, tetanus, whooping cough (pertussis), polio and HiB (*Haemophilus influenzae* Type B) and Hepatitis B. Vaccination against Pneumococcal Disease is also administered at this time in a separate injection.
- At 4 months, the 6 in 1 is again administered along with a vaccine against Meningococcal C in a separate injection.
- At 6 months, the 6 in 1 is administered for the last time along with separate vaccines against Pneumococcal Disease and Meningococcal C.
- At 12–15 months: The MMR (measles, mumps and rubella) vaccine is administered along with a vaccine against Pneumococcal Disease.

In relation to other affluent countries, the uptake of immunisations in Ireland has not been good (UNICEF 2007). In 2006 the overall immunisation rate for 12-month-olds was 86%. [In 2012 this rate had risen to 90%.] (Greene 2009)

In Practice

'A person carrying on a pre-school service shall ensure that suitable, sufficient, nutritious and varied food is available for a pre-school child attending the service on a full-time basis' (Article 26 (1) of the Child Care Regulations 1996)

Food and Nutrition Guidelines – Key Recommendations:

Start with healthy eating for infants:

- Offer a wide variety of foods.
- Offer suitable sized portions.
- Offer healthy food choices and tooth-friendly drinks frequently.
- Accommodate special food needs of individual children.
- Plan healthy, varied meals and snacks.
- Help children learn to eat.
- Foster good dental health.
- Prepare food in a clean and safe way.
- Develop a healthy eating policy. (HPU 2013)

Our next factor is 'social services', but since this was dealt with in Chapter 6 we will consider it only briefly here.

SOCIAL SERVICES

UNCRC Article 26: Social security
Children – either through their guardians or directly – have the right to help from the government if they are poor or in need.
UNCRC Article 27: Adequate standard of living
Children have the right to a standard of living that is good enough to meet their physical and mental needs. Governments should help families and guardians who cannot afford to provide this, particularly with regard to food, clothing and housing.

As we can see, the UNCRC recognises the role of the State in supporting children, their development and outcomes. 'Social services' is a very broad category and typically refers to services provided by the government for the benefit of its citizens, for example education, housing and services to those who are especially vulnerable, such as the young and the elderly. Chapter 4 looked at the social work system and how failures in that system led to very negative outcomes for the children involved, e.g. in the Roscommon abuse case. A failure of social services is a risk factor; conversely, when social work departments are well run, adequately funded and meet the needs of vulnerable people, this is a protective factor. (For more on social services as a factor in outcomes, see Chapters 5 and 6.)

Access to education is also identified as a factor; as this book has made clear, education plays a pivotal role in influencing the lives of children and in their wellbeing. We have seen evidence of this in policy developments, where early education has become increasing prominent, and in initiatives such as the introduction of a free pre-school year and the implementation of Aistear, the early years curriculum; and we have seen the benefits accrued from ECCE in all aspects of child wellbeing.

Employment and social welfare entitlements that expectant parents and parents of infants can avail of include:
- Maternity leave and benefit
- Adoptive leave and benefit
- Parental leave
- Social assistance
- Child benefit and early childcare supplement.

For more information on these entitlements, see Greene (2009).

The resources and services made available by the State to its citizens have a real and tangible effect, especially in the realm of poverty. Child poverty is an indicator or measure used by GUI to track child wellbeing. So let's take a look of the impact of socio-economic status on development and wellbeing.

SOCIAL STATUS

UNCRC Article 6: Survival and development
Children have the right to live. Governments should ensure that children survive and develop healthily.

Socio-economic status (SES) is generally defined as the social class or standing of an individual or a group. It is often measured by a combination of income level, education and occupation. The impact of poverty on a child and their family can affect all areas of development; physical health, learning, social and emotional development. But is child poverty an issue in Ireland? Let's look at the figures.

Child Poverty:
- Almost 19% of children in Ireland aged 0–17 years are at risk of poverty.
- 8.7% of children are living in consistent poverty.
- In 2009, 210,000–220,000 children lived in households that were experiencing poverty.

According to the OECD:
- Government objectives should ensure that child benefits provide adequate income support for different family types and complement parental career prospects and publicly provided childcare.
- Ireland continues to spend well below the OECD average on family and in-kind services.
- The cost of childcare more than doubles the effective tax rates faced by low-wage parents and is a major barrier to work. (Social Justice Ireland 2011)

Poverty or low income levels are often cited as a critical factor. To illustrate this we are going to look at two powerful pieces of research that highlight the relationship between SES and low birth weight.

Low Birth Weight and Social Inequality

A report entitled *Unequal at Birth* (McAvoy 2006) outlines that social inequalities are shown in the incidence of low birth weight (LBW). In the report the indicator used for low birth weight babies was a weight less than 2500 grams (5½ pounds).

Certain women are especially vulnerable to poverty and social exclusion and are therefore likely to suffer health inequalities in relation to their pregnancy and their babies. These groups were identified and include teenage mothers, lone parents, disabled women, Travellers, refugees and asylum seekers, other ethnic minority women, women prisoners and homeless women. (McAvoy *et al.* 2006, p. 28)

It is evident that women in lower socioeconomic groupings are more likely to experience a teenage pregnancy and, as young mothers (aged 19 years or less), they are more likely to deliver a low birth-weight baby. Teenage pregnancies are associated with prematurity and the preterm delivery rate of teenagers far exceeded matched controls of women aged 20 – 24 years in one Irish maternity hospital. Almost ninety percent of attendees at a Dublin Adolescent Antenatal Booking Clinic were recorded as being in the lowest socio-economic group and most had poor educational attainment. 87% of these mothers had left school. It is also well recognised that pregnant schoolgirls suffered from poor housing, overcrowding and high unemployment rates (McAvoy *et al.* 2006, p. 23).

Using data from *Growing Up in Ireland*, Madden examined the relationship between LBW and SES: children who are LBW have poorer outcomes, including 'foetal and infant mortality, as well as with short- and long-term morbidity. In addition, there is fairly extensive evidence that LBW is also regarded as a risk factor for a number of health and non-health outcomes in later life' (2012, p. 2). In the table below, Madden analyses birthweight by social class, with 'no class' signifying that the person has never worked. Intrauterine growth restriction (IUGR) – poor growth of the baby in the womb – was also included, along with pre-term delivery and LBW.

BIRTHWEIGHT BY SOCIAL CLASS

	Professional, Managerial	Non-manual, Skilled manual	Semi-skilled Unskilled	No class
LBW (%)	5.18	5.49	6.89	9.35
Pre-term (%)	5.72	6.68	8.18	8.71
IUGR (%)	1.87	2.01	2.01	3.94

Source: Madden (2012).

As you can see from the table, these conditions are more prevalent in groups from lower SES. In relation to IUGR, Maddens points out that there is relatively little difference between the first three social class groupings, but there is a substantial jump for those who have never worked (no class). Overall, those in the 'lowest' SES are at higher risk of having a baby born with LBW or IUGR.

These pieces of research show how powerful social factors such as SES can be and how they can impact not just the individual, in this instance the mother, but also her baby – before it is even born. So, as we have seen, income, education, areas of poor housing or high unemployment can have a detrimental influence on an individual. A myriad of factors can influence a myriad of different outcomes and areas of development.

How do we measure these factors and track child wellbeing? We use **indicators**. For example, when the Census is held (every four years), we are asked to give information to help the statisticians create a 'picture' of our society, including how different outcomes, such as poverty, population figures and so on, affect the population. The study also uses indicators to track child outcomes.

INDICATORS OF CHILD HEALTH AND WELLBEING

At their simplest, indicators are measurements of the impact of a factor. For example, if we were looking at child health we might consider immunisation a factor that can influence a child's health outcomes. An indicator measuring immunisation would look at the percentage of children being immunised or the rate of measles, for example, to gauge the impact of the factor (immunisation) on children's health.

In developing *Growing Up in Ireland*, indicators measuring child wellbeing were chosen so as to obtain the best picture of child wellbeing. Below are the indicators initially chosen for the longitudinal study. The majority relate to general wellbeing; the remaining five relate to demographic patterns.

CHILD WELLBEING INDICATORS IN *GROWING UP IN IRELAND*

Abuse and Maltreatment	Enrolment in Education/Completion of School	Quality of Childhood Care and Education
Accessibility of Basic Health Services for Children and Young People	Environment and Places	Relationship with Parents and Family
Attendance at School	Health of the Infant at Birth	Relationships with Peers
Availability of Housing for Families with Children	Immunisation	Screening for Growth and Development
Children and Young People in Care	Mental Health	Self-Esteem
Chronic Health Conditions and Hospitalisation	Nutrition**	Self-Reported Happiness
Community Characteristics	Parental Time with Children	Sexual Health and Behaviour
Crimes Committed by Children and Young People	Participation in Decision-Making	Things to Do
Economic Security*	Pets and Animals	Use of Tobacco, Alcohol and Drugs
Enrolment in Childhood Care and Education	Public Expenditure on Services for Children and Young People	Values and Respect

* includes relative and consistent poverty

** includes eating habits, feeding practice and nutritional outcomes

Socio-Demographic Indicators:
- Child Population
- Family Structure
- Parental Education Level Attained
- Child Mortality
- Children and Young People with Additional Needs

Further information on the development of this set of child wellbeing indicators can be found in Hanafin and Brooks (2005), the National Children's Office (2005) and the most recent *State of the Nation's Children* report (2012).

BRONFENBRENNER'S ECOLOGICAL THEORY

Urie Bronfenbrenner (1917–2005) developed a theory that helps us make sense of the different layers or circles of factors that influence an individual's development. As you can see from the diagram, the nearest circle is that which has the most direct influence on the individual, their family. The circles move increasingly away from the individual, reflecting more indirect and subtle influence. So the circle after family contains peers and school. The next circle out contains community, with the circle furthest out including factors such as cultural attitudes or government policy that affects a child indirectly.

FIGURE 7.3 BRONFENBRENNER'S CIRCLES OF ENVIRONMENT

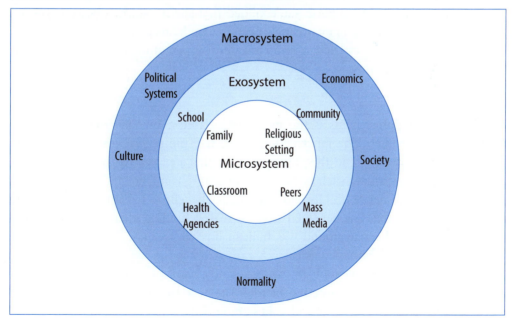

An ecological approach can be seen in the whole child perspective adopted by the National Children's Strategy (see Chapter 1) to understand children's development. The really clever aspect of this approach is that it encompasses the immediate environment of the child (parents, siblings) and more distant influences at the outer circle (ECCE policy, for example). By using Bronfenbrenner's model we can start to understand how distant and immediate factors can intertwine in influencing a child's outcomes. Let's look at a case study to illustrate this.

Case Study: Ecological Understanding and Interplay of Factors

Lily is 3 years old and lives in a neighbourhood that falls under DEIS: it suffers from economic and social deprivation, including high unemployment levels, addiction and poverty. Lily lives with her mum and younger brother Darren who is 1. Lily's dad isn't around and she misses him when the other children talk about their fathers. The flat they live in is damp and cold – Lily's mum, Susie, struggles to find the money to pay for heating. Lily has had continual chest infections and was recently diagnosed with asthma. Susie cannot work because: Lily is often sick; childcare is too expensive; and she would lose her benefits for no financial gain. It is difficult enough for her to feed and clothe the children as it is. Susie can't afford to buy her children many treats, like toys, and the playground that was built in the area has been vandalised.

Lily has started to attend your crèche under the free pre-school year, but she misses days due to being sick. Lately you have noticed Lily has become quieter and withdrawn; when you mentioned this to Susie she confided that she herself had been diagnosed with depression and is feeling increasingly overwhelmed. Susie has few social supports or friends and is feeling isolated. You are aware of a parenting support intervention available in the community.

External Influences

- **Government policy:** This is the most distant factor, but one that affects Lily's wellbeing outcomes. The introduction of the free pre-school year has given Lily the opportunity to attend the crèche. Why is this a protective factor? Child and parenting interventions, such as Early Start or Springboard, are initiatives that could have a direct influence on Lily and a secondary benefit to her through supporting her mum. The area has benefited from increased funding after being designated a DEIS area; and a playground was built in line with *Ready, Steady, Play!* to give children outdoor play experiences.
- **Community and pre-school:** In this case study, would you identify 'community' as a **risk factor** or a **protective factor**? The risk factors include poverty, high unemployment and low levels of cohesion, and these are associated with poorer outcomes. There is a lack of play opportunities in the area since the playground was vandalised. Poor housing is a risk factor and is contributing to Lily's health

problems. Can you see anything protective in Lily's community? Well, there is a high-quality crèche, which is protective; and there are family interventions in the community that could be accessed.

Immediate Influences

We can see that the circle of influence closest to Lily has the most direct impact upon her. Let's look at this from a few different angles:

- **Relationship with parent:** What are the protective influences? Are there any negative aspects?
- **Physical health and wellbeing:** Lily's physical environment in her home is not conducive to general wellbeing. Is this a risk factor? Is it contributing to her health problems?
- **Social relationships:** Susie doesn't have a strong social network of family and friends, so Lily is missing out on what can be a protective factor. However, now that she is attending the crèche she has the opportunity to develop friendships with other children.
- **Poverty:** Lily lives in an impoverished family and in a community of social and economic deprivation. In her home she sometimes goes cold and doesn't have a lot of toys to play with as her mum can't afford much. In her community the playground that was built has been vandalised, so she has no real outdoor space to play in. Living in poor housing has led to her health problems, which in turn means that she often misses pre-school; this could impact on her learning potential.

Can you see the different layers of factors and influences intertwining with each other and affecting Lily's outcomes? A lack of expenditure at government level has led to poor housing, which in turn has directly affected Lily's physical health.

Hopefully you can use this approach to understand how influences that appear distant, such as government policy and funding, have a real impact on child wellbeing; and that factors interplay with one another rather than operating in isolation. The policies you studied earlier in this book should now seem more relevant to child health and wellbeing.

References

Brady, B., Dolan, P. and Canavan, J. (2004) *Working for Children and Families: Exploring Good Practice*. Dublin: Department of Health and Children, http://health.gov.ie/wp-content/uploads/2014/03/Working-for-children-and-families-exploring-good-practice.pdf

Bronfenbrenner, U. (2005) *Making Human Beings Human: Bioecological Perspectives on Human Development*. London: Sage

CECDE (Centre for Early Child Development and Education) (2004) *Strategy for Strengthening Families*. Dublin: CECDE

CECDE (2006) *Síolta: the National Quality Framework for Early Childhood Education*. Dublin: CECDE, http://www.siolta.ie

Commission on the Family (1998) *Strengthening Families for Life: Final Report of the Commission on the Family*. Dublin: Department of Social, Community and Family Affairs

Costello, L. (1999) *A Literature Review of Children's Well-being*. Dublin: Combat Poverty Agency, http://www.combatpoverty.ie/publications/ALiteratureReviewOfChildrensWellbeing_1999.pdf

CSO (Central Statistics Office) (2012) *Religion, Ethnicity and Irish Travellers*, Profile 7. Dublin: Stationery Office, http://www.cso.ie/en/media/csoie/census/documents/census2011profile7/Profile,7,Education,Ethnicity,and,Irish,Traveller,entire,doc.pdf

DCYA (Department of Children and Youth Affairs) (2006, 2012) *State of the Nation's Children*. Dublin: DCYA. 2006: http://www.dcya.gov.ie/documents/Publications/SONC_final.pdf; 2012: http://www.dcya.gov.ie/documents/research/StateoftheNationsChildren2012.pdf

DCYA (2014) *Better Outcomes Brighter Futures: The National Policy Framework for Children and Young People 2014–2020*, http://dcya.gov.ie/documents/cypp_framework/BetterOutcomesBetterFutureReport.pdf

DES (Department of Education and Science) (1999) *Ready to Learn*: White Paper on Early Childhood Education, http://www.education.ie/en/Publications/Policy-Reports/Ready-to-Learn-White-Paper-on-Early-Childhood-Education.pdf

DES (2009) *Developing the Workforce in the Early Childhood Care and Education Sector: Background Discussion Paper*. Dublin: DES

DoHC (Department of Health and Children) (2000) *Our Children – Their Lives: National Children's Strategy*. Dublin: Stationery Office, http://www.dcya.gov.ie/documents/Aboutus/stratfullenglishversion.pdf

Elder, G.H. (2001) 'Human Lives in Changing Societies: Life Course and Developmental Insights' in R. Cairns, G.H. Elder and E.J. Costello (eds), *Developmental Science*. Cambridge: Cambridge University Press

ESRI (Economic and Social Research Institute) and TCD (Trinity College Dublin). *Growing Up in Ireland: National Longitudinal Study of Children*. Dublin: Department of Children and Youth Affairs, http://www.growingup.ie

Fahey, T., Keilthy, P. and Polek, E. (2012) *Family Relationships and Family Wellbeing: A Study of the Families of Nine-Year-Olds in Ireland*. Dublin: University College Dublin and the Family Support Agency, http://www.ucd.ie/news/2013/01JAN13/docs/Family_Relationships_and_Family_Wellbeing_Dec_2012.pdf

Gilligan, R. (1995) 'Family Support and Child Welfare: Realising the Promise of the Child Care Act', in H. Ferguson and P. Kenny (eds) *On Behalf of the Child: Child Welfare, Child Protection and the Child Care Act*. Dublin: Farmer

Greene, S., Williams, J., Doyle, E., Harris, E., McCrory, C., Murray, A., Swords, L., Thornton, M., Quail, A., Layte, R., O'Dowd, T., Whelan., C.T. (2009) *Growing Up in Ireland: Review of the Literature Pertaining to the First Wave of Data Collection with the Infant Cohort at 9 Months.* Dublin: ESRI, TCD, OMCYA, http://www.esri. ie/Childrens_Longitudinal_Study/news_publications/publications_-_infant_coh/ Review_of_the_Literature_Pertaining_to_the_First_Wave_of_Data_Collection_ with_the_Infant_Cohort_at_9_Months.pdf

Griffin, S. and Shevlin, M. (2007) *Responding to Special Educational Needs: An Irish Perspective.* Dublin: Gill & Macmillan

Hanafin, S. and Brooks, A.M. (2005), *Report on the Development of a National Set of Child Well-Being Indicators in Ireland.* Dublin: National Children's Office, http:// www.dcya.gov.ie/documents/research/ReportonDevelopmentWelBeingIndicators. pdf

Holt, S., Manners, P. and Gilligan, R. (2002) *An Evaluation of the Naas Child and Family Project: A Springboard Initiative.* Kildare Youth Services and South Western Health Board

HPU (Health Promotion Unit) (2013) Food and Nutrition Guidelines for Pre-School Services, http://health.gov.ie/wp-content/uploads/2014/03/Food-and-Nutrition-Guidelines-for-Pre-School-Services.pdf

HSE (Health Service Executive) (2013a) *Immunisation Guidelines for Ireland.* Dublin: HSE, http://www.hse.ie/eng/health/immunisation/hcpinfo/guidelines/

HSE (2013b) *Healthy Ireland: A Framework for Improved Health and Wellbeing 2013–2025,* Dublin: HSE, http://www.hse.ie/eng/services/publications/corporate/hieng.pdf

Irish College of Psychiatrists (2005) *A Better Future Now: Position Statement on Psychiatric Services for Children and Adolescents in Ireland.* Dublin: Irish College of Psychiatrists, retrieved from: http://www.rcpsych.ac.uk/files/pdfversion/op60.pdf

Irwin, L.G., Siddiqi, A. and Hertzman, C. (2007) *Early Child Development: A Powerful Equalizer: Final Report for the World Health Organization's Commission on the Social Determinants of Health,* http://www.who.int/social_determinants/resources/ecd_ kn_report_07_2007.pdf

Madden, D. (2012) *The Relationship Between Low Birthweight and Socioeconomic Status in Ireland,* Working Paper Series 14. Dublin: UCD Centre for Economic Research, http://www.ucd.ie/t4cms/WP12_14.pdf

Maycock, P., Bryan, A., Carr, N. and Kitching, K. (2009) *Supporting LGBT Lives: A Study of the Mental Health and Wellbeing of Lesbian, Gay, Bisexual and Transgender People.* Dublin: Gay and Lesbian Equality Network and BeLonGTo Youth Services

McAleese, M. (2011), address to the Tallaght West Child Development Initiative (TWCDI) event, The Story So Far, 19 September

McAvoy, H., Sturley, J., Burke, S. and Balanda, K. (2006) *Unequal at Birth: Inequalities in the Occurrence of Low Birthweight Babies in Ireland.* Institute of Public Health in Ireland

McPherson, K., Kerr, S., McGee, E., Cheater, F. and Morgan, A. (2013) *The Role and Impact of Social Capital on the Health and Wellbeing of Children and Adolescents: A Systematic Review*. Glasgow: Glasgow Centre for Population Health

National Children's Office (2004) *Ready, Steady, Play! A National Play Policy*. Dublin: Department of Health and Children, http://www.dcya.gov.ie/documents/publications/NCOPlayPolicy_eng.pdf

National Children's Office (2005) *The Development of a National Set of Child Well-Being Indicators: Executive Summary*. Dublin: National Children's Office, http://www.dcya.gov.ie/documents/publications/Executive_Summary_Child_Well_Being_Indicators.pdf

NCCA (National Council for Curriculum and Assessment) (2009a) *Aistear: the Early Childhood Curriculum Framework*. Dublin: NCCA

NCCA (2009b) *Aistear: Guidelines for Good Practice*. Dublin: NCCA, http://www.ncca.biz/aistear/pdfs/guidelines_eng/guidelines_eng.pdf

NCCA (2009c) *Aistear: Principles and Themes*. Dublin: NCCA, http://www.ncca.biz/aistear/pdfs/PrinciplesThemes_ENG/PrinciplesThemes_ENG.pdf

NCCA (2009d) *Aistear: Building Partnerships between Parents and Practitioners*. Dublin: NCCA, http://www.ncca.biz/aistear/pdfs/Guidelines_ENG/Practitioners_ENG.pdf

NESF (National Economic and Social Forum) (2005) *Early Childhood Care and Education*, Report 31. Dublin: NESF

Nic Gabhainn, S. and Sixsmith, J. (2005) *Children's Understandings of Wellbeing*. Dublin: National Children's Office, http://www.omc.gov.ie/documents/research/ChildrenUnderstandingofWellbeing.pdf

OECD (2004) *Thematic Review of Early Childhood Education and Care Policy in Ireland*. Dublin: Department of Education and Science, http://dccc.purposemakers.net/wp-content/uploads/2009/12/OECD-Thematic-Review-Early-Childhood.pdf

OMC (Office of the Minister for Children) (2006) *Diversity and Equality Guidelines for Childcare Providers*. Dublin: OMC

Pavee Point Traveller and Roma Centre (2010) *Our Geels – All Ireland Traveller Health Study*. Dublin: Pavee Point, http://www.paveepoint.ie/resources/our-geels-all-ireland-traveller-health-study/

RCN (Royal College of Nursing) (2004) *Transcultural Health Care Practice with Children and their Families*. London: RCN, http://www.rcn.org.uk/development/learning/transcultural_health/transcultural/childhealth/sectionone

Social Justice Ireland (2011) *Child Poverty Policy Issues: Briefing for Joint Oireachtas Committee on Health and Children*. Dublin: Social Justice Ireland, http://www.oireachtas.ie/parliament/media/committees/healthandchildren/J20-Social-Justice-Ireland---Briefing.pdf

Start Strong (2010) *Planning Now for the Future: Children's Early Care and Education in Ireland*, http://www.startstrong.ie/files/Children_2020_Planning_Now_for_the_ Future.pdf

Sylva, K., Melhuish, E., Sammons, P., Siraj-Blatchford, I., Taggart, B. (2004) *The Effective Provision of Pre-School Education (EPPE) Project: Final Report.* London: Institute of Education

WHO (World Health Organisation) *World Health Statistics.* Geneva: WHO Global Health Observatory

CHAPTER 8

The Development of the Professional Practitioner

INTRODUCTION

A clear understanding of the requirements for professional practice and personal learning and development are key to the provision of quality childcare, so in this chapter we shall go beyond the basic requirements of Module 6N of the Childhood Social, Legal and Health Studies course. You will find that there is considerable overlap with **Work Experience 6N1947**, which is a mandatory module, and **Personal and Professional Development 6N1949**. We will cross-reference to enable you to use the work you undertake for other modules.

As an early years practitioner you must first have an understanding of what is required; then undertake an assessment of your current knowledge, skills and attitudes in relation to identified criteria; from which you can then draw up your learning goals and what you need to do to achieve those goals.

There is an ever-expanding body of knowledge in this field, and we do not have space in this book to give it justice. We view this chapter as a starting point from which we encourage you to go and explore the wealth of knowledge available to you.

In Chapter 1, we referred to the emergence of the role of the childcare worker as a professional. Historically the childcare worker was seen very much as a carer/childminder; the role was not to provide formal education for the child/children but to 'mind' them in a safe and caring environment.

With the development of the sector and also our understanding of the needs of children, this is most definitely no longer the case. Recognition of the value of the role played by early years practitioners has certainly increased. Barnardos cite work by Graham (2008), Melhuish (2004) and Mathers *et al.* (2007) in support of this. As we have seen in this book, many national and local initiatives have contributed to the quality and professionalisation of the sector; these initiatives include City and County Childcare Committees, Aistear, Síolta and the expanding role of voluntary organisations such as Barnardos and Early Childhood Ireland.

The role of the early years practitioner is to work in partnership with parents/carers to identify each child's uniqueness and the needs they have as a person. Síolta encapsulates in its Standards (particularly Standards 3, 4, 5, 11 and 12) a core emphasis on the importance of professional practice and partnership in supporting the child's holistic development.

We are all in no doubt that our aim is to provide a service in which the children are seen as unique people with individual needs which we work towards achieving in our daily practice. The child's needs are paramount and the environment we provide for them must be inclusive and constantly supportive to both them and their families. A love of children and a fascination for how they think and behave are vital requirements for anyone working in the childcare field. In addition, a vast body of knowledge supports the view that education and training are essential to enable the early years practitioner to become the 'expert' needed to manage the demands of the service today. The Tickell Review of early childhood education (Tickell 2010) highlights the link between a strong, experienced, well-qualified supported workforce and educational outcomes of the children in the service.

Siraj-Blatchford (2000, cited in Barnardos) stated that 'pedagogy requires shared knowledge and also practical experience which includes opportunities for reflection and the vital role of working in collaboration with all stakeholders including parents and families.'

KEY DOCUMENTS

We will begin by reviewing a number of documents which help to highlight key areas in relation to knowledge and skills for development. It is **imperative** that you as a childcare practitioner have the **knowledge, understanding and ability to see how you can apply the proposals for 'best practice' in your ECCE setting**.

1. *Model Framework for Education, Training and Professional Development in the ECCE Sector* (DJELR 2002)
2. *Workforce Development Plan for the Early Childhood Care and Education Sector* (DES 2010)
3. *Right From the Start* (DCYA 2013)

1. Model Framework

The *Model Framework for Education, Training and Professional Development in the ECCE Sector* (DJELR 2002) identified core values and standards for the profession. The aim was to facilitate the development of a unique professional identity for all practitioners, while allowing for and respecting the diversity of service provision and professional practice that currently exists.

FIGURE 8.1 AREAS OF CORE KNOWLEDGE AND SKILLS FOR AN EARLY YEARS PRACTITIONER

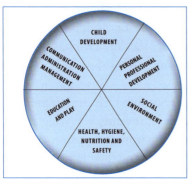

Figure 8.1 identifies the core knowledge and skills that an effective early years practitioner needs. The modules included in the FETAC awards in Early Years Care and Education Levels 5 and 6 address all these areas.

We will take the theme of child development in the *Model Framework* to demonstrate the depth of knowledge and understanding required. It is important that you spend time reviewing this document further to increase your depth of understanding of the level of knowledge required for the different levels of practitioner.

Child Development
Child development includes:
- The study of theories of development and learning, including the domains and stages of development from conception through to age eight
- The study of the process of development in both normative and atypical development
- Study of the influence of environmental, biological, social, and cultural influences on growth and development
- The roles and responsibilities of parents and early childhood educators in providing developmentally appropriate experiences to facilitate the potential development of each child
- Methods and importance of child observation
- Education and play, including:
  - Theories and processes of learning in early childhood
  - Approaches to curriculum for early childhood
  - Processes involved in curriculum development
  - The role and importance of play. (DJLER 2002)

Recommended knowledge includes the following.
Education and play:
- Theories of education and play and the process of children's learning
- Pedagogy

- Curriculum development
- The role of play in the child's learning experience.

Social environment:
The significance of social knowledge and experiences in the development of social competencies in children, including the following:
- Social skills
- Initiating interactions
- Maintaining relationships
- Dealing with conflict
- The role of early years practitioners and parents in supporting the child's social and emotional development by acting as positive role models.

Health, hygiene, nutrition and safety:
- Knowledge of relevant theory and legislation related to promotion of welfare and well-being of children
- Knowledge and ability to implement the relevant health safety and hygiene policies
- Planning and promotion of a safe and secure environment
- Knowledge of and ability to complete appropriate record-keeping procedures, e.g. documenting and reporting accidents, procedures for reporting and recording of illness and child protection issues.

Personal/professional development:
- Independent learning skills
- Ability to identify and engage in opportunities for ongoing reflection and sharing of knowledge with colleagues and others
- Development of key skills, e.g. literacy, numeracy, independent learning skills.

Communications management and administration, including:
- Understanding the importance of interaction with babies and young children in ways that encourage them to communicate their thoughts and feelings
- Planning an environment that provides materials and activities to promote communication skills
- Maintaining effective two-way communication between staff and families
- Efficient record-keeping systems that provide confidential information about children and their families.

The *Model Framework* emphasises that initial education is only the starting point – it covers the many different kinds of knowledge and understanding in the field of ECCE – but continuing professional development (CPD), which includes time to reflect on practice, is vital for the development of the professional practitioner (Fisher 2002).

In Practice

Reflect on the core knowledge and skills above in relation to yourself and your colleagues and identify key areas that you consider to be lacking in your early years setting. Then identify possible strategies for meeting these areas of deficit.

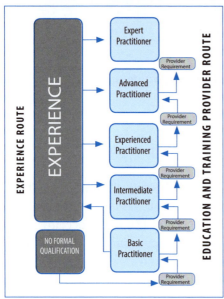

FIGURE 8.2 A MODEL FRAMEWORK FOR EDUCATION, TRAINING AND PROFESSIONAL DEVELOPMENT

In undertaking a self-assessment, which we will explore later in this chapter, the *Framework*, in particular Figure 8.2, provides us with some very clear guidance on the breadth and depth of knowledge the practitioner at each level should have. The second document we shall consider offers suggestions on how the early years practitioner can be supported to achieve the level of education required.

Table of occupational profiles and descriptors

Occupational profile	Intellectual skills/attributes	Processes	Accountability
Basic Practitioner	Elementary understanding of core knowledge areas. Ability to apply solutions to familiar problems. Ability to receive and pass on information.	Ability to carry out routine tasks. Basic competence in a range of clearly defined operations.	Directed activity under supervision. Reliance on external monitoring and quality control.
Intermediate Practitioner	Broad range of core knowledge with some depth. Ability to interpret and reflect on information. Well-developed range of practical skills.	Ability to carry out varied range of tasks in a limited range of different contexts.	Responsibility for own actions under direction. Some responsibility for quality of services within prescribed guidelines.
Experienced Practitioner	Broad range of core knowledge with greater depth. Ability to acquire specialist theoretical knowledge in one area. Ability to access, evaluate, compare and interpret information. Well-developed range of skills and ability to employ in complex non-routine situations.	Ability to select from a broad range of skills appropriate to context. Present information to audience.	Operate with full autonomy with broad guidance/ evaluation. Responsibility for quality of services in accordance with specified standards. Limited responsibility for work of others.
Advanced Practitioner	In-depth understanding of comprehensive body of knowledge. Expertise in particular area of knowledge. Generate responses, demonstrating some innovation, to challenging situations. Analyse, evaluate and interpret a wide range of information.	Perform effectively in a wide range of contexts involving creative and non-routine activities. Use judgement in planning, selecting or presenting information, methods or resources.	Full autonomy and responsibility for own for actions and those of others. Responsibility for meeting required quality standards.
Expert Practitioner	Mastery of complex theoretical knowledge. Ability to critically evaluate knowledge, concepts, and practice. Expertise in research, policy development.	Apply diagnostic and creative skills in a wide range of situations. Engage in planning, policy development, and management. Engagement in research, publication and dissemination of knowledge and skills.	Complete autonomy in professional activities. Responsibility for achieving personal and group outcomes. Accountability for all decision-making.

FIGURE 8.3 OCCUPATIONAL PROFILES

2. Workforce Development Plan

The *Workforce Development Plan for the Early Childhood Care and Education Sector* (DES 2010) states that:

> The early years workforce should be supported to achieve qualifications (appropriate to their occupational role and profile) that equip them with the skills, knowledge, competencies, values and attitudes to:
> - Deliver high quality, enriching early childhood care and education experiences for all children aged birth to six years.
> - Work effectively with parents and guardians in a mutually supportive partnership towards achieving positive outcomes for children.
> - Engage in interdisciplinary professional work practices designed to support the delivery of consistent quality in the early childhood service provision experiences of young children and their families. (DES 2010)

In Practice

Five years on from the publication of the document, do you think that your service is meeting these expectations?

3. Right from the Start

Right from the Start (DCYA 2013), a strategy document developed by the Expert Advisory Group, deals with a wide range of issues pertinent to the ECCE setting and, in particular, highlights implications for training and continuing development. As you read through our highlights of the document you will gain an insight into the key areas of focus for development. The document is a comprehensive piece of work, providing a great deal of guidance and recommendations for the care and education of children aged 0–6 years.

The strategy identifies key themes for the next five years:
- Theme 1: Economic rationale for increased investment
- Theme 2: Supporting families
- Theme 3: Health and wellbeing
- Theme 4: Access to services and inclusion
- Theme 5: Quality in services and supports
- Theme 6: Training and professional development
- Theme 7: Regulation and support
- Theme 8: Governance
- Theme 9: Information, research and data
- Theme 10: Implementation

In dealing with Theme 6: Training and professional development, the Expert Advisory Group recommends the following:

- **Implement the recommendations of the recent Core Report**, in particular through moving to a situation in which at least 60% of those working in pre-school early care and education services are qualified to degree-level, including equally those working with under-3s and those working with over-3s.
- **Introduce a training fund** to enable those working in early care and education services to gain additional training and provide for regular, funded non-contact time to ensure staff can engage in continuing professional development.
- **Undertake and follow through on a review of the extent to which Ireland has a 'competent system' in early care and education**, including in relation to training requirements for service managers (leadership and management) and in relation to the qualifications and training of trainers themselves (teaching as well as early education qualifications), with a view to ensuring a systemic approach to achieving higher quality standards.
- **Support professionalisation through higher wages in early care and education services by requiring adherence to an agreed salary scale as a condition of public funding**, e.g. through reform of the higher capitation grant. The salary scale should encompass all levels of practitioner, with graduate salaries comparable to those for related professionals, including primary school teachers.
- **Review graduate training options and requirements for all professionals working with young children and their families** (including nurses, doctors, all children's inspectorates, early care and education workers, managers and primary school teachers) to ensure that appropriate specialist training is available, including training that is specific to early childhood and to the management and supervision of staff working with young children.
- **Ensure that all those working with young children and their families are required and supported to undertake regular continuing professional development** to ensure that their knowledge of international standards, best practice and current national policy changes are up to date. Ensure that funded support structures are in place so that all those working with young children and their families can take part in continuing professional development. (DCYA 2013)

In Practice

What effect do you think implementing the above recommendations will have on your early years setting? Are the opportunities for training and development adequate to meet these recommendations? Can you suggest anything that would improve opportunities for early years practitioners in your setting?

KEY KNOWLEDGE, SKILLS AND ATTITUDES FOR PROFESSIONAL PRACTICE

Recent policy developments promote the importance of regarding the early childhood period from birth to six years as a continuum in a child's life, during which the child has both care and education needs. *Ready to Learn*, the White Paper on Early Childhood Education (DES 1999), made a clear commitment to:

> Support the development and educational achievement of children through high quality early education, with particular focus on the target groups of the disadvantaged and those with special needs. (DES 1999, p. 14)

It goes on to identify the characteristics of this early education as being underpinned by quality, built on existing provision, and in partnership with parents, providers and interested parties. Early intervention is identified as essential, particularly for those children at risk of educational disadvantage (DES 1999, p. 5).

Emergence of a Professional Association

An important development in ECCE practice in Ireland was the emergence of a professional association. In 2007, the Association of Childhood Professionals (ACP) was established with the following aims:

- To define a professional identity for people working in the early years and school-aged childcare sector
- To form a body to which workers can affiliate
- To advocate for the rights of its members to equitable pay and work conditions
- To promote, develop and support the continuing professional development of childcare professionals.

In Practice

Were you aware that that there is a professional association for early years practitioners? How do you think such an association can enhance the development of professional practice?

Síolta

Síolta (CECDE 2006) is the **Quality Framework** which must guide and be overtly evident in every aspect of our practice in the early years setting. Síolta's Standard 11 deals with professionalism in the sector.

Standard 11: Professional Practice
Practising in a professional manner requires that individuals have skills,

knowledge, values and attitudes appropriate to their role and responsibility within the setting. In addition, it requires regular refection upon practice and engagement in supported, ongoing professional development.

Achieving this standard requires that adults are encouraged and appropriately resourced to engage in a wide variety of regular and ongoing professional development.

Component 11.1 All adults working within the setting can provide evidence that they have achieved levels of skills and knowledge appropriate to their role and responsibilities

Signpost for reflection: What levels of qualifications have been attained by adults working in the setting?

Component 11.2 All adults subscribe to a set of core principles, which inform all aspects of their practice in early childhood care and education settings.

Signpost for reflection: What are the key principles which guide and determine practice in your setting?

Component 11.3 The setting supports and promotes regular opportunity for practitioners to reflect upon and review their practice and contribute positively to the development of quality practice in the setting.

Signpost for reflection: What processes are in place to allow practitioners time to reflect on their own practice, in order to identify areas where obtaining additional knowledge or changing approaches is necessary?

Component 11.4 Adults within the setting are encouraged and appropriately resourced to engage in a wide variety of regular and ongoing professional development.

Signpost for reflection: In what type of professional development activity do adults working in the setting participate? (CECDE 2006)

In Practice

What resources are available to support staff development in your work setting? Can you suggest what further opportunities need to be available to staff to enable them to fully implement Síolta?

UNDERTAKING A SELF-ASSESSMENT

It is necessary to undertake a range of assessments in order to determine what skills and knowledge you have at this point in your professional career and then plot what you need to develop further as a professional practitioner. You will need to undertake a skills and knowledge inventory and from that set your learning goals.

Levels of Learning

First it is helpful to spend a little time exploring the concept of 'levels of learning'. In the 1950s, Benjamin Bloom, an educational psychologist, came up with a taxonomy (categorisation) of learning, which was further developed in the 1990s by Anderson and others (see, for example, Anderson & Krathwohl 2001). It provides us with a useful way to examine categories of knowledge, skills and attitudes. The idea is that you must achieve each level before you can move up to the next rung on the 'ladder' of learning.

FIGURE 8.4 BLOOM'S TAXONOMY OF LEARNING

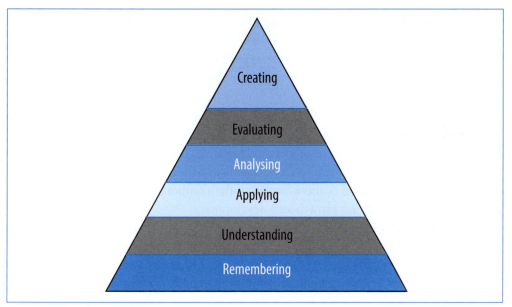

Source: Overbaugh & Schultz

On the bottom rung is **remembering** – we learn something and retain it in our memory. The next level is **understanding** – we not only remember but understand the relevance of the information. Level three is **applying** – we remember the information, we understand it and we can apply the information in a practical way. At the fourth level – **analysis** – we are competent in the first three levels and can now understand what has happened when we look back at an action, e.g. what went well, what went wrong, how it could be improved. The level of **evaluating** follows analysis – we can determine the success of what we have done and decide what we will do should the same situation arise to help ensure a more positive outcome. **Creating** is much more complex – we develop a new concept based on what we have learned.

Here are some examples:

Example 1: Fire Evacuation

- **Remembering:** The ability to recall the policy in case of fire.
- **Understanding:** Being able to explain the policy to another person, including the steps to be taken in the event of a fire
- **Applying:** Being able to put the policy into practice when a fire evacuation is necessary.
- **Analysing:** Reflecting on how the evacuation went and whether the policy worked in practice.
- **Evaluating:** Deciding what changes need to be made to the policy to make it better.
- **Creating:** Rewriting the policy so that it works more effectively.

As our cognitive ability develops, we ascend the ladder.

Example 2: Nutrition

We can also use the ladder to look at meal time for a group of children aged 1–3 years.

- **Remembering:** The practitioner remembers that it is very important for children to have a good lunch.
- **Understanding:** The practitioner studied nutrition in the Child Health and Wellbeing module Level 5 and is aware of the components of a well-balanced diet and their importance for growth and development.
- **Applying:** The practitioner knows that not all children like the same foods, so a range of foods must be offered to children to ensure that they do actually eat a well-balanced, nutritional meal. He/she will encourage children to choose what they would like from a range of foods and supervise them to ensure they eat.
- **Analysing:** One child is not eating their lunch, despite being encouraged to do so. The practitioner sits beside him and observes him closely; she does not assume that he does not like the food or does not feel hungry – he usually has a good appetite. She notices that he is a little pale and when she takes his hand it is hot. She asks him if he feels unwell and he says yes.
- **Evaluating:** From the information she has gathered she judges that the child is sick.
- **Creating:** The practitioner will offer the child a cool drink and some light food, which may tempt him to eat. She does not want him to become dehydrated and knows that even though he is unwell he needs some calories to provide him with energy to fight the possible infection.

So we have identified that cognitive ability develops over time with increasing knowledge and experience. FETAC have produced a most valuable tool which identifies the range of abilities at FETAC level 5 and 6. Here we suggest that you consider what you can do/achieve already and what you wish to achieve.

LEARNING STYLES

There is a considerable body of knowledge about how individuals learn most effectively. Having some basic understanding of how we learn can help us plan learning opportunities and identify the learning method most suited to each of us. It is also very important to a facilitator to support the learning of others (students and practitioners on the team) to better understand their needs.

The most common classifications of learning styles are: left and right brain; and auditory, visual and kinaesthetic.

Left and Right Brain

According to Rose and Nicholl (1997), the left side of the brain specialises in academic thought, e.g. maths and language, logical thought, sequence and analysis; the right side is concerned with creative activities such as music, rhythm and visual impressions. The table illustrates how the two sides of the brain differ.

LEFT AND RIGHT BRAIN

Left (Analytic)	Right (Global)
Predominantly left-brained people prefer a slow step-by-step build-up of information; they are sometimes called 'linear' learners	Predominantly right-brained people need to see the big picture, to have an overview; they are the 'global' type of learner
Successive hemispheric style	Simultaneous hemispheric style
Verbal	Visual
Responds to word meaning	Responds to tone of voice
Sequential	Random
Processes information linearly	Processes information in varied order
Responds to logic/logical	Responds to emotion/intuitive
Rational	Holistic
Objective	Subjective
Analytical	Synthesising
Plans ahead	Impulsive
Recalls people's names	Recalls people's faces
Speaks with few gestures	Gestures when speaking
Punctual	Less punctual
Looks at parts	Looks at wholes
Prefers formal study design	Prefers sound/music background while studying
Prefers bright lights while studying	Prefers frequent mobility while studying

Source: adapted from www.mathpower.com/brain.htm; www.funderstanding.com/right_left_brain.cfm

Most individuals have a distinct preference for one style; a minority of people are equally adept at both.

Auditory, Visual and Kinaesthetic

FIGURE 8.5 AUDITORY, VISUAL AND KINAESTHETIC LEARNING STYLES

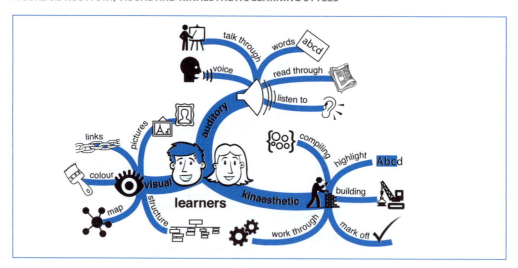

Research by Bandler, Grinder and Grinder (1990, cited by British Council (website)) identified three distinct learning and communication styles: auditory, visual and tactile/kinaesthetic.

Visual Learners

Visual learners absorb information most effectively when it is in a written format, e.g. notes, diagrams and pictures. These learners need to see the tutor's body language and facial expression to fully understand the content of a lesson. They may think in pictures and learn best from visual displays, including:

- Notes on a flip chart
- Handouts to follow during class
- Text books with illustrations
- PowerPoint presentations
- Videos reinforcing information

Visual learners tend to find it most helpful to absorb information if they take detailed notes at a lecture, even when they are provided with lecture notes. Visual learners make up around 65 per cent of the population.

Auditory Learners

Auditory learners learn through listening. They learn best through spoken lectures, discussions, talking things through and listening to what others have to say. Auditory learners listen carefully to tone of voice, speed, pitch and other subtle cues in an oral presentation. They often benefit from reading text aloud and using a tape recorder. They will tend to listen to a lecture and then make notes afterwards, or rely on printed notes. Auditory learners make up about 30 per cent of the population.

Tactile/Kinaesthetic Learners

These learners learn by moving, doing and touching; they learn skills by imitating what they see and practising it, which is particularly useful when teaching/learning a skill. They learn best through a hands-on approach, can find it hard to sit still for long periods and may become distracted by their need for activity and exploration. Predominantly kinaesthetic learners can appear unresponsive, in that information is normally not presented in a style that suits their learning methods. Kinaesthetic learners make up around 5 per cent of the population.

All of us use all three types of learning, but most people display a preference for one over the other two. In early life the split among the overall population is fairly even, but by adulthood the visual side has become dominant. (Adapted from www.fastrak-consulting.co.uk/tactix; www.ldpride.net/learningstyles.MI.htm.)

As stated above, most of us use a blend of a range of learning styles, so an effective learning experience is one that comprises a variety of learning opportunities. However, students who have a strong leaning towards kinaesthetic information processing can get bored very quickly and respond better to interactive and hands-on learning experiences. Learners who have a blend of learning styles need to use a range of methods. For example, explaining the daily routine in a room will probably involve quite a lot of information. This is probably best communicated by: providing a brief outline of the routine in writing; then giving more details orally, allowing the student to refer to the outline and encouraging them to take notes.

In Practice

Work experience diary entry: Reflection. Explore what you have learned and how you could use this learning in your practice now and in the future.

REFLECTIVE PRACTICE

Reflective practice is one hallmark of a professional. In this section we shall explore some of the theory behind the vital role of reflective practice in our development as professionals.

Reflection is something we do all the time, but we tend to focus more on situations that have not gone well and try to identify how we could have brought about a more positive outcome if we had handled the situation better (see Lia (n.d.) and University of Kent website).

FIGURE 8.6 GIBBS' REFLECTIVE CYCLE

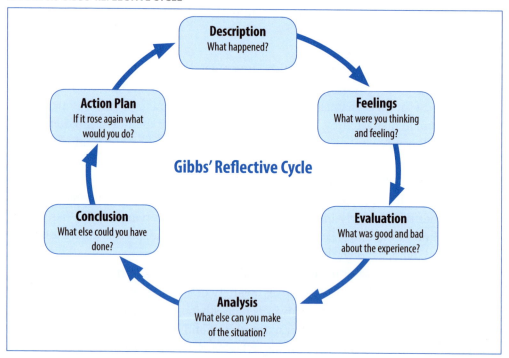

In reflective practice, practitioners engage in a continuous cycle of self-observation and self-evaluation in order to understand their own actions and the reactions they prompt in themselves and in learners. The main aim of reflection in ECCE is to encourage the early years practitioner to continuously examine their practice. Reflective practice is a journey in which the practitioner develops skills and then refines these skills through further exploring their research-based practice.

Mhic Mhathúna and Taylor (2012) remind us that developing the ability to become a reflective practitioner, like learning any new skill, takes time, practice and commitment. Sometimes it can be uncomfortable or even painful to reflect, and we may be inclined to mentally 'sweep it under the rug'. You as the learner (and those you supervise) may need support to reflect. Time spent with your college tutor discussing your experience generally or examining a specific incident (critical incident analysis) can prove most helpful in developing the higher-level learning identified by Bloom. You can look at something that went particularly well or something that did not go well. Beneficial reflection is a skill we develop with practice.

The reflective diaries you are required to keep as part of your work experience aim to provide you with the ability to develop reflective skills which will enhance your professional practice throughout your career.

There are many definitions of reflection and reflective practice and of course the depth of reflection can vary greatly. We think the following definition offers some insight in to what we are aiming for:

> Reflection is an in-depth consideration of events or considerations outside of oneself. The reflector attempts to work out what happened, what they thought or felt about it, why, who was involved and when, and what these others contributed.

The Value of Reflection

In Chapter 2 we examined the legislation which guides our day-to-day practices. By reflecting on how we implement these requirements every day, we can see what factors affect our ability to do so. For example, the Child Care Regulations clearly state the ratio of staff to children. Critically reflect on how these regulations are met and what factors might affect full compliance. Critical incident analysis, in which you focus on a particular incident in detail, can help you decide what measures can be in place to prevent it happening again. For example:

- **What happened?** Insufficient members of staff to meet regulation ratios.
- **How did you feel?** In control of the situation? Not in control of the situation?
- **Evaluate.** What led to the situation arising (e.g. a member of staff off sick)?
- **Conclusion.** Why was it a problem? Because we were in breach of regulations.
- **Action.** What action can we take now and in the future to prevent this situation arising again?

WORKING IN PARTNERSHIP WITH PARENTS

It is well recognised that working in close partnership with the child's parents/guardians greatly enhances the outcomes for the child. There is a significant body of research to support the view that effective partnership with parents/guardians and using practices that promote parental involvement is beneficial for all concerned (Martin & Fitzpatrick 2002; Epstein & Sheldon 2002). As we saw in Chapter 7 (page 156), Aistear highlights a number of benefits for all stakeholders of working in partnership with parents (NCCA 2009a).

Chaboudy *et al.* (2001) identified that parents with higher levels of involvement in the early years setting also devote more time at home to providing a supportive home learning environment.

Barriers to Effective Partnership

There are a number of issues that can prevent effective partnership between parents and the early years setting:
- Lack of clear and consistent policies on partnership and parental involvement
- Parents' own negative experiences of education and their perception of 'teachers'
- Parents' lack of confidence, preventing them communicating effectively with the placement
- Lack of time
- Language difficulties
- Perception that the setting is not inclusive or respectful of a parent's ethnic, religious or cultural background, physical disability or sensory impairment.

Whalley (2001) found that factors within the setting itself can lead to barriers in the development of a partnership. The factors she identified are:
- Lack of leadership and commitment to partnership
- Lack of structure and resources to support this work
- Lack of skills and knowledge by educators to engage effectively with parents and external agencies
- Lack of confidence in their knowledge of the curriculum by early years educators
- Use of professional language and jargon by educators, which can be off-putting to some parents
- Negative perceptions and attitudes by educators towards parents, such as being critical or judgemental
- Lack of equality and anti-discriminatory policies and related staff training
- Staff concerns and fears that parents will 'take over', 'want their own way', etc., making it difficult for staff to 'be in charge'.

Moloney (2010) found that staff can experience a lack of professional identity and clarity and feel that they are treated more like babysitters than professionals. Research by Batey (1996) and Alexander *et al.* 1995 (both cited in Lane 2012) highlights the importance of the early years setting having sufficient room for staff to actually meet with parents one to one, and also for parents to have somewhere to meet for information evenings, etc.

> ## *In Practice*
>
> In your Work Experience module, reflect on your own experiences and examine the relationship between practitioners and parents/carers. Did it work? Was it a positive relationship? What factors contributed to success? What factors created barriers? Can you suggest any improvements and how to carry them out?

What do Parents Want?

From the parents' perspective, research by Riordan (2001) and French (2002) has highlighted the following points about what parents want.

- Support that meets their information needs at different times. They particularly identified the need for accurate and relevant information about child rearing and parenting, health-related issues and support in the community
- Emphasis on building their existing skills, which helps parents to understand and feel more confident, enabling them to enjoy the whole parenting experience more, rather than feeling inadequate and anxious
- A need for more focus on providing support rather than education, e.g. using terms like 'parent groups' rather than 'parent classes', which would focus more on the parents' needs and less on skills
- More opportunities for parents to participate in a less structured and formal way so that they do not feel 'stigmatised' when unable to do so; 'open access' services which are available to all parents
- Help with overcoming barriers to accessing the support offered by the setting, e.g. offering times when working parents can attend, arranging for their children to be cared for while they attend, encouragement and understanding for parents who may lack confidence
- Openness and transparency from services about their purpose, policies and procedures
- Having a say in relation to the support they receive and being offered choice when possible.

Encouraging Parental Partnership

There are no hard and fast rules about how a positive partnership should develop, but there are a number of guidelines worth exploring.

Pugh (1989) has identified five possible dimensions in parental involvement.

PUGH'S DIMENSIONS OF PARENTAL INVOLVEMENT

Non-participation	Parents have consciously opted not to play an active role in the setting
Support	Parents help with practical events such as fundraising, outings, sports days
Participation	Parents participate in the setting by taking part in the daily classroom routine, as helpers in the daily routine
Partnership	Parents are involved in a working relationship defined by a shared sense of purpose, mutual respect and the willingness to negotiate They may also attend meetings and workshops to learn about their own child and develop their knowledge around childcare. e.g. behaviour management
Control	Parents determine and implement decisions and have administrative responsibilities, e.g. participating in staff recruitment, managing resources

Pugh suggests that we should use these dimensions to evaluate the level of partnership in our setting. It is important to point out that the Control dimension is unlikely to be relevant to any Irish settings as they are predominately privately owned; while it would not be out of the question to have parents involved at this level we have not yet reached that stage. Control is certainly happening in publicly funded early years setting in the UK, which are more common than here in Ireland.

Epstein (1992, cited in Lane 2012), an American researcher, has proposed a six-dimension model.

EPSTEIN'S ACTIVITIES IN PARENTAL INVOLVEMENT

Parenting	Helping families establish supportive learning environment for children at home. This may involve inviting parents to information evenings on subjects such as supporting child's learning, offering a lending scheme for books and other educational material
Communicating	Designing effective forms of two-way communication, e.g. notices, memos, newsletters, 1:1 meetings with parents
Volunteering	Recruiting and organising parental help and support, e.g. help with outings, parental representation on committees, planning groups, helping day to day in the setting
Learning at home	Supporting learning activities at home by providing families with information and ideas on how to help their children at home
Decision making	Including parents in the setting's decisions, encouraging and developing parent leaders and representatives
Collaborating with the community	Identifying possible resources in the community and integrating them in the setting to enhance the experiences for the children and their families

According to Lane (2012), areas for skill development include:
- Developing partnerships with parents and families
- Relationship building
- Communication skills
- Anti-discriminatory practice
- Child welfare and protection
- Record keeping and report-writing.

Role of the Key Person

A key person policy in the early years setting promotes and supports working in partnership with parents, children and families. A specific member of staff is identified as the main contact between the child and the family/home. This practitioner takes special responsibility for the child and communicating with the parents/family, other practitioners and other stakeholders.

Lane (2012) identifies specific responsibilities for the key person:
- Assisting the child and family to 'settle in'
- Identifying and understanding the child's unique needs
- Planning the interventions most appropriate to support the child's development and learning
- Taking part in the child's review
- Monitoring the curriculum offered to ensure that it meets the child's needs, abilities, interests and unique personality
- Having an understanding of any specific cultural needs the child/family may have, including learning a few key words in their language.

Tús Maith

Tús Maith, a Barnardos initiative, is a centre-based model of early years care and education for children aged 3–5 years. It is designed for families living in areas of disadvantage where the children are not meeting their developmental milestones. Parents are actively involved in supporting their child's participation in the programme, where there is great emphasis on the vital link between the early years setting and the child's home. The model used is an integration of the High/Scope curriculum and the research-based developmentally informed programme (REDI), and it is based on achieving specific measurable outcomes (www.barnardos.ie).

The Da Project

In 2003 Barnardos set up the 'Da Project' in conjunction with the Barnardos Cherry Orchard Family Support Project. Its aim was to engage more fathers in the services and to support parent–child relationships.

Making a concerted effort to engage with fathers and offering fathers a space in the early years setting requires encouraging practitioners and a welcoming environment. Some of the strategies we can use to involve fathers include:

- Displaying images of fathers on walls, in leaflets, etc.
- Ensuring that all written materials, such as letters, notices, etc., clearly include fathers
- Building relationships with fathers when they come to the setting to drop off or collect their child
- Asking fathers to become involved in the setting and encouraging them to put forward ideas
- Encouraging fathers to become volunteers
- Recruiting male staff.

In Practice

Can you identify other ways in which you can involve fathers more in your setting?

Other Stakeholders

Síolta Standard 10, 'Organisation', defines stakeholders as children, parents, staff and other professionals. Stakeholder consultation is a feature of national developments in relation to ECCE in Ireland. We have already considered the role of parents within the ECCE context, but a range of other professionals will potentially be involved in the ECCE setting: public health nurses, social workers, educational psychologists, therapists, counsellors, etc.

Síolta Standard 10 emphasises the importance of teamwork in supporting children's development. It is through understanding each role that the early years expert practitioner can fully appreciate what they offer and also realise the importance of involving these professionals in the child's care.

References

ACP (Association of Childcare Professionals) (website) www.acpireland.com

Anderson, L.W. and Krathwohl, D.R. (eds) (2001) *A Taxonomy for Learning, Teaching and Assessing: A Revision of Bloom's Taxonomy of Educational Objectives*. New York: Longman

British Council (website) 'Learning Styles and Teaching', http://www.teachingenglish.org.uk/article/learning-styles-teaching

CECDE (Centre for Early Childhood Development and Education) (2006) *Síolta: the National Quality Framework for Early Childhood Education*. Dublin: CECDE, http://www.siolta.ie

Chaboudy, R., Jameson, R. and Huber, R. (2001) 'Connecting families and schools through technology', *Book Report* 20(2), 52–7.

DCYA (Department of Children and Youth Affairs) (2013) *Right from the Start: Report of the Expert Advisory Group on the Early Years Strategy*. Dublin: Government Publications, http://www.dcya.gov.ie/documents/policy/RightFromTheStart.pdf

DCYA (2014) *Better Outcomes Brighter Futures: The National Policy Framework for Children and Young People 2014–2020*, http://dcya.gov.ie/documents/cypp_framework/BetterOutcomesBetterFutureReport.pdf

DES (Department of Education and Science) (1999) *Ready to Learn*: White Paper on Early Childhood Education, http://www.education.ie/en/Publications/Policy-Reports/Ready-to-Learn-White-Paper-on-Early-Childhood-Education.pdf

DES (Department of Education and Skills) (2010) *A Workforce Development Plan for the Early Childhood Care and Education Sector*. Dublin: DES

DJELR (Department of Justice, Equality and Law Reform) (2002) *Model Framework for Education, Training and Professional Development in the Early Childhood Care and Education Sector*

Epstein, J.L. and Sheldon, S.B. (2002) 'Present and accounted for: improving student attendance through family and community involvement', *Journal of Educational Research* 95(2).

Fisher, J. (2002) *Starting from the Child*. McGraw-Hill

French, G. (2002) 'Principles of best practice in parent education', *ChildLinks*, Spring

Lane, F. (2012) *Can We Help? A Guide to Supporting Children and Families in the Early Years Services*. Dublin: Barnardos

Lia, P. (n.d.) 'Using Gibbs' Reflective Cycle', http://www.kcl.ac.uk/campuslife/services/disability/service/Using-Gibbs-Reflective-Cycle-in-Coursework.pdf

Martin, S. and Fitzpatrick, A. (2002) 'Parents as Partners in Early Years Services in Ireland: An Exploratory Study', paper presented to OMEP Ireland Conference, DIT, 20 April

Mhic Mhathúna, M. and Taylor, M. (2012) *Early Childhood Education and Care: An Introduction for Students in Ireland*. Dublin: Gill & Macmillan

Moloney, M. (2010) 'Professional identity in early childhood care and education: perspectives of pre-school and infant teachers', *Irish Educational Studies* 29(2), 167–87

NCCA (National Council for Curriculum and Assessment) (2009a) *Aistear: Building Partnerships between Parents and Practitioners*. Dublin: NCCA, http://www.ncca.biz/aistear/pdfs/Guidelines_ENG/Practitioners_ENG.pdf

NCCA (2009b) *Aistear: the Early Childhood Curriculum Framework*. Dublin: NCCA

NCCA (2012) *Annual Report*. Dublin: NCCA

Overbaugh, R. and Schultz, L. (n.d.) *Bloom's Taxonomy*, http://ww2.odu.edu/educ/roverbau/Bloom/blooms_taxonomy.htm, accessed 9 October 2014

Pugh G. (1989) *Working Towards Partnership in the Early Years*. London: National Children's Bureau

Riordan, S. (2001) *Supporting Parenting: A Study of Parents' Support Needs*. Dublin: CSER

Rose, C. and Nicholl, M.J. (1997) *Accelerated Learning for the 21st Century*. Delacorte

Tickell, C. (2010) *The Early Years: Foundations for Life, Health and Learning: An Independent Report on the Early Years Foundation Stage to Her Majesty's Government*. London: UK Department of Education, http://earlylearningconsultancy.co.uk/eyfs-news/

University of Kent (website) 'Reflective Learning', http://www.kent.ac.uk/learning/PDP-and-employability/pdp/reflective.html, accessed 9 October 2014

Whalley, M. (2001) *Involving Parents in their Children's Learning*. Sage

Appendix A: The United Nations Convention on the Rights of the Child

The Articles that make up the UNCRC are as follows.

Article 1: Definition of a child
Article 2: Non-discrimination
Article 3: Best interests of the child
Article 4: Implementation of rights
Article 5: Parental guidance and the child's evolving capacities
Article 6: Survival and development
Article 7: Name and nationality
Article 8: Preservation of identity
Article 9: Separation from parents
Article 10: Family reunification
Article 11: Illicit transfer and non-return
Article 12: The child's opinion
Article 13: Freedom of expression
Article 14: Freedom of thought, conscience and religion
Article 15: Freedom of association
Article 16: Protection of privacy
Article 17: Access to appropriate information
Article 18: Parental responsibilities
Article 19: Protection from abuse and neglect
Article 20: Protection of children without families
Article 21: Adoption
Article 22: Refugee children
Article 23: Children with a disability
Article 24: Health and health services
Article 25: Periodic review of placement
Article 26: Social security
Article 27: Standard of living
Article 28: Education
Article 29: Aims of education

Article 30: Children of minorities or indigenous peoples

Article 31: Leisure, recreation and cultural activities

Article 32: Child labour

Article 33: Drug abuse

Article 34: Sexual exploitation

Article 35: Sale, trafficking and abduction

Article 36: Other forms of exploitation

Article 37: Torture and deprivation of liberty

Article 38: Armed conflicts

Article 39: Rehabilitative care

Article 40: Administration of juvenile justice

Article 41: Respect for existing standards

For more information on the UNCRC, consult the following website: www.childrensrights.ie/sites/default/files/UNCRCEnglish.pdf.

Appendix B: Legislation Relevant to ECCE Settings

The HSE recommends that ECCE settings should consult the following pieces of legislation and regulations.

Child Care Act 1991

Child Care (Pre-School Services) (No. 2) Regulations 2006 [S.I. No. 604 of 2006]

Child Care (Pre-School Services) (No. 2) (Amendment) Regulations 2006 [S.I. 643 of 2006].

Child Care (Pre-School Services) (No. 2) Regulations 2006 and Explanatory Guide to Requirements and Procedures for Notification and Inspection (DoHC 2006)

National Standards for Preschool Services (DoHC 2010)

Other relevant material:

Building Legislation and Regulations and Planning Acts (available at www.environ.ie)

Children Act 2001

Child Care (Amendment) Act 2007

Child Care (Amendment) Act 2011

Children First: National Guidance for the Protection and Welfare of Children (DCYA 2011)

Children First Bill 2012 – Draft Heads and General Scheme

Child Protection and Welfare Practice Handbook (HSE 2011)

Criminal Justice Act 2006 Part 15 – Miscellaneous – Section 176 – Reckless endangerment of children

Data Protection Acts 1988 and 2003

Disability Act 2006

Freedom of Information Acts 1997 and 2003

Health Act 2004

Health Act 2007

Health and Safety Authority (HSA) publications

National Vetting Bureau (Children and Vulnerable Persons) Act 2012

Our Duty to Care: The Principles of Good Practice for the Protection of Children and Young People (DoHC 2004)

Protections for Persons Reporting Child Abuse Act 1998

These pieces of legislation are particularly important, but they do not include every regulation required to operate a childcare service. This list is extensive; the City and County Childcare Committees and Barnardos are useful sources of information. The Clare County Childcare Committee has an excellent, comprehensive guide to key legislation involved in running a childcare setting: 'Operating a Childcare Service: A Guide to Key Legislation', available at www.clarechildcare.ie/zdocs%5CLegal%20 Booklet%20%282%29.pdf.

Index

Page numbers in **bold italic** indicate tables and diagrams.